Reading Classes

The Prickly Song
by Scurvy Burr

Bouncy.

Thistles and thorns and por - cu - pines and

ur - chins under the sea

all get into a prickly mood,

just like me!

(Try singing this song as a two- or four-part round.)

NOTE: This is the only song approved by Scurvy Burr!

4. The Thorn Patch: There are lots of thorns here— I mean LOTS! There is also a secret spring hidden somewhere, but only the rabbits know where it is.

Lots of thorns!

5. Dragonfly Swamp: Snakes, salamanders, and snapping turtles live here. All kinds of spiny plants grow in the water. But don't fall in!

6. Craggy Cave: This cave is filled with stalactites and stalagmites, which are pointy and sharp. Nearby is my favorite tree in the forest, the prickly ash!

Prickly Ash

READING CLASSES

On Culture and Classism in America

BARBARA JENSEN

ILR PRESS
AN IMPRINT OF
CORNELL UNIVERSITY PRESS
ITHACA AND LONDON

First published 2012 by Cornell University Press
First printing, Cornell Paperbacks, 2012
Printed in the United States of America

Library of Congress Cataloging-in-Publication Data

Jensen, Barbara, 1953–
    Reading classes : on culture and classism in America / Barbara Jensen.
        p. cm.
    Includes bibliographical references and index.
    ISBN 978-0-8014-4476-0 (cloth : alk. paper) — ISBN 978-0-8014-7779-9
(pbk. : alk. paper)
    1. Classism—United States.   2. Working class—United States—
Social conditions.   3. Social classes—United States.   4. Social
stratification—United States.   I. Title.
    HN90.S6J46 2012
    305.50973—dc23   2011051728

Cornell University Press strives to use environmentally responsible
suppliers and materials to the fullest extent possible in the publishing of
its books. Such materials include vegetable-based, low-VOC inks and
acid-free papers that are recycled, totally chlorine-free, or partly composed
of nonwood fibers. For further information, visit our website at www.
cornellpress.cornell.edu.

Cloth printing   10 9 8 7 6 5 4 3 2 1
Paperback printing   10 9 8 7 6 5 4 3 2 1

This book is dedicated to my wonderful family members, Jensens and Mittelmans alike, and especially to my mother and father, Alice and Fred Jensen. I never had a chance to tell you how grateful I am for all you taught me.

Contents

ACKNOWLEDGMENTS

This book took a village. While I wrote and rewrote, others in my life were left to deal with my constant lack of free time, my hasty visits, the family events I didn't make it to, the graduations and holidays I missed, the dates I cancelled, the weeks I took off work to write, and the calls I forgot to make. Thank you for your patience.

To all the people who read the book or parts of it and gave me feedback—Laura Ayers, Carol Barnes, Shirley Carlson, Renny Christopher, Tom Copeland, Bess Donahue, Lary Dunsmore, David Emerson, Nancy Hammond, Kate Hanning, Lily Neilon Jensen, Sharon Kahn, Sherry Linkon, Alfred Lubrano, Roger McKenzie, Marin Peplinski, Kristine Smith, Thorin Tatge (for reading several chapters as well as research assistance), Felice Yeskel, Janet Zandy, and Michael Zweig—Thank you. Thanks to the women in my writers group: Sue Hedley-Keller, Barbara Parisian, Elizabeth Runge, Vicky Lofquist, Sharon Emery, Kathy Zalonni, Charlene Knox, Barbara Haselbeck, Antonia Krueger, and especially our fearless leader, Margot Galt.

Special thanks to Holly Menino Bailey for her keen eye, excellent editing, and kind heart.

Thanks to all family members who let me record their work histories and thoughts about class in America, or who fed me after I interviewed their spouses: Nancy Houg, Rick Jensen, Eugene and Shirley (Pete) Jensen, Mike Larson, Don and Carol Jensen, Cindy (Jensen) Koslowski, Lily Neilon Jensen, Luella and Bob Sharpe. Thanks to all the others, and to Aunt Shirley and Uncle Bob Jensen, for a lifetime of love and winks.

Thanks to Mark Mendel for years of technical assistance; for transcription, Nate Bucklin and Kate Hanning; for indexing, Karen Babich.

For years of patience, I thank the teaching staff and students at Loring Nicollet Alternative School as well as all of my private therapy clients, you know who you are.

For emotional support and encouragement above and beyond: Nicky Bredeson, Tom Copeland, Lary Dunsmore, Lily Neilon Jensen, Margie Lessinger, Mark Mendel, Greg Schmitz, Thorin Tatge, Felice Yeskel, and, especially, Lori Zuidema.

I want to thank my champion Fran Benson for years of believing in, and fighting for, both the book and me. Thanks also to Katie Meigs, and to Katherine Liu and Candace Akins at Cornell University Press for their excellent work on this book.

Finally, my deepest gratitude to Jack Metzgar for extraordinary support on every level, from reading every chapter as I went through the first draft, to page-by-page feedback on two versions of the manuscript, for yelling at me when I needed it, and, especially, for his exceptional depth of compassion and ability to "get it" from the very start. At the end of the 2011 Chicago Working Class Studies Association conference, he had me jumping up and down with him; "We made it!" he shouted. I would never have made it without you, Jack.

READING CLASSES

Prologue

What Part of Fridley Are You From?

My big brother, Eddie, retired from the post office at fifty-five and had a party. He started as a mail carrier and worked his way up to postmaster. His girlfriend, Lynette, threw the party at a park in Elk River, a northwest suburb of Minneapolis where they lived. Since my husband and I had just separated, I went to the party by myself, dreading telling my bad news to my aunts and uncles. Getting married was one of the few normal things I had ever done, even if I had done it at forty, instead of twenty, in a fancy old hotel, not a scrubbed-white Lutheran church, with a judge, not a minister. My family was used to me being "different," a catch-all term in Minnesota for anything you can't say something nice about.

Eddie played rockabilly guitar at that wedding and sang "The Battle Hymn of Love," which the pianist reprised as we left the altar, deftly switching into a rocked-out bit of Beethoven's "Ode to Joy." My large extended family of Danish and German Lutherans joined me for a reception and dance in Red Wing, Minnesota, in the Summit Room of the Saint James Hotel, which had a wall of glass overlooking the Minnesota

River—not the usual American Legion or VFW halls. My cousin Dave Jensen, who lives in Fridley, another northern suburb, played real good rock 'n' roll with his band. It seemed then to me I had finally blended my two lives, my middle and working class selves.

The news of my impending divorce was going to make my relatives sad, and I didn't want that. It was only my second extended-family event since my father had died the year before. Arriving at Eddie's party, I hugged him and our younger brother, Jim. Missing my dad, I then joined three of his four remaining brothers, who looked so much like him. Jensen men are very large. They stand out and up in a crowd. Of my father's brothers, there's not one of them as small as six feet. Their noses are large and beak-like, set in faces with big angular features. They have striking blue eyes and pale skin. Their once brown heads of hair, blond when they were kids, have now turned white. When they sit down together they spread out their knees and elbows; they take up a lot of space. They are physically formidable, but this is tempered with a great tenderness of heart. Gentle giants, they always seemed to me. That day, I noticed they were getting slightly shorter in old age, their Scandinavian skin even whiter, and their blue eyes sometimes filled with tears.

"Would you tell me about the work you did when you were young, when you lived in Minneapolis?" I asked my uncles. I love to hear their stories about old Minneapolis. My father's generation of family members were the only other relatives to have lived in "The City." Uncle Gene told me he had worked with my father collecting trash when they first moved to Minneapolis (after my dad had lived with my Jewish mother in Brooklyn for five years . . . but that's another story).

"Now, Barbie, you gotta understand that back in them days, there was nothing wrong with hard work," said beefy, sunburned Uncle Gene. He had spent most of his life working for the railroad and still wore the cap and overalls. Only my uncles and aunties had retained the right to call me Barbie. At forty-nine, it was particularly odd for me to hear it, but also somehow comforting.

Uncle Donnie piped up, "Oh yeah, Zucherman, he was your dad's boss, too, Barbie. Yeah, bosses liked us plenty 'cause they got such good work out of us. You know, it was easy for us 'cause we always worked hard all our lives. We got up at four in the morning. Every day. We'd work ten, twelve, fourteen hours. Out there on the farm, Barbie, it ain't like now."

Uncle Donnie leaned back in his folding lawn chair, spilling out of it as Nordic giants do, ready to hold forth at length.

Uncle Gene cut in, and Uncle Donnie stopped without rancor: "Yeah, that's right, Barbie, some of them men weren't so reliable as us. He was glad to have us. He started us at five in the morning, but that didn't bother us none. We were used to it. We worked all morning, and then we got us some lunch."

"Oh yeah, that place there on Lake Street," Uncle Bobby cut in next, wearing his NASCAR billed cap with the adjustable plastic strap. The youngest of the three, Uncle Bobby was a farmer and a trucker who always had a big smile and a wink for children. I remembered the thrill of having him swing me up onto his shoulders and carry me around when I was little. "That one with them great hamburgers and sandwiches. Five cents apiece, Barbie. You can't even get McDonalds for that. What was the name of it?" My family always talks about what things cost, especially back then.

"Angie's?" Uncle Donnie asked, hand over his eyes to keep the sun out. "Over there on 4th Avenue and Lake Street, don't ya think?" I remembered Uncle Donnie singing soulfully with my father and Uncle Gene, their heads tilted together with the same earnest look in their eyes. I remembered the sweet cigar smoke of those long-ago holidays at Gramma and Grampa Jensen's house in Glenville, Minnesota.

"Yeah," said Uncle Gene, the best singer of them all, picking up right where he had left off. "You kids don't know about them days. But we got up every day, and whatever job we had at the time, we worked harder than anyone ever does nowadays." He shifted in his plastic folding chair.

My father, their big brother, had died the year before of a sudden and terrible cancer; we were all brokenhearted. He took his detailed stories about his life with him. When I was a teenager, battling my parents, Eddie once told me that Dad had collected trash when he first moved to Minneapolis. Later, when I asked Dad if he had collected trash, he said, yeah, because he wasn't "ashamed of hard work."

My uncles amazed me, as my father always did, with the amount of detail in their memories. The way they spoke was at least as interesting as the stories they told: piping up whenever they felt the urge, amicably interrupting and arguing with each other. The warmth and eagerness in their eyes, their honest combination of pride and self-effacing humor—all this opened my heart and reminded me of my dad. Their vivid details and occasional moral endings ("Nobody said life was fair!") sounded so much like my father that I knew he was still alive, in all of us. I regretted the years I hadn't asked about their stories, years I had spent busy becoming something that took me further and further away from them.

Of course the aunties sat elsewhere, talking about the important stuff among themselves. You can talk with uncles without revealing anything about how you are feeling. Not so with aunties, who are tuned like hawks to feelings and the details of peoples' lives, always ready to care. I sat down with aunties Carol, Bev, and Pete. "We're just separated," I lied, and my eyes flushed with involuntary tears. Their love made me want to hope that my husband would love me again, too, the way my family loves.

Next, I met my brother's karaoke friends. Although Eddie had worked his way up from mail carrier to postmaster, he was still, culturally, almost completely a blue-collar guy, for all his New York verbal charm and wit. His friends implored me to come back for karaoke that night at Muny's, the municipal bar in Elk River. My brother was the local karaoke king, they said. I remembered the times he brought his girlfriends and daughters to see me sing and play guitar in folk-rock bands in the City. I said, "Okay," wishing I had brought evening clothes. I dreaded the long drive back to the City and out to Elk River again, but the smile on my brother's face made me determined to come back anyway.

So I asked my ex, David, to join me for the long drive back to Elk River. Though we had separated, we were trying to be nice to each other, to help each other out, and he missed my family. We drove from my house on the south side of Minneapolis, through the once-familiar northside and northern suburbs of my childhood. My father, his brothers, and his sister Mary, my godmother, had all settled north of the Twin Cities and raised families. It was cheaper to buy homes and farms there, while the southern suburbs attracted wealthier people.

At Muny's, it was clear, my brother was karaoke king. He burnt up the stage with his soulful versions of songs by Hank Williams and Johnny Cash. The crowd cheered. As usual, my brother embarrassed me by introducing me to all his karaoke friends as "my little sister, the psychologist." Nearly everyone was dressed in blue jeans, brightly colored shirts and blouses, and billed or cowboy hats. I felt a bit odd dressed in black sparkly stuff that I had bought in New York. In our usual black dress-up clothes David and I looked like FBI agents, undertakers, or, worse, city snobs.

Bringing my handsome cosmopolitan husband to family events, I had been able to feel that my own, very different, life was finally a bit visible, even enviable. David's now-temporary presence helped me feel this way again and, as always, a little cocky as well. David strode confidently to the microphone to sing karaoke, something we had previously disdained as "real musicians." A child prodigy on the piano by the age of four, he sang off pitch and didn't even know it! I couldn't help but smile a little; I had so revered his musical genius and classical training. I picked a Mary Chapin Carpenter song that I had already performed in concert and just barely made it through. We both left Elk River with a new respect for karaoke singers, more humble than when we came.

Back in Minneapolis at 2 a.m., we stopped at Little Tijuana, an all-night diner near the Minneapolis College of Art and Design. Here we blended in nicely with our arty black clothes. As always, it felt good to be back in the city, no longer different. We slid into a booth in front of a large table of similarly arty young people. I remembered how exciting it had been to be a young art student with a whole new life ahead of me. I remembered, too, my eagerness to move into the city as soon as I graduated high school. I grinned broadly at them; they smiled back. Not one of my Jensen cousins has lived in the city. Most of them would not even drive through the city. In the quiet awkwardness of "trying to be friends," while David and I waited to order, I overheard a young man from the table behind me "dissing" someone.

"So I said to him, 'What part of *Fridley* are *you* from? I mean where in *Anoka* did you grow up?'" My eyes popped wide in shock. Those were the northwest suburbs of the Twin Cities we had just driven through, where much of my extended family still lived, including the uncles, aunties, and cousins that I felt so grateful for that difficult day. Fridley is where Dave Jensen lived, Uncle Gene's son, whose excellent band played at our wedding dance. Uncle Donnie and Auntie Carol and my deceased godmother, Mary Jensen Larson, lived in Anoka.

The guy behind me went on, "What trailer park in *Spring Lake Park* are you from? What part of *Columbia Heights*?"

"Yeah," another guy joined him as our waitress came, "What rock in *New Brighton* did you crawl out from under?" New Brighton was my childhood mailing address. I skated at the roller rink in Spring Lake Park; I got my first job there in a bakery at fourteen. I sputtered through my order while these two guys behind me riffed on, besting each other's epithets, to a table of people laughing. Every one of their epithets were the places where my father and much of his family (and, later, my cousins and their families) had proudly bought homes and farms and settled down with skilled working class jobs. The shock and irony of hearing their blatant classism when I had just been out there left me speechless. Suddenly my head was spinning with rage. It made me crazy to juxtapose the tenderness and triumph of the day—and my own complicated cultural history—with this casual and complete contempt for the places my family called home.

David dismissed them, "They're just blowing hot air. They could be talking about anything." But they weren't talking about anything. They were talking about my family. Of course, they had no idea that someone from those "low class" places was sitting in the booth behind them. In my black clothes and cat's-eye glasses, I could be one of their teachers; indeed, I do teach at a local university and have even taught art in the past. David was right, I suppose, they were only using popular idioms and insults of the day. Still, their words hit my chest like buckshot. They desecrated my family, and my heart, with their casual, playful speech.

I could still see my uncles telling their colorful working class stories. I could hear my brother belting out Hank Williams, proud to show off to his little sister, the "fancy-pants psychologist." The sweetness of my uncles, the love in my aunties' eyes, the reach beyond my own knee-jerk class prejudice against karaoke bars to hear Eddie singing and to meet his friends—all this had resurrected a deep sense of family intimacy, of belonging, again. Despite the loss of my parents and my marriage, despite all the years I aimed myself away from the life they expected of me. For a little while I had enjoyed freedom from the confusing fragility of my own uneasy psychological truce of selves: southern and northern Minneapolis, educated professional and fun-loving tough girl, professional middle class and working class.

"What part of *Crystal* are you from?" I heard. Uncle Gene and Auntie Pete lived in Crystal.

"What pickup truck in *Mounds View* did your mother drop you in?" I just popped up then and glared at the guy who was talking—Mounds View was my town. I was surprised to see he was Asian American. He was surprised I glared at him. Fuming, I walked to the restroom.

When I returned, David told me that the other guy talking was the big white guy with the baseball cap. They left as we ate our meal. When we left the restaurant, they were out front. I saw the Asian American kid again and I looked him in the eye. He looked right back at me, a wary look. Mostly, I tried to catch the eye of the white guy, to glare at him, but to no avail. His gaze didn't rest on me long enough to register anything at all. He kept on blathering as we walked away.

In the car, David told me that the white guy had done most of the talking.

As I went into my house, and David didn't anymore, I could hear the slow crunching of new tar, gravel, and our exciting cosmopolitan life beneath his tires. Tears suddenly rushed from my eyes; I fought my grief by willing back precious images of the day. Then I heard those kids talking shit about my family's hometowns, and I tried to picture the big white kid with the billed cap in my mind.

My anger came unbridled. I shouted at my house of ghosts, "What rock in Fridley did I crawl out from under? Every rock in Fridley! Every part of Mounds View, Anoka, Columbia Heights, Coon Rapids, Crystal, Spring Lake Park! *I am Fridley*!" I felt thirteen again, wishing life was simple enough that a physical fight could resolve something once and for all. Wishing my own insides were that simple.

I walked back outside and stood on my porch in the summer air. I watched David's red taillights drift away and, with them, the anchor my marriage had been. I belonged nowhere. Again. I saw the white kid from the restaurant clearly now; he was a lot bigger and beefier than the other artists, and his cap, though streaked with black and gold, had plastic nubs in back to adjust it. Just like the caps my uncles get at feed stores or Menard's. Then I realized: he looked way more like a guy from places he was slamming than the art students he was trying to impress. Bingo!

My anger deflated as suddenly as it had erupted. I knew it wasn't just the casual classism of strangers that made me so angry, but *my* classism, the years of running away. I felt shame and sorrow for the embarrassment I felt for my parents, back then, with my educated new friends. A sharp slice of memory dances in my mind, and I hear myself arrogantly correcting my parents' colorful English. I had inhaled and exhaled classism as naturally as air, as I swam ecstatically into my "life of the mind," correcting the voices I would now give anything to hear just one last time.

I stood on my porch. It was July. A north wind blew through the Mississippi River Valley, and I caught a fresh breeze on my face. I looked at the crazy patchwork life I have fashioned, belonging nowhere but also almost anywhere. I knew I would always be suspended between worlds: between Minneapolis and New York City; between theater, literature, world travel and the rooted, easy-going, and enduring pleasures of my working class life.

I stood on that porch a long, long time.

1

Getting Class

Welcome to my worlds. Both of them.

I come from a stable, solidly working class neighborhood and large extended family. On my dad's side, the Jensens, nine brothers and sisters survived to adulthood, married, and had children. I now have an extended family of over 140 people; many still get together to celebrate Christmas each year and a slew of graduations, confirmations, bridal and baby showers, weddings, anniversaries, and retirement celebrations. We still have a family picnic every summer. My family is real, funny, and wise. The uncles and aunties in my prologue started out their adult lives dirt poor and worked very hard to move on to stable, skilled working class jobs, a mobility that makes them proud.

I worked hard, too, and have also moved up the class ladder in America. But instead of going from a job in a poultry plant to a good union job as a railroad worker, a security guard, a meat cutter, or working in a school cafeteria, I worked my way through a lot of school (with a variety of working class jobs) to become a psychologist. My uncles and aunties didn't have to change cultures to change jobs; I wandered into a whole new world where few of the rules from my first world—their world—apply. I also entered a world where people view my wise, funny, and loyal family as something quite different from what they really are.

Now I am in my mid-fifties, and I am a professional counseling and community psychologist, a university instructor, and a scholar—in short, a member in good standing of the upper middle class in America. As an official member of the professional middle class I have framed degrees, licenses, certificates, and awards displayed in my office, proving my membership. I am a working class to professional middle class "crossover" or "straddler" who really enjoys many aspects of each class-related culture I know (Lubrano 2004).

Unlike many people who have crossed this class divide, I enjoyed growing up working class and remain in relatively close contact with my extended family. I still love ball games in the street, roller-skating, playing country music on my guitar, and belting out rock 'n' roll songs. Conversely, I have developed a taste for Chilean sea bass and pine nuts, Beethoven, exotic travel, and the kind of theater that leaves many people frowning and scratching their heads.

Growing Up Working Class

My dad was a meat cutter and my mom a telephone solicitor (long before they were upgraded to "telemarketers"). Everyone we knew was working class. In my childhood, we were often driving across the state to see more relatives. With dozens of cousins, aunts, and uncles, I got to stay in many different houses, saw different ways of living, had different kinds of fun, and saw different kinds of difficulty—all of them working class. At the farms belonging to my Dad's brothers and sisters we had animals, huge fields of corn and soybeans glistening in the summer sun, barns, haymows and attics within which to play. Being one of the oldest children in the Jensen family, I often told stories to my younger cousins, as my big brother, Eddie, had told stories to me. I was as close to my cousins as I was to my neighborhood pals in Mounds View.

My big family gave me a sense that my world was very large and included more people than I could possibly count who were either related to Dad, friends from jobs he had worked, or friends from the many places they had lived as he grew up. My childhood map of the world was mostly in Mounds View, and then mostly four streets: Pinewood, Terrace, Oakwood, and Hillview. But Dad was always driving us somewhere else, and Minnesota seemed a very big place, with endless new landscapes and towns. Glenville, where Grandma and Grandpa Jensen lived with Uncle Ricky in that long-ago little white house with a back porch and deep yard, outdoor clotheslines running the length of it. Alongside the house, there was a small hill and at the top was the railroad track, just off Main Street in Glenville. There was an outside toilet that people used even when the one inside worked. Glenville was the center of the Jensen family, way back when Grandma was still alive and I was little. We spent nearly every holiday there and all Dad's brothers and sisters and, as they were gradually added, new spouses and more cousins still went there as often as possible.

My childhood map also had two very far-away lands: Denmark, where Grandpa Jensen came from, and New York, where my mother was raised and where Grandma and Grandpa Milstein still lived. Not just New York, we knew, but Brooklyn, New York.

There wasn't much happening in our little village of Mounds View, just quiet rows of identical tract houses (there were two types, small and medium) and tiny trees planted by hopeful young couples. Now I can't help but laugh when I say the name Mounds View: there were no mounds to view. It was dead-flat prairie and even swampy in parts. There was no town center, no library, no town, actually. My best friends were Terrie Blanchard, Marie Butler, and Rene McDonough, and we had plenty of time to invent our own fun.

There were half-done housing developments to play in, mountains made of dirt to climb, big bumpy laps of sprawling old oaks we climbed into in the school yard across the street from our house, the slurpy bog you went through to get to the woods, and an even slurpier expanse of black peat to explore. We had the farmer's yard on Hillview Drive with a tire swing we loved to ride, countless games of dodgeball and statue-maker in McDonough's yard, led by Rene's older sister and brother, a record player and a passel of 45 rpm records in their basement that all of us took turns pantomiming to each other. There were countless overnights in each other's houses, and many more whispered stories and secrets between us. Things weren't always easy for our parents—some of them worked too hard at difficult, often multiple, jobs, and every once in a while their frustrations rocked our wood-frame houses and shattered the quiet suburban air. But we were not alone in the world. We always had "us."

In our neighborhood there was one primary school—Pinewood Elementary. In first grade, kissing Mrs. Johnson's old papery-white cheek as we left school each day, I dreamed of being a teacher's pet, but I never was. I loved books, but there weren't any in our house, or in Pinewood Elementary. (They finally got a library just as I was leaving sixth grade for junior high.) My godmother's house had a piano, because their Pentecostal religion said they couldn't have a TV, and I begged my parents and pined for a piano and lessons all through grade school. I never got them. One sad lesson I learned at the time: try not to wish for things you can't have, it only makes you feel bad. As my father always said, "You can't have everything." Also, as everyone in Minnesota still says, "It could be worse."

I'm sure no one read books to me in the 1950s and '60s, because I still remember getting my first and only books in childhood. Two of them. I remember being surprised, and a bit disappointed, to open them under the Christmas tree. They were fairy tales I eventually came to adore and imitate. Mostly, I read the grisly stories in the *National Enquirer, The Star*, and *Weekly World News* at a neighbor's house with horrified fascination. I then wrote stories about mutilation and brutality, and my mother praised my writing skill. The only books I saw adults read were the Bible (and then only my godparents Mary and Milton) and what I later learned to call "potboilers," like Harold Robbins's *The Carpetbaggers* or Willard Motley's *Knock on Any Door*, that my mother read and that I eventually learned to plow through. Also, my mom made sure we always had lots of magazines.

Sometimes I awoke to Mom's sobbing in the night, "I want to go home!" I had no way to know what she meant by "home," since our house on Pinewood Drive was the only home I had ever known. I remember going into the new living room Dad had built and finding him sitting on the edge of the couch, his miserable head in his hands, until I said, "Dad?" And he looked up, surprised and, for a moment, truly lost.

"Mom's had a little too much to drink, Barbie," he said, looking like my ever-confident, competent dad again. He said, "Go to bed, it will be better in the morning." But Dad didn't look convinced. I know now that she missed New York, but then I went to my bedroom afraid and deeply puzzled, while Mom's noisy sobs shook the house.

And it would be better in the morning, and better still by Friday night when we relaxed into another long car ride and cruised up Highway 65 to the cabin. Dad bought my brothers and me a handful of candy bars to choose between, and he let us listen to rock 'n' roll on the radio. Long car rides turned quiet and intimate as we eventually lost radio reception and began to sing. Everyone had special songs to sing, and we took turns, the more tender the lyrics the better. Dad sang "Rocking Alone in an Old Rocking Chair." Mine were "Patches," a tragic tale of class prejudice, and "Scarlet Ribbons," a magical tale of a little girl whose faith brought her gifts beyond human comprehension. And when we didn't know the lyrics, we all made goofy ones up together, and we laughed out loud.

There was a spaciousness to life, and it seems to me now that people in my childhood heard *inside* of words. Words were buoys, instead of building blocks—buoys floating in a world dense with shared images: farms and factories, haymows, shanty towns, and neon city streets; cows, horses, pigs, dogs, and chickens; shining meadows, swamps, and fields of corn; dense forests of birch, pine, and oak; a wonder of pheasants, grouse, deer, moose, and black bears. The meaning in our lives changed together, like weather. Everyone in the neighborhood watched together as good times and bad times, odd times and usual times, came and went.

Then came sudden events, all in a tumble, like the Tornadoes of '65 (sixth grade) that flattened two blocks of houses. A rush of people and danger and excitement. We always knew there were frightening things beyond our understanding, beyond our control: we saw shattered houses and scattered treasures. But we already had seen hands with a missing finger, people whose faces had burn scars, animals struck and bloodied by cars, and other great, troubling mysteries of childhood. We also knew that, mostly, people like us survive. Everyone came around to help and rebuild. Eventually, those battered streets ended up having the nicest houses in the area. Then we coasted again through another endless summer.

If we were deprived, we didn't know it. Later, as an upwardly mobile young adult, I would curse and mourn the lack of good literature, art materials, and music training in my childhood, how far "behind" I felt among my new middle class friends. But, at the time, in our relatively homogenous suburb, we were unaware that anyone else had anything we did not. I enjoyed being a working class kid, riding my bike all over Pinewood and beyond to Greenfield and Red Oak neighborhoods, making new friends and finding new adventures.

Adventures in Adolescence: Discovering Class

In junior high we got a school library, but I wasn't looking for books to read anymore. (Okay, I did sneak a few Beverly Cleary books home.) I was far more interested in getting more and more cool, as my brother Eddie had six years before me. Some of the teachers even called me "Little Jensen," remembering my brother and expecting me to be a hood too. I did not disappoint them. I exhibited bravery, sheer nerve, willingness to face consequences (detention), and humor—sometimes at the teacher's expense—in front of the whole classroom.

When Terrie, Marie, Rene, and I were twelve, we started going to Teen Night at the Bel-Rae Ballroom every Tuesday. It was always packed with kids and live bands that played songs of the '60s like "Let The Good Times Roll." "Heat Wave" by Martha and the Vandellas was the song that always made everyone get up and flood the dance floor. We freely smoked cigarettes. The management didn't even try to stop us. I don't know if I ever missed a Tuesday night from age twelve through my high school graduation at seventeen.

I was a most unlikely candidate for college.

But when I was fourteen (in 1968) an old friend from Pinewood whom we saw every week at Bel-Rae, Jeanie, started inviting me to her house. My parents' dream neighborhood had only been a stopping place for her family. They had moved into a real middle class neighborhood in nearby New Brighton—a real town with a library, a couple of restaurants, a post office, a bank, and different classes of people. Mom went there often for a "smidgen of civilization," as she called it.

On my first visit to my friend's house I had a "we're not in Kansas anymore, Toto!" experience. This house had books galore, special "reading" lamps, no TV in the living room (the object around which every living room in Mounds View revolved), and a component stereo system with no cabinet her brother had brought back from Vietnam at the end of his first tour. Her parents were divorced (that was *different*), her oldest sister was a model, and her other older sister had my name, Barbara, and went to the University of Minnesota. Her mother was also attending the U to get a master's degree in library science. They welcomed me into their family.

My own family was in trouble. By the time I was in high school, my parents and I were fighting all the time. My mom had become increasingly dark and stormy as the years wore on in Minnesota. Six years older than me, Eddie had married his high school sweetheart and moved a mile down County Road I; he was trying to help me understand my parents. Eddie and I had many talks about our family while parked in the driveway where no one would hear us, exhaust pluming up around his car like ghosts in the winter air. Mom fought an unintelligible battle that only started to make sense when Eddie finally told me, when I graduated high school and left home at seventeen, that Mom's parents were Jewish.

Since I was not getting along in my family, I more or less took up residence in New Brighton. Staying with Jeanie's family changed the course of my life forever. In particular, her older sister Barbara reached out and brought us to the West Bank (of the Mississippi River) by the University of Minnesota campus, where she lived with other students.

The streets of the dilapidated West Bank neighborhood inhabited by skid row alcoholics and cockroaches was now packed with university students with long silky hair or gigantic tousled curls, flowing East Indian Nehru shirts and long billowy skirts of brightly colored prints. Barbara was completely at home there, with her long straight hair, blue jeans, and sweatshirts. She was a protester of the war in Vietnam, a natural foods eater, and an athlete who worked with kids every summer. She had a big and ready smile and always talked to me like I was an adult.

I remember my first night on the West Bank with her, going up a long flight of stairs in an old house to the Coffeehouse Extempore. We gave a donation at the door to a small man with black hair in two long pigtails, while I tried really hard not to stare at him. This may be hard for people born after the 1960s to imagine, but boys and men back then always had short hair. This room was full of men with long hair, women in tie-dyed clothes, cigarette smoke, and the smell of coffee. I had never seen anything like it; I was fascinated. Wandering in, I found a room where a guy played guitar and sang folk music on a small stage while people sat at tables and listened. Everyone was very friendly and sweet, loving even. This was quite different from my tough-guys neighborhood, because I was a stranger and yet they treated me like one of them (though I was only fourteen and dressed like myself—a working class tough girl in black shorts with make up and long black wings painted on my eyelids).

Where I came from people treated me like family, but they didn't invite strangers into the community quickly. An extrovert by nature, and coming from a family that was forever visiting others, I found it easy to endlessly hang out and visit in this strange new place. Young college people were everywhere, talking about everything from politics to weaving. Jeanie and I started hanging out at Barbara's apartment; then her mom let her live with Barbara one summer, and I more or less lived there, too.

The day after my sixteenth birthday, on October 15, 1969, I marched in the nationwide moratorium against the war in Vietnam, along with thousands in Minneapolis and millions across the country. Laura Nyro was singing "Save the Children" on the radio: "Babies in the blinking sun / Singing 'We Shall Overcome'." Being welcomed into a community of bright, defiant, and idealistic young college students who believed that people could get together to change things, to stop the authorities who were sending young men to die and kill for no good reason, infused me with a sense of belonging, hope, and purpose. I was at once given an outlet for my gathering anger and embraced by a community where "all you need is love." That solidarity, the huge symbiotic wave of us—singing and chanting down power and death—that sense of belonging and hope has never left me.

Eventually, Barbara moved into a collective household where Jeanie and I were regular guests for elaborate vegetarian dinners, political discussions, a wonder of books (like *Do It!*, *Steal This Book*, *Native Son*, *Stranger in a Strange Land*, and *The Hobbit*), oil painting, another incredible stereo system, tons of underground and folk music, and all the other cool things they did. Barbara liked to tutor me in cooking natural foods, cooperative economics, ecology, and anything else. I was rapt, listening to her talk about anything—even cooking, in which I had had no previous interest. I went from being rebellious against authority in general to rebelling against more specific authorities, like the U.S. Congress and President Johnson.

My high school boyfriend, John, was from the opposite side of the Twin Cities, a much wealthier southern suburb. We had met at the Minnesota State Fair, in St. Paul. He and I embraced the counterculture together. We took my mother to task for replacing the old metal ice cube trays with plastic ones: "It *never* biodegrades, Ma! Your ice cube trays will be here forever! Where are they going to put all this junk, Mom? The planet is filling up with plastic junk."

"Bio-de-what!?" Mom exclaimed with a wry grin. "You're telling me my buying ice cube trays is going to destroy the planet?" and she laughed in her sarcastic New York way. "Well, now that I've already bought them, should I send them to the planet to be junk? Since they're going to last forever, wouldn't it be okay if I used them for a while?" Then she laughed her husky cigarette laugh. It was hard to not laugh with her when she talked that way.

When I graduated from high school at seventeen, in 1971, my parents gave me one month's rent money to leave home and stop fighting with my mother. My idol, Barbara, went off with her guy to live on a farm, as so many of the counterculture did, along with other friends who bought land nearby. Within five months I made a year-long move to Anchorage, Alaska, with a new, older, and terribly intellectual boyfriend, where I worked in a ceramics factory and a restaurant.

Passing: Class in the Counterculture

Coming home a year later, I immersed myself in the life Barbara had had by becoming a university student and joined the heart of the counterculture by working for years in the burgeoning co-op movement of the 1970s. Those were years when grants and student loans were readily available. I attended the U of M full time studying studio art and political science, and worked at the co-op for a year without pay, while working in a downtown bakery for money. When the co-op finally was able to offer four people a very minimal wage, I felt lucky to be working in the movement for actual money. I dropped out of the U. In the co-ops, the camaraderie of being "freeks" together, practicing communal values, was not so unlike the white working class neighborhood where I grew up (though political views seemed almost diametrically opposed), which made this transition possible for me.

In the counterculture all you needed were jeans, sweatshirts, and the long antique dresses we found for quarters at a local rag store. The tribal spirit was so strong you could almost feel it embrace you. This type of rebellion was one my developing mind could embrace without having to change my sense of being something of an outlaw. And the enemy appeared to be roughly the same, authority in general, but this time I could fight with focus and solidarity, and I was armed with facts. I still had plenty of community; but this one had focus and power. And it gave me a new path to the future, something my working class life limited to getting married and having kids. I wanted, in the words I found to use at the time, "a life of the mind." Maybe it was all those movies about New York that I watched at night with my mother, but I knew there was a very big world out there with untold mysteries. I wanted at it.

I flourished within these intentional communities. We created dozens of community food co-ops, bakeries, and warehousing "collectives" (businesses run by and for those who work there). We developed many practical talents together (e.g., growing and distributing food), and also created collectively run cafés, where we built stages for people to play music and read poetry. I joined a co-op community newspaper and learned all the skills involved in production, developing my writing ability in a collective of budding writers. I had been writing since I was a small child; now everything I wrote came out in print and went to hundreds of people. These cooperative businesses inspired a lot of fun, good will, and more community. At that time, for all my other leftist politics, *I* thought I was middle class. I thought everyone was, except the poor and the rich, as I had been told.

But I knew I wasn't middle class like some others in the movement, and I believed I wasn't as smart as they were. I knew my brain worked okay, but they knew more, lots more, and I wanted what they had. They often referred to authors I had never read or even heard of. They used words I didn't understand, and they often talked about their college experiences, worldly travel, orchestral music, and other things with which I had little opportunity and experience. They appeared to all understand one another, but sometimes I just pretended I understood, and then I felt ashamed of both not knowing and pretending. By then my parents had enough money to buy lots of things, but money couldn't buy what I wanted, nor did they show any interest in helping me with "this *college* deal"—with emphasis on *college*, to point out it was a silly idea.

By my mid-twenties, mainly through my involvement in the grassroots women's movement, I had figured out that having a meat-cutter for a dad and a mother who sold stuff on the telephone made me working class. In the women's movement, class was an issue that was dealt with in a less abstract manner than in the rest of the New Left, since the personal was considered political. By the time I discovered I was working class, it was considered a good thing—in the upside-down middle class world of the counterculture, the women's movement, and the New Left at that time— so I was unashamed of the fact. I even got a bit of clout for it. Still, even as these college kids rejected their class's focus on individual achievement in favor of community, they had been so steeped in the culture of the professional and managerial middle class, and personal achievement and "self-actualization" were so much a part of how they approached life, that I slowly learned, within the community-oriented counterculture, to develop my individual abilities, to be an individual. I read. I made oil paintings, wrote poetry, played guitar and sang in our co-op cafés. I worked on several community newspapers, and toured the upper Midwest in a collective feminist theater group. I didn't walk, I *flew* into this new world. I became, as a poster I had in the 1970s proudly proclaimed, "a woman giving birth to herself."

Because I was still ashamed of all the more intangible aspects of my upbringing—my speech, spelling, energetic and emotional personal style, my inability to read sheet music, even, and sometimes especially, my own family—I was reinventing myself. I was becoming a middle class leftist, a feminist, and a class warrior who had shame for all the cultural, psychological, and linguistic aspects of her own class! These cultural leftovers of my working class upbringing did not fit in this new world, however alternative to the real middle class it was supposed to be. Since that time, these conflicting values or ways of life—communal belonging versus individual blossoming or "becoming"—have been an ongoing internal struggle. This book is one of the fruits of that struggle.

The Inner Life of Class

I was twenty-two when I first read Lillian Rubin's *Worlds of Pain* and Richard Sennett's *Hidden Injuries of Class*, two groundbreaking books about the inner lives of working class people. An already repressed pain suddenly blossomed into consciousness. The differences between working and middle class people were obscured in the movement, as we all wore faded jeans and sweatshirts, few had cars, and we ate cheap whole foods from co-op groceries and cafés. I had learned that if you speak the way other people do, they assume you are one of them. The down side of this was that I was privy to what they thought about people like my family. I admired and respected these downwardly mobile college students. I wanted to be smart like them. But at the same time I felt inferior and shameful for my working class habits of speech and "manners."

The political activist group I was eventually drawn to most was called Movement for a New Society. I liked MNS because (unlike the rest of the New Left) it fostered a deep sensitivity to process issues, feminism, human feelings, and, especially, the inner life of oppression issues that I had only seen previously in terms of real world justice. In MNS we used a kind of peer counseling that was in fashion at the time: Re-evaluation Co-counseling (RC). Like other humanistic therapies of the mid-twentieth century, there was a stress on "discharging" strong emotions, pounding pillows, crying, and the like, but with the addition of a strong cognitive piece: "clearness" or clear, rational thinking after emotional discharge.

Oppressed people were encouraged to counsel on the subject of their oppression in front of a group, letting people from the oppressor group listen and learn about the inner experience of being, say, a woman who is afraid of rape whenever she is out and alone at night. MNS and RC organized "speak-outs" where all the members of an oppressed group (like the few working class folks) were encouraged to say anything they chose to say, or feel, about their experiences in life or in MNS or RC. For me, these experiences meant coming to understand that I was working class and not just inferior. At the same time, I was being encouraged to feel and say everything I could about it, which turned out to be a lot.

In the speak-outs of RC and MNS, working class people said they didn't like being preached the gospel of simple living by middle class leftists whose parents routinely gave them so much: brand-new gas-saving automobiles, while we drove huge, ugly beaters that produced clouds of nasty blue smoke; college tuition; multiple medical necessities; and sometimes even the up-front cash to buy the big old houses wherein we gathered and lived collectively. People talked about feeling stupid when others corrected their grammar and spelling, and were angry that—even in the counterculture— Standard English was still considered the way that smart people speak.

Working class activists talked about how the meetings and actions we organized seemed middle class. These speakers made our group's implicit middle class rules explicit, so we could look at them—the reserved politeness and quiet tone of our events, the "wait your turn" nature of all our discussions, the fear and squelching of conflict within the group. We were tired of being regarded as too loud, too confrontational, too direct, too mouthy—too working class. We countered that our fellow middle class activists knew how to use silence to judge and hurt others. "I'd rather someone just yell at me and get it over with," someone said. Working class MNS folks also talked about not having anything to fall back on: the money to buy new glasses or for getting their rotting teeth fixed, as well as how often they felt they paid their fair share at a restaurant, while others with far more resources would find ways to get out of paying for things, like by ordering a whole lot for themselves and then saying, "Let's just divide it evenly."

We thought they were obsessed with picky details like making sure everyone used the correct terms ("women" not "girls," "young people" not "kids," "men" not "male," etc.) or having meetings start exactly on time. We felt they overplanned, and they didn't seem to know how to make meetings fun. Indeed, we felt that "fun" must have very different meanings in the world they came from than our own. We cried and laughed loudly, and enjoyed breaking the unspoken rules. In essence we were developing a critique of middle class cultural norms.

These experiences gave me an extraordinary opportunity to learn about class from the inside out, hearing the inner lives of dozens of others who were encouraged to speak about being raised poor and/or working class. This method also produced a proportionate amount of middle class guilt in folks raised with what I now call "cultural capital," that is to say, they had knowledge that came from being raised in the culture of the professional middle class. After the joy of solidarity, it was very painful to admit the differences between myself and my middle class New Left peers; and, clearly, it was hard for them to hear. But I really can't imagine a more supportive way to question the psychological dynamics of class difference between working and middle class people or to expose the often-subtle expressions of *classism*, or prejudice against working class people, including their lifestyles and cultural norms.

Class shame gradually turned to pride as I realized that it *was* intelligence that allowed me to be able to "pass" as middle class without any of the training they had received. It helped to find out my new friends from the real middle class had already completed college, their parents had bought them their cars, and that they grew up speaking the ways I had only just learned. They could play piano because they had been *forced* to take lessons as a matter of course. It wasn't that they were smarter, or better, it was that they had had privileges I had not. I moved away from a sense of individual shame, and blame, to seeing class as cultural, not just about economic injustice.

I was painfully aware that I was switching back and forth between two very different worlds. I began to realize that the invisibility of working class culture is part of the larger injustice of class in America (alongside concrete issues like workers' rights, fair pay, decent benefits, and control on the job). This missing personal and cultural dimension of class seemed glaring to me when I was among left-wing radicals who would champion working class liberation, then make fun of rednecks and trailer trash. Just as having to punch a time card or ask permission to go to the toilet can be an erasure of one's humanity, so too the invisibility of working class life—the warmth, loyalty, belly laughs, spontaneous fun, and shared tragedies—erases the real lives of working class people.

College, Culture, and Community Psychology

After a couple years of being very jealous of my middle class friends and comrades—"It's my turn!" I had wailed in a speak-out—I got my ass in gear, buckled down, and went back to college in my late twenties and early thirties. I was more than ready to tackle college again, and I sailed through with a 4.0 average. No longer an art student, I concentrated on getting job skills. The confidence and skills I gained in these cooperative communities, where I was allowed to be a leader though I was without professional qualifications or even a college degree, prepared me to handle almost anything in the middle class, except perhaps the eventual loss of community.

In my early thirties I wrote my graduate thesis, "The Invisible Culture: Psychotherapy and the Working Class Client." I focused on class, culture, and classism. I set out to find the facts that would support or disprove the experience-based subjective knowledge that came from my own and others' life experiences (Belinky et al. 1986). I found very little research on the inner life of class, but what I did find firmly supported, and expanded, the subjective knowledge I had received (Bernstein 1971; Jones 1974; Meltzer 1978; Heath 1996; Ryan and Sackrey 1996).

Perhaps not surprisingly, I became a counseling and *community* psychologist. In my development as a young psychologist, I went from undergraduate intern to full-time lead therapist in a therapeutic psychiatric community for twenty-four young adults. While continuing my involvement in both the cooperative and women's movements, I joined a therapy staff at Janus Treatment Residence that was full of other aging alternative types and operated as a collective. We offered whole foods cooking with other independent-living skills, art therapy, drama therapy, dance therapy, and dream therapy in addition to family, addiction, and other talk-based psychotherapies. When I look back I am struck with how much healing and joy was possible within that community.

Around this same time, I began what would turn out to be a half-a-lifetime of pilgrimages to New York City to connect with my mother's sister, Flora, and her family. This family had books, art, discussed sociology and history, and valued college education—everything I had worked so hard for so long to grasp! Flora had put her husband, my Uncle Milton, through school, and he was an academic at Hunter College in New York City.

It was as if some dream from childhood in which I fantasized being reunited with my "real" parents, who I thought had been stolen from me by these angry strangers who had taken their place, had come true. After many years of silence between my mother and her only sibling, Flora welcomed me with open arms. I began going to New York for Thanksgivings and Passovers and as many other times as I could manage. Here, it was finally "normal" for me to want to be a professional, to love art, to read as many books as I could get my hands on, to dine on Thai food, and to go to the theater. I fell in love with New York, the city my mother had mourned the loss of throughout my childhood.

I have struggled long and hard to bridge my Aunt Flora's cosmopolitan world with the working class world of my mother and father. I have struggled even longer to integrate my working class and middle class selves: Barb, the tribal or pack animal (as a work colleague once called me) and Barbara, the individual with honors and distinction. My ongoing membership in these two very different cultures has led to a lifelong balancing act. Since I began my private practice in 1989, I have often worked with middle class people from working class backgrounds, people who are currently working class, and with many couples in which each person hails from a different class background than the other. I have also worked for decades in an inner-city alternative high school with young people from a variety of class backgrounds, and I frequently mediate discussions between kids from different classes.

In my clinical work, as in my experiences as a young adult crossing the class divide, I have found dramatic demonstration that working class and middle class folks come from different cultures. Yes, we are all American and share certain characteristics of American culture. But I have repeatedly found those same differences of inner life that I saw so vividly illustrated in MNS and RC speak-outs in my counseling work.

My particular profession, counseling psychology, all too frequently considers working class people and cultures unhealthy in and of themselves. By that I mean that to help the working class folks that come to see us, we encourage them to "get ahead" by going to college, to find meaningful work, as we see it, and to actualize (use) their abilities. In short, to become more middle class. Among professionals in general, just the fact of someone being in the working class is considered a sign of failure to achieve, at least in the "socioeconomic status" model. This model sees class in the United States as having steps on a ladder and that those who work the hardest move to the upper rungs while those nearer the bottom belong there and are thus granted much lower pay, power, and control in their work lives (Torlina 2011).

This view is pure bullshit. My personal and professional lives, as well as the research reported in this book, contradict this commonly accepted middle class assumption. My family members are the hardest workers I know. Also, I have encountered some folks on the upper rungs—psychologists, college teachers, lawyers, doctors, executives, and other professionals—who do not work very hard. They got where they are because they *started* on the upper rungs. As Jim Hightower put it: they were born on third base but think they hit a triple!

Border Patrol

So, here I sit, in between my two worlds. I am in the upper middle class, at least culturally (if not economically). I watch people from my present world make fun of people from my first world on my Facebook page. I also see people from my first world make fun of the people in my second world. I try to mediate, but no one seems to be listening.

On one side of the class boundary, there are the real lives of working class people, however varied they are, that is all but completely invisible to anyone not of their class. And the disinterest goes both ways—they don't care what *people like that* think of them. The trouble is that the people they don't care about administer so many of the invisible particulars of their lives, deciding whether there are jobs or not, what they get paid at work, whether or not there are layoffs or forced overtime, the kind of education their children will receive in school, their ability to fact-check what crooked politicians and preachers holler at them, and much more.

On the other side of the class boundary, in my middle class world, there are the ones who really believe they deserve so much more than the working class. They don't talk about what they make because it is considered rude in the middle class to do so. But, while they may make anywhere from $20 to $1,500 an hour, they are the stockholders who vote to take away $2 an hour from people who make, and try to support a family on, $10 an hour. They work hard, too. They are not the upper class, the ultimate masters of the American universe. But they routinely dismiss and denigrate working class people, laughing at their language, making fun of their political views, and denigrating their religion.

I have developed a dual vision in which I can't help but see things from the points of view of both of my classes. I also have two voices, one I use in my family and with other working class folks, and one I use in my professional life and with middle class friends. I have learned in my double life that working and middle class people value disparate communication styles: they use words and explain things very differently. Within these language styles we find the distinct cultures they represent. This leads us to the subject of this book: class and culture and the way they conspire to aid and abet *classism*, that is, prejudice against working class people, including their language, cultures, and communities.

I do not blame middle class people for their ignorance of the working class, nor am I trying to divide people into good guys and bad guys. I ascribe no malice to middle class people who may believe they are superior due to their knowledge of high culture, their positions of power and responsibility, their relative material success, or anything else. Very good people can have substantial class prejudice. Class is enormously mystified and complex in the United States, and largely hidden from view. On either side of the class divide, what we know and have been taught is our "normal." All of us are peppered with prejudices, with "them and us" mentalities, with the sense that our people are the best ones. Working class people, too, can puff themselves up with a sense of moral superiority to those farther down the class hierarchy, and sometimes those above them (Lamont 2000; Torlina 2011).

I offer this book toward repair of class divisions that, I believe, leave both individuals and our nation psychologically, culturally, economically, and politically poorer than we should be. In it I use both of my voices and different ways of thinking to give voice to the silent inner life of working class people in America. I challenge the myth that most Americans are middle class. I uncover a wide cultural divide between the professional middle class, who mostly use their minds to work with symbols such as writing, designing, and teaching, and the working class, who use their hands and heads to make and work with things, such as building houses and growing or cooking food. I also suggest that class has parceled out different aspects of humanity to different groups; everyone loses and gains something important as a result.

I hope to show aspects of working class life that are invisible to most middle class people, and perhaps to working class people as well. I also want to show how people in working class life fare within our larger society. I especially want to give voice to hidden aspects of working class cultures. I want to show and explain working class experience from a psychological and cultural point of view, as these aspects are least likely to show up on the radar of the upper class and professional middle class.

In particular, I want to show how class becomes class*ism*. Class says, "These people will do the work that is low paid, dangerous, or deadening." Class*ism* pipes up to say, "They will do it because it is all they deserve; other people deserve more freedom, control, respect, and money than these people do." Classism stereotypes and stigmatizes working class people simply for doing manual labor, from the hardest and dirtiest jobs to highly skilled work, such as machining, that involves incredible skill and intelligence. Without this work the United States could not function. But there are moral values many working class cultures hold that indirectly and invisibly point working class people away from the middle class.

I want to show what may not be visible when one looks through the lens of middle class culture. To do this, I use my own life, as well as the lives of my students, therapy clients, and relatives, as cases in point for the anguish of class issues in our society. I use these stories, alongside academic research, as a lens to bring into focus the clash between personal and community development and our larger society's expectations of working class folks. I examine child rearing and schooling—of very young children, of elementary school children, of high school age adolescents, and then of college students and young professionals—as practiced by different classes. I do this in sequence so that we can see how, at every point in their personal development and educational history, working class children are misunderstood, ignored, or disrespected by the middle class people who administer the particulars of their school and work lives.

2

THE INVISIBLE ISM

We are a nation born of idealism as well as the desire to abolish near-absolute class differences in particular. In America the fact of distinct classes is a contradiction of our basic value of equality of opportunity. Perhaps that is why it is so hard for Americans to admit we even live in a society that is divided into different classes, or to see how drastically class divisions have increased over the last thirty years.

Class can be broken down into more subtle categories within both the working and middle classes (Labov 1970; Vanneman and Cannon 1987; Fussell 1992; Lareau and Conley 2009). There are significant differences between, say, the lower and upper middle class, just as there are between the upper and lower working class—or between the working and poverty classes. These distinctions are beyond the scope of this chapter, and to a large extent, this book. I prefer a vernacular approach to defining class in America: rich, middle class, working class, and poor, though some very good arguments have been made for other definitions, for example: capitalist class, middle class, and working class (Metzgar 2005; Zweig 2005, quoted in Russo and Linkon 2005).

The kind of cultural differences and societal injuries I describe in this book are true for people within the broader categories of working and middle classes. In other words, I am favoring a *categorical* use of the terms working class and middle class, rather than a *gradational* or socioeconomic status one. I believe class-related family and cultural practices clearly cohere into foundational psychological patterns within these categories (Lareau 2003; Lareau and Conley 2008; Torlina 2011).

For individuals looking to define class in their lives or backgrounds, I favor definitions that are based on, though not necessarily limited to, lived experience and common sense. For my purposes, working class people work at manual labor, with both their heads and hands, and middle class people work mainly with symbols, mental products, and processes. In preparing for this book I interviewed my father's siblings on their work histories and thoughts about class. Every one of them identified still as working class when given a choice between working class and middle class. Education is also a class indicator as, after high school, most working class people do not obtain a college education but, rather, go to trade or tech schools, no schools, or to community colleges. In middle class life, getting at least a four-year college degree is expected (and saved for), and it matters a lot whether one goes to the "best" schools, best being defined by how much prestige the school has in the work world.

Let me be clear: I believe economic power, not culture, is the spine of class in the United States—what holds it up and in place. In 2007, the wealthiest ten percent of households owned 73.1 percent of all household wealth in America (Zweig 2012). While this book is about cultural divisions, it would be entirely missing the forest for the trees to ignore the economic conditions that produce and reproduce class in America. If culture is the medium through which class inequality is recreated—the arms, hands, and legs of class—it is still economic power that is its spinal column—the core of class in America. Nor are class divisions static; they are dynamic "living fighting entities," and the borders and boundaries between all four classes change with the times (Zweig 2005, from Linkon and Russo 2005). The top 20 percent of the U.S. population in terms of wealth gained about 89 percent of the wealth created by our nation between 1983 and 2007; the remaining 80 percent of households gained just 11 percent of that wealth (Zweig 2012).

The upper fifth of the population (by wealth) increased its net worth by some 70 percent from 1970 to 1995, according to economist Michael Zweig

(2000), and the greatest portion of that wealth went to the top 1 percent. In 1983 the wealthiest 1 percent had an average net worth of $9.1 million (adjusted for inflation); by 2007, the average had more than doubled to $18.5 million. At the same time the bottom 40 percent of households saw their average net worth drop by 62 percent, and their indebtedness, excluding homes, increased by 160 percent as they scrambled to make ends meet on an average annual income of $20,200 in 2006 (Zweig 2012). That is all to say that there has been an enormous redistribution of wealth in the United States since the years when I was growing up in my stable working class community. The top 1 percent of the population in terms of wealth collectively received 1.35 *trillion* dollars in 2006, according to Robert Frank (2007, 3), more than the entire economies of France, Canada, or Italy. Then our top-heavy economy started to fall apart.

Knowledge about the inner life of class should not replace or be disconnected from knowledge of the very concrete and drastic inequality that class itself creates in America. Economic power, and the social control it can buy, is very real. In the early years of the twenty-first century class has heaped enormous rewards on people who do certain kinds of work: professional, corporate/managerial, and especially the upper, or capitalist, class. Others have to fight just to see a doctor or get an education, while in other civilized (and less wealthy) nations these things are offered to all citizens as basic rights. The economic fact that most working class people have had lower wages for four decades, which has led to significantly more inequality than when I was young, is crucial to understanding working class experience today.

Even so, it is a mistake to reduce working class experience to nothing but jobs and justice. A small, ordinary example of power in cultural action is found in Sennett and Cobb's *The Hidden Injuries of Class* (1972), in which they describe two men, a construction worker and a schoolteacher. They were next-door neighbors, friendly, and their incomes were roughly the same. Nevertheless, the schoolteacher called the construction worker by his first name and the construction worker called his neighbor "mister." In our larger society, the dominant (middle class) culture awards far more status and money, for example, to middle class work and individuals who demonstrate outstanding verbal or mathematical ability, while it ignores or vilifies those who do manual labor and come from traditional communities of care and deep life-long connections (emotional intelligence).

Class is an injustice that says some Americans deserve much more time, leisure, control, and far more financial reward than others. Class*ism* is the set of myths and beliefs that keep those class divisions intact, that is, the belief that working class cultures and people are inherently inferior and that class itself demonstrates who the hardest workers and the rightful winners are. My concern in this book is to highlight how culture plays into class, and especially class*ism*. By "culture" I mean a constellation of accepted values, customs, mores, attitudes, styles, behaviors, and, especially, worldview—the shared *unconscious mind* of a community, to put it in psychological terms.

Class-Based Cultures

Cultures are the medium through which class inequality manifests itself. To give you an example of how culture works, I offer a story that illustrates my particular region's divisions based on class and culture. These specifics are not intended to be universal, as working class cultures vary greatly by region, ethnicity, gender, race, and other factors (though, as we will see, they do share some fundamental factors).

I went to two Lutheran confirmation celebrations in the late 1990s— same day, same town, same white clapboard country church. Though living only a few miles from each other, the two families were worlds apart. One of the two girls was working class, one middle class, though the single mothers throwing the parties, an executive secretary and a nurse, earned roughly the same amount of money. Two Lutheran confirmation parties with two different social *meanings*.

At the working class celebration, my aunties and uncles and most of my cousins and their spouses showed up, as they do for most of our many family events. When I arrived, my cousin Linda shouted across the living room, where the aunties and other women were visiting, "Hey Sunshine! You finally got out of bed and decided to grace us with your presence!" She laughed her great big laugh, traversed the tangle of people, and gave me her bear hug.

"Nice to see you, too!" I retorted and made my way into the room hugging various aunties and cousins. Everyone was complimenting the hostess on her new split-level house she had bought with a divorce settlement. It was large, had a new deck in back, and a prominent beer stein collection above the kitchen cupboards. The women were dressed in slacks or newer jeans. They wore casual knit cotton-poly tops that had big flowers and other patterns on them. They wore clean tennis shoes or other comfortable shoes. Their hair was generally curled, some in tight home permanents. Voices were often raised in exclamation. We were all "catching up," and sometimes the noise level got too high to hear well. People frequently called out across the room to one another.

Though the men were mostly gathered in the large clean garage, they traipsed through the living room and kitchen regularly to get food and drinks. Cousin Linda and I called out mouthy comments to them as they passed. They wore jeans or comfortable cotton pants, casual button-down shirts; my dad and big brother wore silver bolo ties and belts with large silver buckles. We ate tuna-noodle salad from a big Tupperware bowl, canned baked beans from a Crock-Pot, and a tossed-fruit salad. The hostess made white-bun sandwiches with presliced ham and Miracle Whip on the spot. Other women also took turns at this task. People were told to help themselves to Kool-Aid, soda pop, or coffee. All through the house, people hugged, laughed, and greeted each other with much affection. The crowd was all family except for the honored girl's closest friends.

Very little attention was paid to the fifteen-year-old girl who had been confirmed, aside from initial greetings and cards with checks in them. She spent most of her time downstairs in the lower half of this new split-level house, sprawled on her boyfriend's lap watching TV with her siblings, friends, and some younger members of the extended family, occasionally going outside to smoke cigarettes. Separate spaces for adults and young people is typical in my family. The others also stared at the screen, though they talked freely and loudly. The confirmed girl was the only one there in a dress. The most common comment made to her was on her dress and how pretty she looked. To which the girl kind of apologized, pulled uncomfortably at the hem and said she felt "weird in it," that she had just bought it the day before, that she never wears dresses.

People were there to "pay respects" and to visit with one another; the checks in the cards were important, something kids in my family count on. I didn't hear anyone ask the girl who had been confirmed anything about her confirmation. It was an expected Lutheran tradition; we all understood it as an accomplishment signaling her movement toward adulthood. All were relieved that she had managed to do it—a couple years behind schedule—after a few years of trouble that followed her parents' divorce and led to her being placed in a foster home for a while. All family events are yet another opportunity for a reunion. At one point I asked her, privately, how she felt about being confirmed. She said, "It took long enough!" and went on to say she was just glad that she finally did it, but she felt embarrassed it took so long. Uncharacteristically, she spoke frankly about herself for a while with me. I felt soft with love for her and grateful she opened up and we connected, as I hadn't seen her for quite a while. I was impressed with her ability to both know and express her inner life.

At the other confirmation party, that of a middle class friend's daughter, a few miles away, the hostess warmly greeted me at the door. This mother's much smaller townhouse was decorated with framed posters of paintings by Miró and Modigliani, hand-painted stenciling along the ceiling, and antique furniture. The first things I noticed on arrival were how quietly everyone here spoke and the absence of laughter. People talked in small mixed-gender groups or pairs, smiled a lot and chuckled occasionally but did not laugh out loud. There were no separate places for men and women; there were no separate places for children and adults. These women generally wore midcalf-length dresses or skirts of linen, silk, or rayon. The outfits were muted solid colors with the occasional tiny pattern. Some women wore "suits" of slacks and matching blouses. Hair was loosely curled or it was short and sharply cut. I was dressed and coifed like these women. Most of the men wore jackets and some wore ties; they wore good slacks; many wore pullover knit tops; the ones with ties wore fancy button-down oxford shirts. No one wore jeans. Everyone wore leather shoes.

In this celebration the girl who had been confirmed was at the center of the living room and the day. She had made several art projects for people to view, including a small "tree" with pictures of her at various ages and a scrapbook with photographs of her and various attendees at her celebration. These were her family members, but also other adults who had been important in her life. Sitting in the living room with the adults, she rose and greeted people as they came in, showing them their photographs in her book. She encouraged people to write their names in a guest book so that she could keep track of who had attended her celebration and send thank you cards. I don't remember seeing any of her peers there.

We ate quiche, a creative version of escalloped potatoes, and wedges of freshly baked ham kept in a warming server. The fruit was sliced and arranged in a lovely pattern on an elegant serving plate. There was a delicious punch the hostess had invented that day, served in a glass punch bowl, along with freshly brewed coffee. In one room sat an artist who had been hired to do caricature portraits as a party novelty.

When I asked this girl what the day meant to her, it was clear she had already spent time thinking and talking about it. "I think of it as a restatement of my baptismal vows," she replied. She went on to explain that those vows had been made *for* her as an infant, but now she was "an adult in the eyes of the Church, and I am able to make that commitment for myself." When complimented on her dress, she replied "thank you" and smiled, though she was not any more prone to wearing dresses than the other girl. I was impressed with this young woman's keen intellect.

These two teen-aged Lutheran girls from Minnesota were raised with different expectations in different cultures. Understanding the role of culture in class-based differences allowed me to enjoy each party in its own right. Each celebration felt normal and right to the people who attended it, and they would likely feel uncomfortable at the other one. We learn our core values and sense of what is proper behavior (who we are and what life is for) from our immediate influences (family, neighborhood, ethnic group). Each confirmation meant the girl was on her way to adulthood, but each has a very different idea of what that "adulthood" should look like.

Since both parties had mostly Scandinavian Americans in attendance, holding ethnicity constant, they are useful for seeing class as culture. Because of my odd ethnic heritage, I can tell you that all Minnesota Scandinavians are quiet compared with New York Jews, but when compared with other people of Scandinavian descent, the working class folks were quite a bit louder than the middle class ones. The trick is to be able to identify cultural differences *in their own context,* instead of merely assuming the superiority of the one that is most familiar.

In this story, the girls' abilities point to the different unconscious emphases of their cultures: the first girl's psychological ability to open up emotionally and connect, her genuineness and lack of personal defense versus the other girl's intellectual ability to conceptualize, articulate, and present the meaning of the event. Both girls were smart and sensitive; I feel each of them was capable of either response. The cultural difference is in which kind of response first "came naturally" (Adlam, Turner, and Lineker 1977).

Style and general attitude differences are obvious in the story, and while they may not apply well to some ethnic groups or regions, they point to differences in values that may occur across ethnicities and geography. In the middle classes some amount of "self-actualization" is expected, and individual accomplishment is admired. Community generally trumps individuality in the working class; being a show off might make others "feel bad," and how you treat others is more important than being a winner.

The story shows many opposing values: tradition versus distinction—the same Kool-Aid and tuna-noodle hot dishes show up at every reunion; extroverted personal warmth and intimacy versus emotional reserve and friendly politeness; conversation about the intimate details of people's lives (the women) and things or activities, especially cars and fishing (the men), versus discussion of ideas and one's special activities—achievements, awards, travel; the importance of being able to just hang out and feel comfortable together versus individual verbal ability and intellectual sparring; hanging out to "see what happens" versus structured activities.

Middle class and working class cultures are not wholly separate categories but are rather like clouds of culture—of learned styles, behaviors, and values—that overlap in the larger sky of American society. But the sun in that sky shines much more brightly on middle class culture, highlighting it and leaving working class cultures largely in shadow. Both cultures share many features of American society in general, but beneath those veneers lay worlds of difference. Each arises from a different worldview, each produce differences in who people are—in how they think and speak, in how they regard themselves and the world around them, in what they consider normal and good manners.

The different expectations in these two Lutheran settings move from class *difference* to class*ism* only with the assumption that the middle class setting is superior, when working class cultures are judged harshly by standards that are not their own. In our larger society this is often the case, especially in crucial avenues of access to success in adulthood: schools and workplaces.

What Is Classism?

In *The Hidden Injuries of Class*, Sennett and Cobb stepped back in history a couple hundred years to find a stark illustration of class prejudice:

In a letter to a friend, Madame de Sevigne writes about a hanging she witnessed one morning. It was striking, she records, to see the condemned man trembling during the preliminaries of the execution when he was only a common peasant. He groaned and wailed incessantly, causing some amusement to the ladies and gentlemen come to see the spectacle; once hoisted up, his body wriggling in a noose, he presented, Madame de Sevigne remarked, "a most remarkable sight." . . . Yet Madame de Sevigne was not a vicious woman by the standards of the late seventeenth century. She, like other aristocrats of her circle, could view hangings with disinterested fascination, because the person being killed was a creature whose inner nature had little relation to her own. (246–47)

In this snapshot of classism, we find the stark skeleton of class-based prejudice that has survived into our historical moment in a more muted and subtle form. Classism in America is based on the assumption of the superiority of middle (and upper) class styles, tastes, attitudes, and values. *Everyone* is taught in school which ones are the "good" manners, "proper" English, the "good" schools, the "best" occupations. Everyone sees the movies and other media telling which are the "normal" people. The assumption that professional and managerial advancement is the measure of human worth is hammered at all of us from virtually every major social institution. Classism delivers its harsh judgments on working class styles, values, and behaviors. These features are seen as having "no class," or being subnormal, by middle class people, but they are really threads in a larger fabric of working class culture.

Classism has been the single most destructive psychological factor in my process of crossing, then straddling, classes. At the heart of the invisible passage from one world to another is the assumption, everywhere in the middle class, that working class life is simply inferior in all ways. This is classism.

Classism is psychologically destructive to people because, once internalized, it can result in a profoundly divided self, the loss of life-long family and community ties, and/or a confusing present where one feels "nowhere at home" (Ryan and Sackrey 1996). It is equally destructive to American society at large because it divides well-meaning Americans, working class and middle class folks, needlessly from each other. It also keeps them from recognizing that together they make up the vast majority in this country, and that middle class and working class people have much more in common, at least economically, than either have with the upper, or capitalist, class.

I want to flag some of the varying forms classism takes, as *cruelty* is only one of these forms. Class-based cruelty, though nowhere near the level of Madame Sevigne's time and aristocratic class, survives to this day. In the early1930s, kids at school made fun of my father for his ragged clothes and shoes and, when he got angry at them, they forced him to sit in an "electric chair" of thorns and other painful items. In 2004, Alfred Lubrano wrote about privileged students at Ivy League colleges who held coins to a flame and then dropped them from a second-story window onto the sidewalk below, laughing at the scholarship students who walked by and tried to pick up the hot coins. In 2007, "sport killings" of homeless people hit the headlines, as did a popular computer game called Bum Killing. In 2011, the phrase "tea-tards" is gaining traction, describing the "retarded" "tea party" sympathies of some—a magnified minority—working class folks.

But the most common form of classism is *solipsism*, or my-world-is-the-whole-world, what I call class-blinders. This is the tendency to assume everyone has had the same experience we have had and to be blind to the experiences of people unlike ourselves. "We made fun of them, the people who lived in those tacky, ugly, little trailers. We said, 'Who would want to live in a metal box?,'" a middle class classism workshop participant confided with remorse. "We didn't understand they couldn't afford houses like ours." Middle class people often disdain or make fun of working class people's styles and behaviors as if we were all raised the very same way and these individuals just don't get it. Societywide institutions, like public education, do the same thing: presume we all think and learn like middle class people do, that we all work best as individuals in competition. American education then punishes kids who have not learned to work best this way.

Solipsism is often accompanied by *judgments of taste*: another form of classism. "Oh my God, she had plastic flowers and the couch was orange plaid! Plastic flowers are so *tacky*. She had no class at all," a counseling client said of her new mother-in-law when they first met, as if a few style indicators said everything there was to know about her mother-in-law. "He was a real Archie Bunker type, you know, a redneck racist pig," another client once said when he first met his adult older brother, who had been given up for adoption as a baby by his teenage mother. As it turned out, they had not discussed race at all. My white, college-educated client simply assumed this guy with a billed cap and nonstandard English must be a racist. As they got to know each other better he discovered that his brother was actually engaged to an American Indian woman and was very close with her family.

Negative judgments and stereotypes of people who have working class styles, values, speech, and behavior serve to punish people for being raised within their own cultures (Bernstein 1971; Bourdieu 1984). But whose standards say that framed prints of paintings by Miró are inherently and absolutely more "tasteful" or "classier" than a beer stein collection? Or that orchestral music is more meaningful than rock 'n' roll or hip-hop? As many have argued regarding ethnic prejudice and racism, judging one culture by the standards of another (dis)misses real people and their real lives.

Classism is also societal or *systemic domination*, and this is the most complicated, and effective, method way of keeping working people at or near the bottom of the economic ladder. For example, responsible working class adults routinely have to ask permission to go to the toilet if the need arises before their mandated fifteen-minute break from work, or to bring in a note of proof if they take half a day off work to see a doctor. Other Americans, in the middle class, would never dream of having to ask, indeed, are not required to do more than tell someone they will be in late because of an outside appointment. Nor do middle class folks have to use a time clock to prove their hours at work. Nor would they be asked to give up 20 percent of their pay, two dollars subtracted from a once ten dollars-an-hour job, *less than they can afford to live on*, simply to give stockholders a few more pennies per share that quarter. In the last four decades millions and millions of working class people have lost their skilled-labor jobs altogether and have only been offered entry-level service jobs (like fast food) that pay minimum wage in return.

Systemic or structural classism is a sometimes deliberate, sometimes inadvertent, dehumanizing and bullying of working class people within institutions such as the workplace and in schools. This happens by way of systematic exclusion and control: the exercise of power over people who cannot afford to resist. Concretely, this involves threats to fire workers who complain about poor conditions, or, more broadly, punishment of working class students who do not conform to middle class cultural norms in American public schools, as I will examine in this book. Class is the concrete division of groups of Americans into varying levels of control and authority, and increasingly unequal reward for different kinds of work. But, again, the *medium* of this control, or *how it works,* is through cultural mediums in everyday life (school and work). Nowhere is this as clear as in public education, the very system designed to produce greater equality of opportunity, perhaps our most cherished American value. Public schools enforce the exclusion and control of working class children through the routine use of middle class culture's assumptions and expectations, that is, expecting them to be from backgrounds other than their own.

That many middle class people believe their attitudes and styles are "normal" and that they tend to look down on working class people would not be a big deal if their class didn't run everything that creates image and policy in our society. Defining one's superiority in opposition to some "other" is hardly unique to the American middle and upper classes. Indeed, working class people and communities can also be stubbornly insular and have their own list of epithets for the middle class: eggheads, sissies, cold fish, pencil pushers, spoiled brats, and bloodsuckers are a few. Nor is classism (against those further down the class ladder) exclusive to the middle class.

But, as Barbara Ehrenreich has pointed out (1989), the professional-managerial middle class, by definition, selects and creates all the images and representations of society that everyone sees. Making movies, teaching, writing, publishing, radio, television—you name it—they are all *professional* jobs, and they define what is considered "cultured" and "normal" in the United States. Likewise, managers and managerial jobs, by definition, tell the rest of us what should and should not be done, said, and valued, at least at work.

Understanding classism is not about finding good guys and bad guys or the correct things to say or not say to working class people. Society, cultures, communities, family, and personality all shape what we think is right or wrong, as being "like me" or as "them." Still, despite our common, and very American, belief in human equality, classism is a powerful emotional experience. People feel fear, anger, disgust, revulsion, and even hatred toward other people they describe as "low class." And, sadly, classism can afflict "upwardly mobile" middle class folks originally from the working class, as much, sometimes more, than people born into relative privilege.

I have seen people on the receiving end cope with classism in a variety of ways: a reciprocal, generalized contempt for "rich people" or "yuppies" (by which they usually mean upper middle class people); a creeping dislike for their own culture and a drive to climb the class ladder; sometimes a paralyzing jealousy and sense of powerlessness. Some purposely embrace everything that might upset middle (and some working) class people, reveling in "outlaw" status, or at least the image of it (bikers, hippies, gangstas). I have seen reactions to class prejudice range from a shrug of indifference to feelings of profound shame and rage. But for those who struggle their way into the middle class, encountering classism can lead to the silencing of one's internal voice—and the whole of one's childhood. That denial, in turn, can lead to serious psychological obstacles inside one's own head and heart.

Three Recipes for Classism

In *Money, Morals, and Manners* (1992) Michèle Lamont investigated the values of 160 upper middle class white men (both American and French) and how they defined their own sense of superiority. I use this book now to better understand the core values and beliefs that fuel classism in America. The upper middle class, as defined by the salaries they command, makes up a relatively small percentage of the population (10–15%). While their numbers are not large, they are nonetheless powerfully influential in American society. "Their lives are held up as a model to the rest of the population by the mass media and the advertising industry. . . . [As] professors, consultants, architects, artists, advisors, psychologists and other 'makers of culture,' the ripples that issue from their powerful lives reach far and wide into American society" (xxiii). As business executives and managers, they have large numbers of people working with and for them.

Their responses clearly cohered into three different points of view or philosophies about their lives as winners in the American Dream and the nature of winning in the United States. Lamont's descriptions of attitudes and values in the upper middle class closely match my own observations as a counseling and community psychologist, as well as my personal experience as a middle class professional from the working class. In my extrapolation, these philosophies are three popular recipes for classism— three different ways to say, "I am better than they are." As we will see later, they arise from three different cultural *ways of becoming*, of self-actualizing, in middle class America. For all three groups the exclusion of people who are not "my kind" was openly discussed without embarrassment or apology.

> The people excluded by our boundaries are those with whom we refuse to associate and those toward whom rejection and aggression are showed, and distance openly marked, by way of insuring that "you understand that I am better than you are." (Lamont 1992, 10)

Cultural Classism

The idea of cultural superiority (and inferiority) is a long-standing feature in western European and American societies. *Culture*, in this usage, refers to the standards of "high culture," and has its roots in European aristocratic society, where Madame de Sevigne developed her view of the world. People unaware of "high culture" are often judged unfairly by those who have and value it. While inspiring some of our society's finest artistic, literary, and even humanitarian efforts, "high culture," and cultural classism, defines itself against "common" people and events. It is a ranking system whereby people, events, activities, and interests are considered "high" or "low" culture, or simply more or less "cultured"—synonymous with better and worse. It emphasizes family of origin, schools, and social standing, or, as an executive assistant friend of mine put it, "breeding, polish, and refinement." Cultural classism involves a host of harsh *judgments of taste*. This classism has no time for people with "tacky" or unoriginal clothing, furnishings, and art.

As Betsy Leondar-Wright put it in her 2005 book, *Class Matters:*

> Few middle-class people would say we have prejudices against working-class or low-income people, of course. Our classism is often disguised in the form of disdain for Southerners or Midwesterners, religious people, patriotic people, employees of big corporations, fat or non-athletic people, [heterosexual] people with conventional gender presentation (feminine women wearing make-up; tough, burly guys), country music fans, or gun users. This disdain shows in our speech. (89)

The sociologist Pierre Bourdieu (1984) popularized the term "cultural capital." His point was that presenting knowledge of high culture affords people respect and authority, as much, often more, than actual material wealth does. Cultural capital is the amount of information, interest, and facility one has with high culture, as opposed to a snobbishly dismissed popular culture. The attitude toward people who do not appreciate high culture is expressed with witty contempt: "philistines," or "the great unwashed." They, like me at one time, were quick to say, "I don't watch television, I'm not interested in pop culture." Fascinating, erudite, edifying, and exquisite are other words I learned to use at that time. People born into, or aspiring toward, this category, generally consider themselves more evolved than other people.

This is solipsism, or the inability to see beyond one's own world. The unspoken assumption is that everyone could know these things but that some are too primitive or unevolved to want to know. This classism is fueled by ignorance. It doesn't understand that not everyone has the same access to this information and, more important, not everyone *values* high culture as they do. There are many kinds of cultures with different values. Coming from a family with many religious members, and who all love country music and grow up learning to use guns safely, I was an unlikely candidate for life among people who value cultural capital.

But then I came in through the back door, through the rebellious student counterculture in the late 1960s at the age of fourteen. I shared the counterculture's critique of its members' privileged lives. These students taught me to enjoy white wine, fine art, classical music, choreography, and Russian and German novelists writing about the meaning of life. I was fascinated with ideas and philosophy, and in my working class world, my new college student friends were part of my own rebellion. They lent me books. As a teenager, I was reading Tolstoy, Dostoyevsky, and Hermann Hesse at night in my little twin bed in our tract house in Mounds View. I felt these authors spoke to my very soul, though I knew I didn't understand it all. I loved art, novelty, Beethoven, and all things creative.

Love of language propelled me further into this world. But this use of language—words where multiple, often ironic, meanings are intended; passages with various clever, high-culture references peppering the message—is for members of the supposed cultural elite alone. I loved this use of language when I found it, though as a young adult I only got about a quarter of the meanings. Even so I, in turn, used sophisticated language in an attempt to best my mother and big brother (who were, as usual, annoyingly unperturbed). Like the young adults in the movies *Breaking Away* and *My Brilliant Career*, I wanted "a life of the mind."

I also liked the antiestablishment students' liberal politics, their radical commitment to justice. They cared about class in economic and political terms, but in personal values and judgments, class was their great blind spot. They had contempt for real people from their idealized "working class." There I was, in a loving and large extended family with people who worked long, hard hours; I loved my family and knew them to be good and smart people. Eventually, my own life gave me a vantage point where I could see cultural classism as ignorant prejudice, even though, for a while, I fell prey to it.

Since this kind of classism is common, indeed is *currency*, in higher education, its reach is very long. Though fewer than a third of the Americans in Lamont's sample fell into this group, the rest of the upper middle class men she interviewed admitted they were most intimidated and insecure around the people and qualities of "high culture." I found an example of cultural classism on the Class Matters website: "I was eating lunch with a friend—someone who's proud to call herself a Massachusetts liberal—and the waitress got her order wrong. My friend treated the waitress just fine, but after she left the table, said to me, 'Well, if she was smart, she wouldn't be a waitress'" (Levison 2007).

William Pelz, a college teacher from the working class, had this to say about liberal arts:

> The point is that, at least for the working class and the mass of common people throughout history, much of the liberal arts are not liberal at all. What they are, even if cloaked in politically correct rhetoric, is profoundly conservative—conservative because while they may question the "meaning in life" or even the "problem" of poverty, they flinch like a vampire in sunlight from a concrete examination of the sources of class oppression. (Quoted in Dews and Law 1995, 283)

Moral Classism

In *Money, Morals, and Manners*, a second upper middle class group that cohered around a perceived superiority were those who defined themselves primarily in moral terms: both that their own hard work showed their moral character and by their moral commitment to use their privileges to help others. These men defined themselves (and their kind of people) by the intensity of their commitment to the powerful American "work ethic." Hard work, in and of itself, was considered a sign of high moral character. They saw themselves as living proof of the American Dream, that good grades and enough hard work enable people to "get ahead" and earn more money and luxury than other (presumed lazier) people. They believed their own efforts earned them their creative pursuit of "the good life," and they felt they deserved it.

They were often the first or second generation in their family to be upper middle class and were generally proud that they judge people by certain personal qualities that they believe can be found in any class. These qualities included competence, honesty, ambition, dynamism, resilience, long-term planning, friendliness, and both the ability and willingness to work very long hours. They knew how to be team players (with the people on their side) but could also be highly competitive, aggressive, and hard-nosed with the competition. The men in this group believed that their superior command of these qualities, along with their moral commitment to hard work, was the reason they were nearer the top of the economic ladder.

Solipsism and class-based geographical separation from anyone not in the upper middle class fuel "moral" classism's belief that people who lack advantages are simply not working hard enough. Classism sneaks in with what they do *not* see: that their preferred human qualities are culturally cultivated within the middle class (and partially in some upwardly mobile working class families). Not all people are raised with an emphasis on individual achievement, ambition, and getting ahead. Not all people have entrepreneurial personalities, nor do all people value them. Thank goodness not all people are hard-drivers with skills that work in a competitive society but not necessarily in a cooperative one. Folks in this group may not see that some people come from cultures that consider individualism and competitiveness rude or wrong. People in this group may also not see the ways they were lucky. Moral classism does not see the fact that there are only so many positions near the top and that privilege rests on a large number of people who work for far less reward in far less personally meaningful work. They may say, "We worked hard, why can't you?"

But many people do work very hard and never get these privileges. The attitude that work, in and of itself, is good for us and that self-discipline and sacrifice build character is, of course, also held by many working class people. My father worked two jobs, built an addition onto our house, wired and plumbed it, fixed our cars, and helped anyone who ever asked him for help. He was the hardest worker I have ever known. And I make ten times per hour what he made. Trust me when I say I know I am not as hard a worker as my dad was. Indeed, my father's tendency to work hard until the job was done, no matter the cost, indirectly inspired me to cross the class divide.

Judgments of taste combine with solipsism that extends the presumption of moral superiority to styles, values, and behaviors. Among those long on ambition but shorter on cultural capital, styles are conservative and described with words like tasteful, clean, and, especially, appropriate. Values about behavior match style factors: as colors are muted, so are voices, opinions, amusement, and anger, in favor of a friendly reserve. This classism harshly judges people who "put on a show" or have a "big mouth," people who come off "too strong" in style, opinions, food, or behavior. While these values may well serve those aspiring to power and fortune in America, many working class cultures put a premium on colorfulness, taking up space, and bein' real, rather than on reserve and diplomacy. Classism sees and judges louder, more expressive and emotional human behavior as flaws of personal character, which is called tasteless rather than customs of class or ethnic cultures.

Class and ethnicity affect people's attitudes about work and leisure. For me, and many in the American middle class, work is highly meaningful and integral to our lives and our sense of personal worth. But in my extended Jensen family, people's real lives are not necessarily what they do at work (though they work very hard jobs). In the oral work histories I conducted with my uncles and aunts for this book—I found out that most of them *work to live.* They are anything but lazy, but they see their jobs as allowing them to enjoy life.

For a reality check on the role of work in life, and the moral superiority of near-constant work, I need only walk my dog down my multiethnic working class Minneapolis street where I can usually find people hanging out on porches and in yards: Hmong, Chinese Americans, folks from Central and South America, blonde-haired Lutherans, aging counterculture types, African Americans, African immigrants, white punk rockers with pierced faces and tattoos, and, recently, the white, black, and mixed-race young adults who live collectively, plant gardens, and play with the kids in the neighborhood. People on my block hang out to chat, to enjoy the summer evening, to watch kids race down the sidewalk on scooters and skateboards. They welcome me to shoot the breeze. On this evening, hurrying home to spend the night writing, I envy them their casual, spontaneous life that is very much like the working class world where I grew up. For middle class people like me, too often, work is our life. Not only is this lonelier, it leads to problems like workaholism and emotional devastation if one loses one's job. These thoughts make it hard to finish my walk, ignore my neighbors, and get back to work.

Socioeconomic Classism

The third upper middle class group in Lamont's study was made up of men who described and defined themselves and their kind of people by their financial success. They believed that material success is an indicator of a person's value; worldly success is admired and achieved for its own sake. People in this group are likely to be first-generation upper middle class. They also valued ambition, hard work, competitiveness, and the drive to achieve, not for their own sake but for their result in visible success. They did not necessarily feel they owed society anything. This group lived in a dog-eat-dog survival-of-the-fittest world, a world of winners and losers. People's worth was judged by external status: professional prestige, financial standing, power, and visibility in prestigious social clubs, boards of directors, and the like. People who are unsuccessful in material terms are simply "losers." This form of classism disdains losers.

This classism dislikes people who do not look respectable, whatever that may mean in a certain community or region. People in this group believe money is the only means to freedom, control, and security. Admitting they strive for socioeconomic success for its own sake does not embarrass people who see themselves as simply being "more honest" than others. Many have worked their way up the class ladder and think others should do the same. Again, they assume that anyone can have, and would want, a hard-nosed, competitive personality, and they disregard the fact that there really are only so many slots near or at the top of the American economy. Lamont found this group was the largest of the three in America, while it was the smallest in France.

This segment of the upper middle class has taken on significantly more meaning since the 1980s and '90s made it shamelessly cool to be rich. I remember the very moment I realized that the look-out-for-the-underdog

1960s and '70s were over. In the early 1980s, I was in a hurry and I was cutting through a poster shop to meet a friend. As I took in the pictures around me one stopped me dead in my tracks. It was huge. A sexy blond woman in a mink coat leaned against a sparkling new Mercedes Benz. Across the bottom, in large bold letters, it said, "Poverty Sucks." I was shocked by the blatant lack of sympathy for poor people and the lording-over of advantage. Almost thirty five years later, I see it was a harbinger of things to come.

In fact, in the United States the *gap between* the upper middle class (to say nothing of the upper class) and the rest of society (including the rest of the middle class) has grown astronomically from what it was in the 1950s, '60s, and '70s. Remember the cheerful song from 1990, "I Wanna Be Rich"? Well, as we saw at the beginning of this chapter, lots of people got rich. The number of millionaires doubled between 1986 and 2006, and the number of billionaires increased from thirteen to perhaps a thousand, while the net worth of everyone else fell by 15 to 20 percent in order to fund this redistribution of wealth (Frank 2007; Zweig, quoted in Yates 2007). Only the upper middle class kept its previous value (while net worth in the upper class skyrocketed by over 70%). In these decades, the "power" 1980s and '90s, with its celebrity CEOs, as in the Gilded Age of robber barons in the late nineteenth and early twentieth centuries, being a winner did not necessarily bring a sense of responsibility toward others less fortunate. Then, as now, this inflation of the upper class eventually led to joblessness and financial devastation for the rest of the population, working class and middle class folks alike.

Cultural classism sees these socioeconomic winners as crass and vulgar; moral classism sees them as selfish because they do not necessarily feel the need to give back to society. But, as Lamont pointed out, people who fall into this group strive for a comfort level in material things that is clearly valued across classes. American advertising constantly sells this comfort and luxury through mass media.

A freelance writer and editor who "makes enough to get by" told a story that illustrates this kind of classism, the belief that material success is an indicator of a person's value. He was talking with his nephew, a law student. The uncle was concerned about his nephew's incessant drive to win every competition, to be

> better, smarter, faster than anyone else. I gently informed him that his competitive attitude would in the end work against him—be

counterproductive—because it consistently alienated the people surrounding him—both family and friends. He was most often described as obnoxious. His response pains me to this very day. He said, without missing a beat, "Why should I listen to anything you say—what have you got to show for yourself?" (Mark 2007, from Leondar-Wright 2011)

Lamont's distinctions about different kinds of superiority offer needed complexity to the concept of classism in America. These three points of view offer three ways to disconnect and dissociate from people who are not winners in any of the competitions described above. They are also three ways for people to avoid guilt by making those less fortunate appear somehow less important, less worthy, less human. As she writes, "Exclusive behaviors are experienced as repugnance, discomfort, embarrassment for the excluder and as snobbery, distance, and coldness by the excluded" (Lamont 1992, 10).

Fierce Individualism

The American men in *Money, Morals, and Manners* generally saw themselves as exceptional individuals whose outstanding efforts or talents or intelligence earned them their superior status. Americans, as a whole, are generally more individualistic than people in other countries; we are proud of our ethic that a man (gender intended) can make his own way in the world, with "no kings or bishops" to whom he is beholden. But a much fiercer individualism has taken hold of the United States over the last thirty-five years. With increasing segregation by class, it becomes more and more possible to ignore the context within which different Americans live.

When I say "individual" I do not just mean "person" or "self." The *social* meaning of "individual" implies independence from others. You are a person all your life, no matter how entwined your life is with the lives of others. But to be an individual you must be (or imagine you are) independent and somehow prove yourself so. In schools it is presented as the proper way to become a citizen. In most psychotherapy, individuality is prized above many other human characteristics. Though many theories of personality have also described a basic need for social connection in humans, psychotherapy is generally preoccupied with creating sturdy individuals.

But rugged independence and individuality do not reflect the lives of most people. It is certainly not a good fit for a mother who devotes her life to raising and keeping her family together, who practices "interdependence" (Kegan 1995). Is she less of a person because her life and identity are tied up with her family? Of course not. But she is less of an "individual" (Gilligan 1982; Belinky et al. 1986; Chodorow 1989).

Individuality, striking and standing out on one's own, is not a good model for most working class people either, who have traditionally worked together to make things happen: clearing land, building houses and barns, sewing quilts, working in factory lines, bringing hotdishes to potlucks. Working class people, who tend to favor human connection, cooperation, and community *over* individuality and personal ambition, like middle class women before feminism, are treated (at best) as if they are underdeveloped people. When the *lens* one looks through is white, male, and middle class, the real lives of women, people of color, and working class people of all colors may be invisible. When a middle class lens is used to view working class people, we only see the parts that correspond, or don't correspond, to the culture of the middle class.

When that middle class lens is taken off we see things we could not see while looking through an individualistic perspective. Not all societies praise the rugged individual as Americans do. Individuality, as a good thing, is a value peculiar to European and North American societies, and it is especially applauded in the United States. In far more cultures than not—and in America, once upon a time in the mid-twentieth century—human community is/was valued over individual achievements. Wealth was considered something that could be shared enough so that regular working people could live decent lives. Affluent people were a little embarrassed by having so much more than others, and certainly they did not boast about it—let alone call less-fortunate people "losers."

For the last forty years, this fierce individualism, with an attending decline in community and collective action, has moved slowly over the United States like a thunderstorm (Putnam 2000; Putnam and Feldstein 2003). Indeed, the unfettered pursuit of individual wealth, as economic winners engineered the particulars of financial markets to win more and more for their class, pushed the U.S. economy into near-total collapse at the end of the first decade of the twenty-first century. The individualism that took America by storm has been ravaging the working class—who find their strength in numbers—for decades. It hit the middle class hard over the last decade, and currently it rains on all parades except the wealthiest ten percent. Not for a hundred years has the United States seen such extremes of wealth and poverty or the lavish flourishing of the upper class while the vast majority of citizens fall further and further away from the American Dream.

Classism says that people with more wealth deserve it because they earned it. It ignores the fact that all of us who work create that wealth. It ignores that some work is paid obscenely well while other, more essential, work gets next to nothing by comparison. It goes on to say that economic class correlates with good character, greater intelligence, and a superior moral sense. It divides the United States, just as the new (unregulated) capitalism does, into big winners and devastated losers. It rewards the winners with obscenely large salaries and bonuses (by comparison to the spread forty years ago) and blames and punishes the working class people who do the majority of the work. They do work without which the United States would neither exist nor keep running.

Combating classism involves a deeper understanding of working class people, their real lives and cultural norms that are not based on individualism and competition but rather on community, caring, and mutual aid.

3

Belonging versus Becoming

The inner lives of working class communities are almost completely invisible to people from the middle class. On the surface, to middle class folks these cultures often appear nothing more than Little League versions of the middle class. Or, as we have seen, they are sometimes seen as altogether contemptible. Small wonder these people do not trust the professionals and other upper middle class people in politics and elsewhere, even when, beneath all their overeducated verbiage and multitudes of commas, they are really on their side. Working class people and their communities have their own histories, values, and cultural logic—ones that are often at odds with the more uniform culture of the middle class.

In this chapter I focus on core differences, and opposing directions, between the cultures of middle class and working class communities. To illuminate these cultural differences further, I want to look at habits of communication, in particular the role of language, in middle class and working class families. As a counseling psychologist, and former babysitter, I see child rearing and child language learning as excellent routes to reach beneath surface differences toward a deeper understanding of the psychology of working class and middle class cultures. As a woman, these routes take me back into my own childhood, focusing and sharpening memories, filling my heart with a sense of going home.

Switching between different kinds of English has been a lifelong hobby for me. My mom was proudly and loudly working class, and she loved ideas and discussion. For her, as for many people in the first half of the twentieth century, being working class didn't mean she was anti-intellect. She learned her love of ideas and friendly argument from her parents, working class Brooklyn Jews. They also believed education was important, though my mother did not and shocked them by dropping out of high school to become a telephone operator. Then she shocked them again by marrying a Lutheran from Minnesota.

She told off-color jokes that made her laugh loudly and deeply, made fun of grades and school, and deftly talked the cops out of giving her speeding tickets and from detaining my big brother or me in our teen years. She was a cool mom. My friends smoked cigarettes with her and confided in her. Though she made fun of academics—she saw them as snobby, abstracted people, disconnected from "the rest of us in real life"—I realize now that her appetite for thought and discussion helped inspire me to attain the higher education she disdained.

Many people in the middle class, including people who were once working class, get upset when they hear me present positive aspects of working class cultures, warning me over and over not to "romanticize" or "glorify" the working class. It makes me wonder: Why are they upset? The middle class is glorified everywhere I look. Every one of these folks has lists of public accomplishments, their glories, which are recited when they meet or lecture others. The lives of celebrities and other outstanding and lucky individuals are glorified all the time. Why is finding good things about working class life considered glorifying it, anyway?

Few voices in America validate that working class people even *have* a culture. When I introduce the idea in workshops that there are basic differences between life in the middle class and the working class and, further, that the values and customs of the working class are likely to be invisible to others, the most common response from working class people is "Thank You!" They volunteer little at first. But, when encouraged, their lists of good qualities about working class life come fast and furiously. Countless formerly working class people who are currently in the middle class tell me they are relieved to have someone see and validate their "real" lives. For those who cross the class divide, almost everything about the process asks you to forget what you knew before. How does one speak of, or grieve, a place that isn't even on the map? Invisible, voiceless, unacknowledged–how does one remember what to remember?

In my mid-twenties I had started to perceive and understand class differences by analyzing my own and others' experiences. Then I presented my ideas in workshops and classes and invited discussion, which then informed and altered the theory I was developing. But health problems stopped me from doing this work and led to my getting welfare in order to survive. In order to receive thirty-four dollars a month, I joined the early morning standing-only lines that lasted half a day or more. The concrete, colorless, windowless room had a cop in a caged loft at the back, who sat on a chair with a loaded gun on his hip. I realized then, with horror, I wasn't playing at being poor, choosing to "live simply" as my noble middle class friends were. I *was* poor. And scared to death. As my health improved, I hustled myself back to college to get a job I liked that paid good money.

At the age of thirty-three (1986), I chose to do my graduate school thesis on working class people in counseling and psychotherapy, "The Invisible Culture: Psychotherapy and the Working Class Client." By virtue of nineteen years in the counterculture and the women's movement, as well as having received two college degrees, I had plenty of middle class "cultural capital." Still, entering a profession felt uncomfortable. I had a vague but poignant sense of leaving home. I felt I was moving much farther away than when I left my parents' house after high school graduation. I also wanted to know how well my and others' subjective experiences of class and culture agreed with or contradicted academic procedural knowledge about working class experience. I wanted to study what kind of treatment working class folks received in the profession I was entering. Researching and writing my thesis was a rite of passage from one life into another. It helped ease the discomfort I felt in becoming a professional psychologist.

To write that thesis I slogged through a zillion psychological abstracts (paragraph summaries of scholarly articles) and photocopied about a hundred academic articles and read them. In 1986, I found just three that spoke to anything of the substance of working class life or psychology, that pointed to working class ways of thinking and seeing the world.[1] The most useful of these was one that led me to the British sociologist Basil Bernstein (Meltzer 1978). Bernstein recorded and analyzed speech in different class groups (working and middle, all English) that pointed to different psychological frameworks and social orientations. Working class and middle class speech samples from his studies were different enough from each other to suggest that the groups used the similar language *for different purposes*.

The middle class groups used language and discussion to think and argue, to display their individual ability, and to uncover differences of opinion and debate them within the group. The working class groups used language and discussion to find agreement within the group and to connect emotionally with one another. Bernstein discovered that middle class and working class speech "selects and makes available" different human qualities "from a range of human capabilities." Class differences in speech were consistent and profound enough to point to different cultures (Bernstein 1962, 1971, 1990).

A meticulous scholar, Bernstein's own language use was even more formal and abstract than that of other scholars I had read, but I read his work as eagerly as I would a good novel. I devoured Bernstein's work because it matched my own experience as a Danish American Lutheran girl growing up in Minnesota. It also brought my dilemma into focus: I wanted middle class skills and knowledge, but I was afraid that if I strayed too far, I would never again feel I belonged in my loving extended family. Worse, I felt that I would somehow betray them.

Sennett and Cobb's *Hidden Injuries of Class* (1972) described a similar cultural dilemma for working class children in primary school (and by extension, adults in the workplace). They found that children felt forced to choose between developing their individual abilities and being part of their peer group: being a teacher's "pet" meant they learned lots of schools skills, but they were ignored or ridiculed by the other children. They called this dynamic *fraternity* versus *ability*. I call it *belonging* versus *becoming*. I prefer a term that includes women and points more directly to cultural characteristics. Other personal characteristics rooted in these same differences were described in the last chapter in the story of two Midwestern Lutheran confirmations. The class one is raised in (among other factors) helps train us to view the world in certain ways, to focus on certain things, as well as to act certain ways.

Bernstein found that middle class language and culture tend to promote individual achievements and competition between outstanding individuals, or people who "stand out." Working class language and communities tend to recreate values of social connection, solidarity, and mutual aid. Bernstein articulated what I have found in my own life—words *do* stuff. The ones you use and the *ways* you use them matter. They get others to do and feel things they might not have; they tell stories that make people laugh, or think; they get you things you want; they actually create feelings and thoughts in others. I understand *words as ways*: the language we use helps create certain ways of thinking, seeing, and living. Perhaps nowhere is this more obvious than with young children and their mothers, in the learning and teaching of language.

Language and Child Rearing

I draw a line between classes at the same place language use changes significantly enough to point to fundamental differences in worldview. I live in an urban neighborhood that is mixed in terms of class, race, age, and ethnicity. On the block where I have lived since 1986, we have about thirty-five children who play in the street, across the yards, and for a decade in a vacant lot. Almost everyone has a front porch. In warm weather Columbus Avenue is alive with music, kids on scooters and bikes, and adults on their porches, kickin' it after work. On my porch one summer I read an article for psychotherapists by Bernstein in which he considered how language was used differently by middle class and working class mothers to teach different cultural skills and values to their children. He warned that unconscious (middle class) therapist bias could sabotage therapy for working class patients. I needed only to sit on my front porch to see an American illustration of these different kinds of language and cultural training between mothers and children.

Just two doors down from my house, I watched my friend Sally raise her youngest son on her porch. At three or four, Jacob liked to push things as far as he possibly could. Sally is from a working class background but has learned the language skills of the middle class. She ran a child-care center out of her home for years, and then she got a degree in social work from the University of Minnesota when she was in her forties. One day, Jacob was banging a toy truck on the porch floor. Sally asked Jacob if he would please play more quietly. Bernstein's example of psycholinguistic training in middle class children starts with a mother who says to her child, "I'd rather you made less noise, Darling." However idealized (and British) this sentence may be, it is a good model of middle class language use (1958, 162).

To demonstrate how culture is communicated through language, Bernstein took the sentence apart to see what it does besides asking the child to be quieter. This sentence has a clear "I" and "you," which helps in the development of a sense of individuality through the negotiation between the "I" of the mother and the "I" of the child. On her porch, when Sally asked Jacob to be quieter, Jacob banged the toy truck a wee bit softer, saying, "Is this less?"

"Not enough, Jacob."

He banged a little softer, "How 'bout this?"

"That's still too loud, Honey."

At this point he started barely touching the truck to the porch floor, "Mom! What about this?"

"That's better, thank you," Sally said.

Don't ask me where Sally gets her patience, but she did run that childcare center for years. Jacob then tapped it louder, repeating his question, "How 'bout this?"

It is not so much that Jacob was concerned with finding the exact amount of noise he could make as that he was taken with the game of negotiation (and keeping his mother's attention). Sally, too, was as interested in *how* they were engaged as she was about the noise Jacob was making. She was concerned with the kind of person her son was to become and how he learned to negotiate conflict, and she was consciously using their conversations as a way to shape that development.

Bernstein's sentence "I'd rather you made less noise, Darling" contains other characteristic features of middle class speech and culture. In addition to the I/you distinction, there is "rather" and "less." Jacob is trying to figure out just how much is "less." More precisely, he is figuring out how much "less" is enough to please his mother. "Rather" is not "must," and again there is the "I" who can decide whether or not he will please his mother.

Throughout this process he was learning the art of negotiation, in general as well as across power hierarchies (parent and child). He is also developing an individual sense of *agency*, his own ability to affect and maneuver the world around him. Learning these cultural skills, for Jacob, was part and parcel of learning to talk.

When Jason pushed too far, even sweet-tempered Sally would tire of the game. "I'd like you to put that toy away now and find something else to do, Jacob. Mom's going to study now."

"What if I don't?"

"Then we will not go to the store for Cherry Garcia ice cream later!" Another feature of middle class speech emerges: a sense of means and ends. Now Jacob has to choose, but the choice is his. In this way, he also learns that he has the means to create the end result he wants. In terms of psychological development, we can imagine how these things can facilitate, even necessitate, the development of internal speech and logical reasoning. Jacob sat silently for a while. "I'm going next door to see Amber!" he suddenly announced and dashed next door, apparently deciding in favor of Cherry Garcia ice cream and removing himself from the temptation of the game.

All of the things I have highlighted—individuality, negotiation, learning how to negotiate across different levels of power, a choice of means to lead to desired, and often delayed, ends—are basic to becoming a person in America's middle class culture. Jason is learning the art of individuality through negotiation with his most significant other. He is "becoming."

Bernstein's work has been corroborated by others. "Discussions between parents and children are a hallmark of middle-class child rearing," Annette Lareau writes in her 2003 book about middle class, working class, and poverty class child rearing in the eastern and midwestern United States. "Organized activities, established and controlled by mothers and fathers, dominate the lives of middle-class children. . . . By making sure their children have these and other experiences, middle-class parents engage in a process of *concerted cultivation*. From this, a robust sense of entitlement takes root in these children" (1–2). Jacob is also learning, implicitly, that he has a right to negotiate on his own behalf, and that adults will respect and respond to his attempts to do so. We will see how important this sense of entitlement is in later life. Two decades earlier, Shirley Heath found the same thing with middle class people she studied in a different region of the United States: "Within these households, there is consistent emphasis on the baby as an individual, a separate person, with whom the preferred means of communicating is talk. Nonverbal means are somewhat limited, since [middle class] townspeople frown on the fondling of babies by any but a very few intimates" (1983, 246).

This is not to say that all is rosy in the socialization of middle class children. There can be negative effects from too much role negotiation and behavior modification. It is not at all hard to imagine a parent less skilled, and less destined for sainthood, than my friend Sally. Therapists find many middle class clients plagued with an inhibiting self-consciousness in adulthood, and I suspect that this may be born of too-close parental monitoring in childhood. Psychologically, it can lead to the development of an inner censor or critic that pops up in one's own head to criticize speech and behavior. Likewise, the expectation of self-monitoring and role negotiation, with an implied acceptance of hierarchies of power, may leave a child less self-reliant or to value being with peers less (though well preparing the child for school and professional life). Finally, the cultivation of the ego-heavy "I" may affect how much connection or empathy a person will feel with others. Lareau found in her study of eighty-eight middle class, working class, and poverty class children that "concerted cultivation places intense labor demands on busy parents, exhausts children, and emphasizes the development of individualism, at times at the expense of the development of a family group" (2003, 13). It may also be the case that excessive early emphasis on children being asked to translate impulses and feelings into formal speech may obscure other kinds of experiences.

This leads to the question of bringin' up working class kids. In a similar situation to Sally's, a child banging a toy truck against the floor, a working class parent might say, "That's enough!" A more gentle approach, on a less harried day, would simply be to guide the child away from the offending truck and distract him with something else. Often, an older child will be pressed to "keep your little brother out of trouble." The first thing that strikes the middle class observer is the *lack* of all those middle class psychological skills: development of self, negotiation in general, means and ends, a sense of individual agency, and role negotiation across power differences, as with parents and other authorities, in particular. There would seem to be little encouragement to develop reason and internal speech in such a situation, and typically developmental psychologists have indeed assumed this.

But, as Bernstein wrote, "one of the difficulties of this [psycholinguistic] approach is to avoid implicit value judgments about the relative worth of speech systems and the cultures which they symbolize" (1971, 186). Working class children, in a mainly working class setting, may not develop reason and internal speech *in the way* that middle class children do. But if we try to look at this from a working class point of view, we begin to see other things emerge.

On the same block where I watched Sally training Jacob, across the street I saw Vicky's nine-year-old boy Rashad whacking the cedar tree in front of their apartment with a plastic bat. The first thing Vicky did was to give her son a long meaningful look. He looked back, hesitated, and hit the tree again. He was angry because his father had come back from jail. His father was a man of few words with a storm in his eyes. Vicky said, "Quit that!" and looked right at Rashad, holding his gaze. Her tone was firm but not angry; there was softness in it because she understood—she was upset, too. The look said everything: she understands but there is nothing she can do about it and destroying the landlord's property is not going to help. He stared into her eyes, then looked down, and then began hitting the tree again. She said nothing and sighed out loud. He looked at her. She looked him in the eye, "I don't *need* to tell you twice." He stopped. He knew she was right. She certainly did not need this right then, and twice was more than enough for this mother and son.

I was struck by both the expectation that the boy would tune in to what his mother was feeling and the fact that he did, despite human development theories in psychology that claim he is too young to develop empathy. The looks this mother and son exchanged were by far the strongest part of the communication. As Bernstein wrote of working class speech, it is not only that what is *not* said is more important than what is said, it is *how* it is not said (1971).

Vicky is teaching Rashad something as crucial to working class success as the middle class ability to articulate and debate is to middle class culture. She is telling him, implicitly, to tune in—to her, to others, to what is happening around him. Working class speech and culture *imply*, they do not spell things out. Children are taught to pay attention to a lot more than words. Words become mere buoys that float on a sea of shared assumptions;

they point you someplace you already know. Vicky cares about the kind of person her son will become, too. In order to belong in their shared world, Rashad must listen past the surface, hear beyond the words into the meaning behind them. He must learn that words are markers that lead into a nonverbal realm of communication and shared meanings. In the working class community she studied, Shirley Heath observed that "though young children often use the same language forms for doing [many different verbal acts], they and their audience recognize that interpretation of these forms derives from intonation and voice quality and from the interpersonal context, not the actual words used" (1996, 83).

In marital therapy, the most frequent complaint I hear from working class people about their middle class spouses is lack of sensitivity to these nonverbal signals. As a therapist I was taught that the correct response to this complaint was to coach the working class person that she (or he) must learn to say exactly what she means and wants. She can't expect her partner to read her mind. But what if her childhood taught her to do exactly that, read minds in the form of multiple nonverbal clues? Psychotherapy is based on upper class and middle class cultural biases: individuality, individuation, psychological mindedness, and ego strength. Is it not just as valid to request that a middle class partner learn to pay attention to nonverbal cues? Or that the partner should take responsibility for the nonverbal cues he or she gives out?

Vicky and Rashad also demonstrate the sense of immediacy that is common in working class speech and culture. "Now" is the time everything is happening. Now he should stop: "Quit that!" Her tone and gaze said *now* is the time consequences could come. In working class life people often get together with others when they feel in the mood, rather than scheduling social dates. This nowness is also seen in the language working class people use. It doesn't navigate different tenses—past, present, future—very well, something that I have long struggled with in my middle class writing.

Middle class culture, through its emphasis on means and ends that are placed farther apart as a child ages, creates a psychology based on delayed gratification that has significant rewards in education and professional work later in life. Working class people may miss out on this in childhood, sometimes to devastating effect in later life, but they enjoy a larger and roomier sense of now. Rashad, who had a lot of time on his hands, liked to start up football and baseball games with other kids on the block in the vacant lot. He was developing different skills—self-reliance, initiative, industry, how to make the best of things, negotiating peer relationships, and how to make his own fun. Lareau found that working class children "tend to take real pleasure in their playtime. The lack of adult attention and involvement in their activities leaves children in working-class and poor homes free to concentrate on pleasing themselves. The children we studied tended to show more creativity, spontaneity, enjoyment, and initiative in their leisure pastimes than we saw among middle-class children at play in organized activities" (2003, x).

As a counseling psychologist, I have had many a middle class client striving for the ability to live in what counseling theory calls "the here-and-now." As one high-achieving patient of mine put it, "I'm always obsessed with *later*. Before I finish one accomplishment I'm already planning the next two. I'm never satisfied!" Indeed, humanistic therapies (Gestalt, client-centered, bioenergetics, and many others) are designed to try to develop in middle class people the very things that we find plentiful in working class communication: body language, emotional empathy, directness, pluck, and enthusiasm. In short, they seek an experience unmediated by formal language and all that close monitoring in early childhood. In expressive therapies they learn to pound on pillows and say "Quit that!"

I am not saying that all is rosy in the socialization of working class children. Another crucial factor is the hard life Vicky and Rashad have had. Most communication between them also implies what my father used to say to me: "Nobody said it would be easy." The lack of resources available for working class people in this historical moment creates significant problems. Most important, the language and other cultural skills middle class children learn give them profound advantages in our larger society, especially as adults in the world of work. But that does not mean working class life has nothing to offer.

In my experience, the higher their status in and the longer people have belonged to the American middle class, the more individuality, competition, the pursuit of public excellence, and having power over others figure significantly into what "feels right." I have found a fair amount of agreement about this among scholars (for example, Bourdieu 1984; Heath 1996; Lareau and Conley 2008; Peckham 2010). Individuality, standing out, and competition are central cultural features· of middle class life. Since Bernstein and others first described them, these characteristics have become increasingly pervasive in the middle class.

These features both reflect and recreate a strong (middle class) cultural value of individuals, needs, desires, improvements; competition between sturdy selves; delayed gratification; the pursuit of individual status, including the achievement of entrance into high-status groups; and the pursuit of excellence. While the benefits of these skills result in well-documented advantages in school and in professional and managerial work, I believe much of professional therapy and counseling was created to alleviate the negative effects of these cultural values. One of the things psychotherapy does is help the people who lose, when someone else wins, to feel they are worthwhile despite their lack of success.

Aspects of working class cultures are less easy to define than those of the middle class because the working class is far more diverse. The middle classes all tend, at least verbally, toward the ethnicity of white Anglo-Saxon Protestants, as this is historically the dominant ethnicity among the upper class, the most economically, culturally, and politically powerful people in the United States. Newly middle class and upper class people who are not WASPs learn to behave more like them. On the other hand, I believe it is in the definition of working class culture to be very diverse.

Working class communities are far more influenced by (non-Anglo) ethnicity, geographical factors (e.g., urban or rural), race or color, gender, and other factors that historically have been great dividers within the American working class. In this sense "culture*s*" is a more appropriate term than "culture." Working class communities may have almost as little relation to one another as they do to the mainstream middle class. While the entire working class is a large group of people, as defined by work and status in our larger society, each community may still be *marginal* to mainstream middle class culture. In working class communities, "them" describes not only the professional middle class (an enduring and cross-ethnic Other) but a variety of other "thems" as well, and only one, very specific, "us." When the working class has organized for better economic treatment, as it often has in American history, it has done so in spite of deep ethnic, geographic, gender, and color differences, forging a new and larger sense of "us."

Still, I have found some similar working class values across radically different ethnicities: caring connections with others within the group, communal values of sharing and helping, trust of feelings and personal stories, loyalty, and family-like bonds with others.

Belonging in the working class is different from belonging in the middle class. Clearly, middle class people value and maintain personal connections and care if they belong or not; and working class folks certainly feel the strain of the larger society's valuing of "somebodies" over "nobodies." And, of course, some working class people strive and work very hard to come to belong in the middle class. But part of belonging, *as a central feature of culture,* is a tendency toward peer relationships (where power is equal) and a tendency to shy away from hierarchical relationships. Children play with other children; workers talk together when the supervisor isn't around; women feel free to leave their men in one room and go off visiting together in another; guys are buddies with other guys who have no power over their work lives. Equality invites human interaction that is relaxed and playful. No hidden power agenda is to be served or suspended. This is particularly clear when contrasted with middle class life, where negotiating across and within established hierarchies of power is common.

I found an example of the working class preference for relationships where power is equal, and for leisure time with equals, in a couples' counseling session I conducted. A middle class husband complained that his wife didn't like to go with him to his networking dinners and other activities that helped him "get ahead" in his high-level sales work. He said if she gave it half a chance, she would probably have a good time. His working class wife said, "You're saying we have to spend our *Saturday night* going out with your boss and his wife for dinner? You work over forty hours a week, isn't that enough? I don't call watching every single word I say with the white-wine set having a 'good time'!"

This self-directed "peerness" among working class children was evident to Lareau, who commented repeatedly about the great playfulness and "boundless energy" that these children shared together when grown-ups merely said, "Okay, go out and play now." In contrast to the concerted cultivation of the middle class families, she called working class child rearing "the accomplishment of natural growth":

Parents tend to direct their efforts toward keeping children safe, enforcing discipline, and, when they deem it necessary, regulating their behavior in specific areas. Within these boundaries, working-class and poor children are allowed to grow and thrive. They are given the flexibility to choose activities and playmates and to decide how active or inactive to be as they engage in these activities. Thus, whereas middle-class children often are treated as a project to be developed, working-class and poor children are given boundaries for their behavior and then allowed to grow. (2003, 66–67)

Lareau noticed that these children, despite significant economic hardships, played more, whined less, and never once complained of being bored (which was common among both white and black middle class children). Her central point was that they clearly were not being given the skills they needed to succeed in the professional middle class, hence the title of her book, *Unequal Childhoods.* But in terms of daily life, she was obviously impressed by these working class kids: "Despite the lack of organized activities, he has no trouble filling up his schedule. He has ideas, plans, and activities to engage in with his friends. Unlike his middle-class counterparts, Tyrec needs no adult assistance to pursue the great majority of his plans" (2003, 81).

Working class adults, at the end of the day, are similarly released into their real lives and the companionship of friends and family who they can generally expect to be loyal and basically supportive. Work is left at work. Living is where you "come as you are," where we can "just be ourselves" and get comfy. Being down-to-earth is important. Our friends invite us back into our selves and our lives. Yes, others may run the schools, the factories, and the government, but in all the smaller ways working class life invites activities that require cooperation between "people like us." Indeed there is often an *anti*status ethic because it threatens solidarity within the group.

My bright and hard-working aunt, Luella (Jensen) Sharpe, put this plainly: "I'd rather be a peon than a boss." Anyone who knows Auntie Lu would laugh on hearing her say that, as she is an opinionated woman, she loves to talk, and is the oldest living daughter of her (and my father's) generation in the Jensen family.

But she was talking about institutional power. She told me a story that emphasized the clear choice of belonging over becoming, as well as the divide between workers and "higher ups." She was promoted to supervisor in a large bakery where she had worked on the line for years. She found herself alone. I asked her what happened when all of a sudden she was above all her former coworkers on the job:

> *Lu:* Well, they just ignored you. They plain ignored you. Like, you know, you didn't go to lunch with 'em cause they didn't want you there. You know?
>
> *Barb:* And before, when you came to work as a regular worker, how did people treat you?
>
> *Lu:* Well *great*—I was everybody's friend. But when you become a boss then you gotta go, I, I didn't go to, wanna go to lunch.

Lu gave up supervising and went back to the assembly line.

> *Lu:* And then, you know, Mr. Emerick [her boss] he come to me afterwards. He said, "Why did you quit?" I told him the truth. And he said, "Well, you know, that's the way it is in this world." He says, "Some move up and some don't." He said, "And we really liked your work, and you shoulda, we thought you'd do a really good job." And I said, "Well, maybe I would have." But I said, "To me friends are important." And I said I lost all my friends. They didn't want to be my friends. Well, you know, he told me that you could be friends with the upper ones too, you know, the bosses. I said, "Well, I think I'm friends with my bosses now" [laughs out loud], and I don't think he liked that very well.
>
> *Barb:* 'Cause he was kinda suggesting that maybe you'd trade? You had these friends, but now you could have these other friends?
>
> *Lu:* Yeah, right.
>
> *Barb:* But you wanted those same friends.
>
> *Lu:* Yeah, right.

She resigned from her supervisor job after just two short weeks to rejoin her friends on the line. Her husband's work was seasonal, and she really needed the money that promotion gave her, but not if it meant losing her friends.

> *Lu:* Well, I liked bein' a worker. I liked workin' with other people. I liked bein' around people, 'cause I'm a people person.
>
> *Barb:* Yeah. I guess that's why that supervisor thing would have never worked out for you, because you really wanted to be with the people.
>
> *Lu:* No, no, I guess that's probably why. I don't like for people to think that I'm, you know, *over* them. I don't like that feeling.
>
> *Barb:* Have people done that, though? Cause you're kind of a natural leader. I mean, you were the oldest kid, you know, you did have power over the other kids.

Lu: Not really. I don't think you should ever have power over people.
Barb: Over another person?
Lu: Uh-uh [No].

I have presented the notion of belonging versus becoming to very diverse groups, and I have been surprised by how many different ethnic groups have affirmed this idea as "common sense." In my years of being a practicing psychologist, a university instructor, and in the many professional seminars where I have presented issues of psychology, culture, and class, many people from and in the working class have testified to having similar experiences. From many immigrants and foreign students I have heard about whole societies that hold "belonging" as a key social value: Southeast Asians, Japanese people, people from Central and South America, many different nationalities from Africa and the Caribbean, Greeks and other southern Europeans. Also English, German, and other northern Europeans raised in the working class have also testified to having (or having had) a strong cultural value of belonging, or community-mindedness, as opposed to developing individuality and competitiveness.

Also, in my teaching experience, minority ethnic Americans have repeatedly affirmed the idea of their working class communities being based more on the psychological experience of belonging than becoming. African Americans have been particularly responsive, in my experience, and expressive about the particulars of their versions of belonging versus becoming. White working class women and men have also generally identified with this as well. Most of these people's lives are webs of connection with dozens of relatives and still more people considered "like-family." Many have also testified that their experiences with the middle class in work stands in sharp contrast to the expectations of their more communal culture of origin. Generally, middle class women (from various ethnic groups) have also sympathized with the idea that belonging may be more important than, and at times is certainly in opposition to, becoming. Many have commented that as family caregivers they have long struggled with contradictions between these value systems, between individual accomplishments and devotion to helping their husbands, children, and aging parents.

Class and Language

Basil Bernstein revolutionized the understanding of class as culture when he discovered class differences in speech profound enough to demonstrate that working class and middle class people were using the English language for different purposes and in quite different ways. I would like to venture a bit deeper into language and how it reflects and maintains class-related cultures and conflicts. In chapters 4 and 5, I explore the effect of both language and culture on children's experience in school. We have seen the cultural underpinnings of these different ways of using words. Now I would like to focus specifically on how class and language work together.

Bernstein was a young college teacher in the 1950s when he was asked to teach a class of working class men. He found they could barely stay awake for his lectures, while his class of middle class students treated the same lectures as he would have expected, taking notes, asking questions, and otherwise engaging with him. He was shocked when he took these same working class students to hear a lecture on auto mechanics. The people he had begun to think were incapable of paying attention became active and enthusiastic toward the speaker.

In an effort to understand class differences in schools, and how to make school more accessible for working class kids and young adults, he began to study the differences between middle class and working class speech patterns. He came to the conclusion that working class and middle class people used different language "codes," unspoken rules that govern how, when, and why a person should speak. There was an "elaborated" or public code in the middle class and a "restricted" or private code in the working class.

In his now-classic early experiments, Bernstein (1962) asked two groups, one middle class and one working class, to discuss their views on a topic of the day: capital punishment. He recorded and analyzed their speech. Let's look at how that worked.

For example, the middle class group often started their sentences with "I think": "I think the evidence shows that capital punishment is not actually a deterrent. I think, in crimes of passion, the offender is unlikely to be thinking about the future." As we saw in the development of Jacob's increasingly sturdy *I*, "I think" is a prefix of differentiation; it separates the speaker from the listeners and invites an opposing "*I* think" from others. "I think" begins a sentence by establishing individuality, first and foremost.

We saw how Jacob was learning that certain kinds of speech and negotiation allow him to maneuver (and manage) the world around him. Elaborated code speech emphasizes and develops verbal acuity. It allows various ways of putting words together (structural options) that are complex and elaborate. The vocabulary is large. This code is designed to make clear and precise the differences between the speaker and the listener, and then encourage debate between two or more sturdy selves. It speaks to a general nonspecific audience and is well prepared to illuminate abstract concepts. It allows—and demands—that people use precise and *explicit* language when they speak. The elaborated code is taught in schools as a linear, formal system. This code finds its fullest expression in academic settings, as to use it well requires many years of education.

By contrast, the restricted code used by working class people is *implicit* rather than explicit. Not one working class person used "I think" in Bernstein's speech samples. Rather, they used what Bernstein called "sympathetic circularity" suffixes, ending sentences with "wouldn't he?" or "you know?" or "isn't it?"—something that would invite agreement and put the speaker at ease. And the others in the group nodded or murmured to say: yes, we are with you, and asking something along the lines of, "Well, what if it was the wrong guy, you know? I mean, sometimes they find evidence later on that can change things, right?" No one in the middle class group used these agreement phrases. Bernstein saw that working class speech was used to connect people, rather than to differentiate them one from another. These suffixes created a *we* instead of an *I*.

Using the common speech and gestures of the group reaffirms membership in the group. Because the speech of working class people has both less vocabulary and ways to put words together, the linguistic code is called "restricted." But, as he pointed out, only verbal elaboration was restricted, while gestures, meaningful glances, variations in vocal tone, volume, and pace were used far more freely than in the middle class group (1971). As we saw with Rashad and Vicky, a certain look in the eye and tone of voice were used to communicate in a moment what would take several minutes to explain in words.

When Vicky said "I don't *need* to tell you twice!" she implied what Rashad already knew (Dad is in a bad mood) and encouraged him to "read" her meaning (he might come out here and belt you) from her tone and their shared situation. In less stressful situations, a point may be made with a long story that appears unrelated to the event it is commenting on, but, and the speaker looks you in the eye, "*you know* what I mean." And the listener works to "get it." Specificity and detailed verbal explication are replaced with well-known metaphors, buzzwords, and gestures already understood by people within a particular group. It may be incomprehensible to an outsider.

Restricted codes boil communication down to essential images and meanings, drawing on, or creating, an intimate connection between the speaker and listener. This is also what good poetry does, and it explains why the use of nonstandard English is so powerful, poetic, and popular in fine literature. The best example of restricted code is teenage slang: cool, bad, the shit. With the advent of the digital age, I am watching them create a new, text-based restricted code: lol, lmao, tafn, imho, or cu l8r. Words, gestures, and symbols in this code are not blocks for building proper sentences, paragraphs, and essays; they are markers pointing to shared meanings and customs. "They're deceptively tiny portals into big feelings and experiences," Frank Bruni (2006, section 4, page 1) said about buzzwords.

The middle class groups used language and discussion to display their individual ability to think and argue and to *uncover differences* within the group. The working class groups, on the other hand, used language and discussion to connect emotionally with one another and to *find agreement* within the group.[2]

Some aspects of Ruby Payne's controversial and popular work on the language of poverty dovetail with Bernstein's language codes and provide another way to describe how language and class function together (1998). Payne employed Martin Joos's 1962 work *The Five Clocks* to describe five different registers, or types, of language. These registers are (1) Frozen: language that is always the same, for example, the Lord's Prayer, wedding vows, the Pledge of Allegiance, legal language; (2) Formal: Standard English, the kind of speech expected in schools and in middle class work with complete sentences and very specific syntax and word choices; (3) Consultative: formal register as used in conversation, discourse pattern not quite as linear as formal register; (4) Casual: language between friends characterized by a much smaller vocabulary; with sentence syntax often incomplete and dependent on nonverbal assists; and (5) Intimate: language between lovers, twins, best friends, or other close family members.

Payne used Joos's work to discuss class differences in the uses of formal and casual registers of language. Joos noted that it is socially acceptable to go one register down in a conversation. To drop two registers or more in the same conversation, however, is to be socially offensive. Payne points out that children who are not from the middle class should not be expected to jump several registers all at once.

Although Payne presents entertaining renditions of working class speech, she nonetheless concludes that a formal or elaborated language teaches children to think sequentially, while casual or restricted language can create "cognitive deficiencies" or have adverse effects on thinking (1998, 123). I mention her work as it has become quite popular among educators, and also because it exemplifies an all-too-common incorrect assumption among scholars: because of these language differences, working and poverty class people can't think as well as middle class people. I disagree. In-depth empirical studies of actual communities show that children of all language communities can (and do) easily learn to use other codes of speech.

Bernstein made it clear that all language systems bring something particular and valuable to those who use them. Unfortunately, Bernstein's work was profoundly misunderstood after some researchers in the United States used his notion of codes, and the term "restricted" in particular, to support a view that poor and working class people, and especially black folks, are raised to have serious deficits in mental ability.[3] On the contrary, Bernstein said that working class speech has a pith and beauty to it that the elaborated code does not. His point was that working class language pointed to a world of implicit meanings, a verbal and nonverbal world of poetic, metaphoric, and emotional references that demonstrate a different kind of cultural learning.

I actually asked Basil Bernstein if he ever meant to say that working class people are incapable of high-order or abstract thinking. "Absolutely not," he replied, "but they do it differently than middle class people."[4] We agreed that some working class people develop "wisdom," while some middle class people develop "brilliance." His point was not that working class children's lives were deprived in some broad general sense, just that they would need a way to learn the elaborated code if they were to succeed in school and have access to middle class work. The trouble is, and this was the thrust of his later work, which spanned the rest of the twentieth century, schools do not build bridges between these uses of language because working class ways with words are not visible to the middle class.[5]

But a description of the language codes used by middle class and working class people only begins to describe what life feels like in cultures with strongly communal values. Because much of working class culture is implicit, and thus hard to explain in explicit language, I need another way to point to what working class community *feels* like.

Belonging and Being

We have been looking at different components of cultures influenced by class position in our larger society. But if we imagine forward into the later lives of Jacob and Rashad, we run into problems. It is relatively easy to imagine the path Jacob can take to being a success. Because his is the dominant culture, his trajectory is in plain view: early childhood prepares one for education, which prepares one for higher education, and higher education prepares you for success in a profession, government, the arts, and other prestige occupations. But what about Rashad? Beyond the basics of survival, it is not clear that there is a trajectory for working class folks, unless it is to take a significantly longer route to the middle class. Indeed, working class cultures do not, generally, tend to be progressive. Rather, they rely on, cherish, and preserve tradition.

I have described two different kinds of child rearing, and language codes, to illustrate differences in culture. You could say the middle class elaborated language code is three-quarters full of words and structural language options designed for precision—mastering these leads to predictable ends, success in schools and professional or managerial work. The working class codes have a lot fewer words and also require much less verbal precision—let's say it is only one-fourth full of words—not literally how much people talk (this depends on many things, such as personal temperament and ethnicity) but how many words are expected to communicate a particular point, and how much verbal precision is required in the *way* one makes that point. But that raises the question: What makes up the rest of working class child rearing, communication, and culture? What fills the rest of that box? Is it just emptiness, waiting for the right education to fill it up with middle class skills? This is a very common assumption among teachers, psychologists, and other helping professionals.

I don't think so. I don't know any more of Rashad's story, since they moved away, but I do remember my own life as I grew into teen years and young adulthood. Jack Metzgar, in *Striking Steel* (2000), talks about displaced steel workers and describes a strikingly similar model to my "becoming versus belonging." He called it "*doing* and becoming" instead of "*being* and belonging." Metzgar's additions fit well with my sense of class and culture and shed light on my question. We have glimpsed the "tuning in," the *being with*, that was expected of Rashad. For him words are buoys in a sea of shared assumptions. Much of working class communication, both alongside and nestled within speech, is nonverbal. One of the best descriptions I have found about working class speech came from an elderly African American woman called "Annie Mae" who was interviewed by Heath:

> He gotta learn to *know* 'bout dis world, can't nobody tell 'im. . . . You think I can tell Teegie all he gotta know to get along? He just gotta be keen, keep his eyes open, don't he be sorry. Gotta watch hisself by watchin' other folks. Ain't no use me tellin' 'im: "Learn dis, learn dat. What's dis? What's dat?" He just gotta learn, gotta know; he see one thing one place one time, he know how it go, see sump'n like it again, maybe it be de same, maybe it won't. He hafta try it out. If he don't he be in trouble; he get lef' out. Gotta keep yo' eyes open, *gotta feel to know*. (1996, 84; emphasis mine)

I can't explicate Metzgar's idea of "being and belonging" any better, but I can *imply* it further by describing *gotta feel to know* in two of my favorite working class activities—making music and roller-skating.

One summer I attended the Winnipeg Folk Festival in Canada. At the festival, I saw a "blues jam" that brought these different orientations toward music into sharp focus. Blues is a quintessential example of working class music. The right feeling is essential or "the blues" just doesn't happen. In this concert, the blues acts that had played individual sets were brought on stage together at the end of the night to jam. The groups took turns starting songs. The contrast of two harmonica players, from different acts, really struck me.

One was an older man who appeared to be a long-standing member of the blues community. His cowboy hat was cocked forward on his head, and his long gray and black hair fell in tendrils alongside his weathered face onto the red and yellow cowboy shirt with silver buttons. He played and blended beautifully with a singer-guitarist in his earlier performance. The other harmonica player was a clean-cut young man dressed all in black, at the center of his own band. Both were white. This player's virtuosity was astonishing, and the audience cheered when his group played, but the other musicians in his group were all but invisible. The musicians in other acts onstage looked down. This young man riffed on and on, doing what he thought music was about—delivering an impressive "outstanding performance" in middle class terms and "showing off" in working class terms. The silver-buttoned harmonica player's face was impassive; he looked out into the distance, as if bored. As other acts took turns starting songs— and ignored the younger harmonica player—his virtuosity decreased as he tried to find his musical way into the larger group. There was a marked change in how he played, as he came to play as a supporting musician, rather than the virtuoso lead. It seemed he was tuning himself to the musicians, and the music, in a new way. As an individual performer he sounded much less impressive, but the music and the other musicians blended better, the songs sounded better.

The process of clashing, then blending styles came full circle when the two harmonica players went into a duet together at the end of the jam. The young man in black first paid his dues by playing a gentle back-up, a musical bow, to the man with the cowboy hat and silver buttons who— for the first time—started improvising with astonishing passion and skill, just wailing on his harmonica. Maybe he hadn't wanted to overshadow the singer-guitarist he was accompanying earlier, or perhaps he just didn't need to show off. The young man in black gradually improvised more elaborately until the two of them flew into an incredible dual solo, with over a dozen musicians supporting them onstage they wailed together into the star-studded Manitoba night. The other musicians onstage shouted out hoots and hollers and the sprawling audience offered up thundering applause or simply got up and danced with joy.

And so it was that the guy dressed in black arts-garb and the old timer with the silver buttons and cowboy hat came together onstage. I don't know what the young harmonica player's class background was (his urban-elegant, East Coast art-world style of dress broadcast an upper middle class, cultural-capital orientation), but it was not difficult to see what class had shaped his approach to playing music.

Some of the middle class musicians I have played music with over the last forty years have bemoaned the way learning rule-bound musical notation from a young age initially squelched their natural ear training and creativity. Some middle class people learn to read music and play an instrument but never *feel* it, never really *join* the music, at least from a working class standpoint. They say they don't know how to "feel to know."

I do not intend to romanticize lack of formal musical training. I am very grateful to have learned both ways of making music and have worked hard to grasp what I call "the grid," seeing music as an intellectual mathematical system. But if I had to choose between what I studied as an adult and what I learned in childhood, I would stick with the ability to make it up. I'd pick the working class music of my childhood because, for me, it's more fun, creative, passionate, and, especially, because it encourages a certain kind of consciousness that I find immensely enjoyable. The working class music I learned was all about *being*—in the music and the moment. *Gotta feel to know.* I really enjoy the kind of knowing you have to feel.[6]

We move one step further in trying to understand the nonverbal part of the working class box when we look at kinds of communication that have no corresponding symbol system. I am thinking about the roller rink of my childhood and contrasting it with the middle class art of ballet, which I have been exposed to as an adult. Most of the graceful boys in the working class suburbs I grew up in would have been very embarrassed to manifest that talent in dancing. Instead, they channeled it into the more socially acceptable art of roller-skating. For both boys and girls, the roller rink met a number of needs at once and well reflects the culture that once elevated it to *the* place to be on a Saturday night. My parents met in a Brooklyn roller rink on a Saturday night, and, while interviewing my aunts and uncles, I found that two of my father's brothers had also met their wives at roller rinks.

There was the institution of the rink itself, a place where people gathered to find each other, meet new friends and lovers, sneak beer and cigarettes, and celebrate Saturday night. Contrast this with the highly structured setting of a dance studio where middle class teens take ballet lessons. At the rink you learn to skate by jumping into the stream of skaters. People just weave around you until you get your bearings and pick up speed. Always there is the group around you, and it is moving; you are in a rushing river of people that is very much like the culture and the consciousness it creates. Everyone moves together, creating a kind of large skating body with many persons within it, each contributing what they can. Within that flow of bodies there is the opportunity to try out new, more daring acts, but it is rather more like the Japanese Suzuki method than a formal dance class where students take (humiliating or triumphant) solo sweeps across the floor to learn a new technique. With skating, you are always contained and tucked within the group.

For the hot shots there was always the option to perform any number of incredible turns and tricks, skate backwards, spin around, but they generally did so within the body of skaters. As such they displayed their special personal talents while also creating the visual embroidery (literally weaving in and out and across the flow of skaters) that makes the whole skating body look good. In my experience, there was much helping of the teetering skaters by the more skillful. A wobbling hand might be grasped and a sudden, steadier companion attached to one's side. Or a brief steadying grasp of the hips or shoulders as the experienced skater paused in her dance, then moved on. A hand was offered to right a toppled soul. Roller-skating is a beautiful art, but it is almost absurd to put it up on a stage for exposition. Almost by definition you have to be there, at least sitting at the side of the rink, drinking a Coke, to appreciate it. Roller-skating is an apt example and metaphor of what I experienced in my working class life. There is room for a person to excel and to be a hot shot. But you do it within the whole, for the whole, and it somehow reflects well on the entire group.

Ways of Knowing

Different social classes influence their members with different *ways of knowing*. Middle class culture, and the worldview it promotes, is driven by formal language and its lengthy, step-wise learning. It both reflects and recreates a culture that prizes individual achievement of excellence and the competition that will (supposedly) force the "best and brightest" to the top. It is a culture designed to facilitate, or at least encourage, "becoming."

In working class culture the details of language are in the backseat rather than at the wheel. In fact, the vehicle of consciousness is not so much driven like a car down predictable avenues, as it is like steering a canoe over a body of water: it must take many elements into account besides distance. "Belonging" necessarily involves paying attention to and being part of the world around one, whether that world is an urban neighborhood, a blues jam, deer hunting in the woods (where deer "tell" hunters—through snapped twigs and tufts of lost fur—"I was here"), a neon city street on Saturday night, or a community conveying cultural practices to its children. What becomes central in communities of mutual aid is a shared consciousness, a *participation of identity*, a living in and through one another. *Me* and *mine* are replaced with *us*. Language is used to shore up a communal way of being, an intimacy beyond words.

Studying language and culture helped me understand and explain intellectually what I felt about class and my life; others have used different methods and measures to arrive at a similar cultural logic (Sennett and Cobb 1972; Meltzer 1978; Heath 1983, 1991, 1996; Bourdieu 1984; Metzgar 2000; Lareau 2003; Lareau and Conley 2008; Torlina 2011, and others). Because working class life is so rarely even acknowledged, and when it is so frequently assumed to be inferior, I have pointed to positive aspects of working class culture. Clearly, this tuning in can fail, particularly during conflict, often between men and women, and very likely in middle class situations such as higher education or business.

My fascination with tracking class and culture through language led me all the way to London. I conducted two interviews with Basil Bernstein in 1998. He was a small gracious man in a black cap, who met me at the tube (subway) stop to make sure I didn't get lost. He took me on a walking tour of the University of London campus. I asked him how he felt about his early work on speech and class-related cultures, which was tragically misunderstood in the United States. He said he still stood by that work. He added, though, that one should not make these generalizations without "the severest of qualifications." I asked if he meant qualifications for issues of race, gender, and ethnicity. "Yes!" he said emphatically.

In America, respect for different ethnicities, colors, and genders, and the inclusion of these new voices in higher education in the late twentieth century replaced the let's-all-blend-in melting-pot philosophy I grew up with in the 1950s. But beyond some concern for those in deepest poverty, class is, mostly, the invisible dimension of inequality in America. For all that our politicians (both left and right) are now hollering about the increasingly desperate "middle class" nobody even mentions the working class, some 63 percent of the American population (Zweig 2012).

When I was very young in the early 1950s, the concept of class in the United States was just being folded into the notion of one big middle class, contrary to what my parents and their parents had experienced as proud, but badly treated, workers building the nation. My parents knew the language of class, and my father's siblings still think of themselves as working class. The memory of a century of large-scale workers' movements and the common use of words and phrases like "working class" and "class struggle," as well a powerful psychological sense of "us" as workers, was obscured by the expanded new middle class. Ironically, the ability to afford houses and vacations, things that once defined the middle class, was made possible only by those working class union struggles, inviting themselves into the American Dream. Now it is as if that history has been entirely wiped from our collective memory.

Now, as forty years of multicultural awareness has opened my eyes to many influences outside of my immediate experience, I struggle to formulate and communicate how class fits into the cultural landscape of America. The African American civil rights movement, the student-led antiwar movement of the 1960s and '70s, the women's movement, all the spontaneous grassroots organizing from which these social movements emerged, along with the scholarship that followed and sometimes led the way, have helped me grasp class in America in a deeper and more personal way than the strictly economic approach I first learned from left-wing politics in early adulthood.

On the other hand, my presentation of distinct class cultures is not a separate-but-equal proposition. Bernstein was always quite clear on this point, and, like him, I have remained a vocal opponent of economic inequality. His five-volume body of work was called *Class, Codes, and Control*. In school settings, he developed his theory about how middle class culture, as an educational medium, reproduced societywide inequality between middle class and working class people. In this chapter I have talked about class as different uses, or codes, of language that reflect different cultural values, mores, and practices. In American society as a whole, the cultural differences I have described are employed to justify serious inequality for working class children and adults. By the time children go to school, these different cultural orientations begin to pay off quite differently for working class and middle class children.

4

Behaving versus Blooming

In elementary school I hoped against hope that I would be chosen to be a traffic monitor when I was in sixth grade. They wore a cool badge and had a flag to put up or down, letting kids know whether it was safe to cross County Road I, which ran alongside Pinewood Elementary School. I lived just across the street, but I knew I would not be chosen; instead I spent most of sixth grade with my desk up front against the blackboard studying chalk dust and the back of our teacher's head. I hadn't been one of the chosen five or six "smart" kids to whom he gave *A Wrinkle in Time*, a real, whole book to take home and read. And, of course, I wasn't chosen to be a traffic monitor either. Now, some forty-odd years later, I just can't pull myself away from playing traffic cop at the class intersection where my precious and wacky life has left me. Little County Road I has been replaced with a sprawling multilane superhighway that directs people every which way—except together. A life lived on borders and intersections can be both exhilarating and very lonely. But, no doubt about it, the view is excellent.

While we have glimpsed that success might mean different things in different cultures, most Americans are glad our education system offers across-class mobility. We believe we should all have the ability to choose how we live, from a fair sharing of the possibilities and options in our country. Equality of opportunity is a prized American value, people around the globe envy our mobility. Further, in the last thirty years, we have come to expect a much wider range of cultural and educational experiences for our children. But class is the diversity few schools seem to covet. Also, since people of color are disproportionately poor and working class, class too often gets equated (by the white middle class) with race. For Americans who are not newly immigrants, invisibly but surely, cross-class mobility is unlikely for all but a very few working class kids. Occupation of parents is still the most reliable indicator of the occupations children will assume as adults in America.

One reason for this is that, as early as grade school, class differences are the source of many misunderstandings between children and their teachers. Shirley Heath observed a simple verbal misunderstanding that resulted from cultural misunderstanding in a first grade classroom. A white middle class teacher asked, "Where's Susan?" Young Lem from Trackton, Heath's rural working class African American neighborhood said: "She ain't ride de bus." The teacher corrected her pupil, "She *doesn't* ride the bus, Lem." Lem answered back, "She *do* be ridin' de bus" meaning she regularly rides the bus, but that she did not today. The teacher frowned at him, then turned away, ending the exchange. Within Lem's community "She *ain't* ride de bus" translated into the Standard English "didn't," not the teacher's assumed "doesn't." Lem was just trying to be helpful. The world children like Lem live in, like their use of language, was invisible to the teacher. She thought he was either too simple-minded to understand the question or that he was trying to be difficult. In fact, Lem understood the teacher's question just fine. It was the teacher who did not understand her student's answer. He persisted in trying to be helpful, and he was rebuffed (1996, 277–78).

Without knowing students' cultural backgrounds, primary school teachers take unfamiliar speech and behavior as deficits to be overcome, not portals into other language systems and cultures. Middle class solipsism (my-world-is-the-whole-world), ignorance of working class experience and its absence in curriculum, combined with wrong-headed education policy and methods conspire to place working class children at a decided disadvantage in school.

In school, class-related skill sets, such as speech and reading, function to reward middle class children, building their sense of competence and self. But the very same teachers and classes unwittingly punish working class kids and challenge their confidence in themselves, their families, and their communities. Working class kids in school practice their usual community-oriented customs and language, while middle class children continue to develop individuality, Standard English, and competitive achievements consistent with their culture. Inequality is profound and poignant as working class children attempt to make sense of and adapt to new middle class rules and roles in school at the tender ages of five and six.

It's not a fair race when some are trained for it all their lives and others are trained for something else entirely. The resulting inequality creates painful problems for working class folks, not only in schools but in later life as well. As we will see, working class kids, both black and white, give up on school too young and too often. In effect, the race is rigged from the start.

In this chapter and the next, I will use, respectively, the work of two outstanding researchers, Shirley Heath and Jay MacLeod, to examine the influence of class and culture on primary and secondary education in the United States. Their in-depth case studies show how the medium of culture creates and recreates inequality (Hollingshead and Redlich 1958; Bernstein 1971, 1977; Bowles and Gintis 1976; Willis 1977; Vanneman and Cannon 1987; Sadovnik 1995; Anyon 1997; Finn 1999; Peckham 2010). These case studies are *not* universal models that speak for all middle class or working class Americans, but they are useful for my purposes. I am looking for general social patterns and currents that interact with other factors such as temperament, personality, family, ethnicity, race, geography, and gender.[1]

Ways with Words

Standard English is the language of power and mobility in the United States. All children should have real access to learning it. We have seen that Basil Bernstein first called it a "public language." A public voice, or elaborated code, requires a lot of education to learn well, and it is necessary if one wants to speak across cultural differences to a general audience. Only when all of our children are taught Standard English can working class people learn how to negotiate for themselves and their people in the places of power where only that language is accepted, for example, in higher education, law, business management, government, and with virtually every kind of professional a person may encounter in daily life. *How* kids should be taught these skill sets is my concern. Is it really necessary to learn that everything a child knew before school about language is nothing more than bad English and ignorance? I think not.

Shirley Heath's ethnography of three southeastern U.S. Piedmont communities, *Ways with Words*, picks up exactly where the last chapter left us: different communities' ways of using words provide windows into different worlds (1983, 1991, 1996). She further illustrated the role of class in language learning, adding the dimension of race, and moves our discussion into elementary education. Eventually she enlisted teachers and administrators to her project with remarkable effect. They found that students from all three communities, black and white middle class, black working class, and white working class, were able to learn the language codes and specific cultural symbols of the other two groups, when approached correctly. For ten years Heath lived with, studied, and recorded the speech of three communities in the Piedmont area: (1) both white and black middle class "mainstream townspeople" from a community she called "Laurenceville"; (2) a rural African American working class community she called "Trackton"; and (3) a rural white working class community she called "Roadville."[2]

Heath found that Laurenceville middle class parents, who were both black and white, all used the same techniques to raise their children. They turned to the same body of secondary sources—advice—of educators, psychologists, and other experts. Two decades later Annette Lareau found and described the same thing with respect to professionals who work with kids and dispense wisdom on proper psychological development to their parents:

> Professionals who work with children, such as teachers, doctors, and counselors, generally agree about how children should be raised. . . . Because these guidelines are so generally accepted, and because they focus on a set of practices concerning how parents should raise children, they form a *dominant set*

of cultural repertoires about how children should be raised. This widespread agreement among professionals about the broad principles for child rearing permeates our society. A small number of experts thus potentially shape the behavior of a large number of parents. (2003, 4)

In this chapter, we will see how these assumptions reflect a middle class bias. Having been trained as a professional psychologist, and having worked as a counselor in an alternative public high school for twenty-two years, I agree that there is a profound middle class bias among most professional advice givers. In an attempt to dispel the popular belief that schools are somehow neutral, and that kids excel, or fail, as a result of personal character, I want to expose the specific skill sets Heath uncovered that children needed to do well in school. The particular patterns of middle class parenting that Heath tracked so meticulously through the 1970s have only accelerated since she did her original study (Rosenthal and Wise 2001; Levine 2006).

Culture and Classrooms

School Starts at Home in Laurenceville

The middle class parents in Heath's study shared a variety of techniques in teaching language and skills of perception that pushed their children seamlessly toward skills that school then reinforced and refined. But, as we have seen, the values and goals public education promotes—*becoming* through individual achievement and mastery, competition between outstanding individuals, the weeding out of all but the "best and the brightest" from the competition—are in direct conflict with norms and moral values in many working class communities. When middle class teachers assume the inner lives and histories of their working class students are the same as their own, they do not learn how to build cross-cultural bridges into their curriculum. The education scholar Jean Anyon (1980, 1981, 1997) has called class bias the hidden curriculum of schools, channeling some children into adult lives as successful professionals and others into lives of supervised manual labor that requires obedience and discourages initiative.

I don't mean to be hard on middle class teachers. They may have the same dilemma as the student. They do not know their students' inner lives and cultural norms any more than the students know their teachers'. They were raised with different worldviews and skill sets. But, in education, the responsibility for bridging the gap between cultures should fall on teachers and the administrators who guide, and increasingly dictate, their curriculum, not on five year olds.

Heath (1996) found that both white and black middle class parents made early childhood a learning laboratory of school-related activities. They believed achievement in school was the foundation on which their children's entire lives would be built, and therefore they devoted an immense amount of time to preparing children for school.

Beyond speech, middle class children were taught literacy skills—reading and writing—from almost the moment they were born. Middle class mothers talked to their children all the time, long before the child could speak. When their babies babbled and cooed at them, they assumed it was *intentional* and represented something specific the baby wanted to say. The mothers then talked "with" the baby to find out what that might be, restating the baby's noises as she believed they were intended. This early focus on speech gave children the idea that someone was trying to "hear" them, and that they should put things into words as soon and as fully as possible.

Reading books to middle class children also began very early (by six months), and parents asked "what" questions about images in books, which children learn to correlate with three-dimensional real-world things. Cloth books with one item per page were used to read with the child. As babies began to walk and talk, these question-and-answer sessions continued and parents added running commentaries. As with Sally and Jacob in chapter 3, middle class mothers used back-and-forth exchanges to encourage conversation and negotiation with their children. "Children are trained to act as conversation partners and information-givers" (Heath 1996, 250). Through these commentaries, mothers linked new and old knowledge.

Between two and three years of age, these children began their own running commentaries about objects and events in their world *and* from books, connecting previous and new knowledge on their own. Adults attended to and encouraged this speech, believing that their children should learn to express their desires and ideas in language, first and foremost. Imaginary tales were also encouraged, and children were taught how to signal when a story was imaginary or real. As children aged, they were oriented toward verbal exchanges of all kinds.

Unlike the working class children in Heath's study, middle class children learned very early to feel comfortable with written and printed text, as they saw adults around them reading print frequently—from how-to instructions to consumer reports on potential purchases to novels, biographies, and "idea" books. Heath's middle class children were trained by their parents to *name, hold,* and *retrieve content* from books and other print materials. They were further taught (1) to ask questions frequently; (2) to expect answers they can understand; (3) to answer questions themselves; and (4) to elaborate.

> It is as though in the drama of life, [middle class] townspeople parents freeze scenes and parts of scenes at certain points along the way. Within the single frame of a scene, they focus the child's attention on objects or events in the frame, sort out referents for the child to name, give the child ordered turns for sharing talk about this referent, and then narrate a description of the scene. Through their focused language, adults make the potential stimuli in the child's environment stand still for a cooperative examination and narration between parent and child. (Heath 1996, 251)

A key difference Heath found between middle class and working class children, in preschool learning and elementary school success, was that middle class kids learned that written words have *a context of their own* that may or may not fit with real-world experiences. They learned the difference between personal real-world knowledge and the knowledge gained from written materials. They learned that words, stories, and ideas don't necessarily have anything to do with one's personal experiences, like fairy tales in "a far away land." The middle class kids learned that written words have their own rules, indeed several different sets of rules. Most important, these children learned to find the context of a story, and which rules apply, *from within the text itself*: "The modes of speaking, reading, and writing are tightly interrelated as children learn to recognize, link, talk about, and 'read' the cow jumping over the moon on the bedroom wall decoration and in the nursery rhyme book, *and* to separate this knowledge from the real-world knowledge they might have which says cows do not jump over moons" (Heath 1996, 256).

In other words, the middle class children learned to name items correctly, identifying "commonly understood" characteristics of a thing—it's a dog, it has a big bite; elaborating knowledge on the subject generally— don't touch dogs you don't know or dogs come in these colors; to state a personal opinion—I like white dogs best; and/or to create an expressive response to the subject—drawing pink and green dogs raining from the sky. All this feels natural for people whose childhoods involved intense one-on-one coaching in these skills. On the other hand, working class speech and stories often depend on having one specific common context, often a unique one that reflects the norms and values of a particular community.

Middle class parents in Heath's study also sent their children, some as early as two or three years of age, to classes at preschools that used "listen-and-wait" book reading, storytelling, and artwork. Children in middle class preschools (but not all preschools) learned to translate skills they have learned one-on-one with parents into group settings. They learned to sit quietly in a circle around a teacher while she tells stories or reads books, and to wait for the teacher's signal that it is time to comment and discuss. "Appropriate" (i.e., middle class) school behaviors are skills that these children learn. By the time they go to kindergarten, gathering around the teacher in a circle and being ready to listen feels entirely natural when the teacher simply says, "Story time!"

Phrases like "story time" or "show respect" have meanings that do not necessarily hold from one culture to the next. Teachers in Heath's study, assuming all students would understand, used indirect phrases from their own middle class lives to guide their students: "Is this where scissors belong?" "Someone else is talking now, we'll all have to wait." "You want to do your best today." Finding familiar language, teaching methods, and rules of interaction in school enables middle class children to feel they belong there and that school is there to help them. Through both imitating their parents and all that one-on-one training they received, middle class children learn the rules of the game that enable them to negotiate with authorities and make the rules work in their favor. This is where middle class kids begin to cash in on cultural capital—their built-in cultural advantage.

Though Heath's initial work is from the early 1980s, in 2003 Annette Lareau found the very same thing: middle class children come to school with skills working class children do not have. "Here the enormous stress on reasoning and negotiation in the home also has potential advantage for future negotiations. Additionally, those in authority responded positively to such interactions. Even in fourth grade, middle-class children appeared to be acting on their own behalf to gain advantages" (2003, 6).

In contrast, the children from both of the working class communities that Heath studied "had difficulty interpreting these indirect requests for adherence to an unstated set of rules" (1996, 280). While middle class kids snapped to the task, the same instructions puzzled children from other cultures who knew nothing of the unspoken context behind the words.

Middle class observers often wonder why working class children lack middle class concepts and behaviors that are so important to school success. They often fault parents for "not doing their job," that is, raising their children to be middle class. They fault communities. "I heard an African American university president say she could not support home-based childcare for low-income families because, 'We have to get those little children out of those neighborhoods'" (Modigliani 2008, from Leondar-Wright 2011).

But we will see how, in context, the lives of both working class children and their parents do not, and could not, prepare them to recognize and follow rules and roles in school that are alien to their own. Working class parents also care deeply about their children and work hard to give them what they think they will need in life.

Comin' Up in Trackton

The most profound differences in Heath's three communities were between Trackton, the rural working class African American community, and the middle class townspeople of Laurenceville. One of the most frequent complaints made by teachers in her study was that the rural black students didn't have normal manners. As we saw briefly, the actual meanings of their speech were often not even understood, nor did the teachers, at least initially, even try to find out what they were really saying.

We have seen that the worldview behind spoken words may differ profoundly from one culture to the next. In direct contrast to the concerted cultivation of middle class children's language skills, the black children of Trackton simply picked up language by being in the constant company of adults and older children who continued their usual conversation topics. Physical, not verbal, connection was considered important for infants.

Babies were constantly on someone's hip or in someone's arms. When old enough to crawl around and get into trouble, they were held on the laps of adults who continued their normal conversations with one another.

Although this African American community, like many others, was a highly verbal culture (more so than either the middle class or working class white folks), adults saw no reason to coach their children to state the obvious. Nor did they dumb down their language. Children learned to speak by jumping into the flow of conversation. It was the child who made what he or she said clear and entertaining enough to get adult attention. Once they could walk, Trackton children were given lots of attention by older children and adults: "Small children are looked on as entertainers, and all of their waking hours are spent in the company of others" (Heath 1996, 77). This was particularly true for the boys in Trackton.

> By the age of twelve to fourteen months boy babies have a special status. They are then accepted as players on Trackton's stage, the plaza at the center of town. . . . Communication is the measure of involvement here. Young boys learn from an early age to handle their roles by getting their cues and lines straight and knowing the right occasions for joining the chorus. They learn to judge audience reaction and response to their performances and to adjust their behaviors in accordance with their need for audience participation and approval. (1996, 79)

For example, Trackton's Ol' Frank puts his face in front of Auntie Mae's grandbaby Teegie: "Hey boy, ain't you gonna talk to me? Gimmie dat drink, I like a bottle too, you know!" Everyone in the plaza watches this challenge with interest. As the baby throws the bottle aside and reaches for Ol' Frank's nose, people laugh and comment: "Baby a toughie, you better look out, Frank, he knock you out" (1996, 79). All signs of aggressive play or counterchallenge bring appreciative hoots and comments from adults and older children. Children in Trackton, as in many other working class black communities, grow up learning they must push themselves into a situation, not "wait their turn."

The African American girls in Trackton did not take the stage like the boys did. Rather, they invented complex and ever-changing rhyme songs, often while jumping rope, in their own display of verbal agility. Both boys and girls learned that actions are messages people will read from your behavior, and that they must also learn to carefully read the behavior of other people. Like Rashad in chapter 3, they appeared to develop empathy and emotional intelligence at a young age. They also learned "fussin," in which they listed their complaints with and to someone who was then expected to listen. Contrary to professional wisdom, Trackton children learned a complex language and the rules of its use and assumed their positions in a highly verbal culture without any of the one-on-one coaching the middle class kids received. They learned to talk and listen appropriately for their context, as well as learning subtle reading and assessing of others' emotional states and relationships.

As one might imagine, these children, acting and speaking the way they grew up in their communities, were not in tune with the linear wait-your-turn rules of speech in elementary school classrooms. Working class children from any talkative, emotionally expressive ethnicity may feel lost and confused by the long periods of quiet expected in a classroom. All their lives they have heard a steady stream of talk in their community. They may burst out in the middle of someone else's speaking, showing they are appropriately aggressive and entertaining. "Entertaining" will be the last word a boy's teacher would use to describe this behavior, however. On the other hand, although eager to interrupt when something exciting occurs to them, kids like Teegie and Lem may be lost when asked a direct question and left in absolute silence to answer it.

Silence to a working class child includes the lack of emotional and other nonverbal signals from the teacher, a lack that is likely confusing. While a middle class teacher's intention is to give space or to act neutral, it will not be interpreted as that by a child who is used to lots of nonverbal responses that tell him or her about the emotional states and needs of others. How can Lem use his skill (and cultural command) to base answers on interpretation of others' desires and expectations when none of the usual signs are present? He may finally mumble, "I dunno." The unenlightened teacher will see only the lack of learning as she or he knows it, the lack of words needed to complete a sentence in her own language code: Standard English. She may think Lem is "slow" or otherwise "disordered" or that his family is teaching him nothing. Indeed, such assessments of working class African American children are common, and untrue (Labov 1969, 1970).

Cultures also instill foundational and unconscious psychological ways of understanding space and time. Personal space and possessions were defined very differently in Trackton than in the other two communities Heath studied. The children learned and were allowed to use whatever was at hand. Trackton kids usually played with other kids, outside. They played together with a variety of things that may not even be welcome inside the house, let alone having a special space for them, where they "belong." A strong cultural emphasis on caring and sharing with others, combined with material scarcity, created a people-over-things value among Trackton residents. Historically, African American folks have been on the short end of the stick economically, as they were in the Piedmont area, and the houses of Trackton were small, run down, and often full of extended family. There was not room for anyone to have a lot of possessions, nor was childhood play focused on store-bought toys.

When a schoolteacher says, "What do we do with things when we are done with them?" the kids are supposed to know what the teacher means: *put them away.* But where is away? *Where they belong.* Where do they belong? *Where you got them from.* Oops, where was that again? Teachers in Heath's study were confused, and annoyed, when these kids left tasks undone to go play with each other, or when they took materials and did the wrong things with them. They appeared to be disobeying the teacher, but they were simply doing what they normally do, just like the middle class children that the teachers praised. Since these kids learned to focus much more on human interactions than on stuff, protecting, preserving, and attending to toys was not necessarily highly valued. When students do not obey, teachers punish them.

Heath provided an example of class-related cultural differences about interacting with objects. She asked some Trackton children to sort thin wooden pieces into two piles of ones that were "alike." The children did not attend to the overall shapes of the cut-out blocks (two-dimensional flat blocks cut to be shaped like real-life things, e.g., pear-shaped) instead they focused on minute details. Each child sorted the wooden pieces into those with glue on them and those without. When she asked them to sort them some more, they sorted them based on lighter or darker grain of wood. They persisted in attending to tiny details of wood and glue.

They also quizzed her about the blocks: "Dese Shannon's blocks?" (Heath's daughter). "You buy dese?" "What you do wid 'em?" "How'd dat git dere [pointing to glue]?" "Can I keep dese?" They were trying to establish a personal connection to this odd, abstract activity. In another example, when she gave them forks to match with other forks, they asked "Why?" and "Who make you do dis?" They were trying to link together the jobs she'd given them, the objects themselves, *and* Heath's relationship to them with people they knew and their own familiar activities. They attempted to translate her "decontextualized" jobs into some recognizable context.

To an outsider from the middle class, the children's failure to do the job that was expected may indicate a lack of intelligence, ambition, cooperation, or worse. But in the highly personal and particular world where Trackton kids "come up," people are primary, things are not separate from people, and *seeing in context*, down to minute details, is important. Unlike the middle class children in Heath's study, these children had not yet been trained to list abstract characteristics (dog-shaped) that make two objects similar or different. However, with all the information her careful ethnography gave about culture, Heath did not perceive this as an intellectual deficit. "They seem, instead, to have a gestalt," she wrote, "a highly contextualized view of objects which they compare without sorting out the particular single features of the object itself" (107). They often volunteered connections between things: "They announce similarities of situations, scenes, personalities, and objects, which reflect not only a gestalt-like sense of whole scenes, but also recognition of minute details as well" (106).

Heath concluded that Trackton children had skills of context, comparison, analogy, and storytelling that they would not need until high school in our education system. In other words, not only did they have trouble understanding her middle class task—their responses indicated a different worldview and way of thinking.

I have seen the same dynamic in my own neighborhood, where some white middle class parents choose to live in a mixed race and class area but are upset when the same black and Latino kids they wanted their children to play with leave toys in the yard, ask to take them home, or talk out of turn repeatedly.

"What is wrong with these kids and their parents?" would best describe the look on the face of one frustrated middle class former neighbor of mine, after attending residents refused to participate correctly in her bicycle decoration competition for prizes at a block party. Knowing I was close with the children, she asked me to help get the kids in line and get people to "vote" by clapping their hands so the best bike could win. No one wanted to favor one kid over another, so every bike, however poorly or elaborately decorated, received much applause. I got the kids to line up and ride down the block three separate times for her, but when she asked I declined to teach the audience to clap more for one than another. In the end she just gave the grand prize to the children she had intended to give it to all along and tossed a few trinkets to the others. What I knew, but couldn't explain to her in a way she could understand, was that the prize of belonging in their cooperative lives every day of the week was of far greater value than competing for tickets to a ballgame.

The sociolinguist William Labov, in his study of African American children in Harlem, found that the artificial (and strange) atmosphere of talking with white professionals, as well as the one-on-one nature of the testing, altered children's speech significantly (1969, 1970). The children gave their interviewers one-syllable answers to questions and were judged slow-witted and verbally inept. When given a black, inner-city interviewer and allowed to have a friend present, the results were very different. In a more familiar cultural context, the children were highly verbal and utilized skills of analogy and other skills considered to be beyond their age level. Similarly, Jonathan Kozol, interviewing in the South Bronx (1995), found children who spoke Standard English with him though not at home or with their friends. So it is not necessarily the case that working class and poor children *cannot* speak Standard English, as that they generally do not. From Labov in Harlem to Heath in the Piedmont Carolina hills, black children were unlikely to speak in their usual way in unfamiliar settings with white strangers.

Notions of *time* were also quite different in Trackton. For the middle class time comes in structured blocks. When middle class grown-ups say, "Time's up," kids learn to abandon an activity and be ready for the next one in a busy schedule. Trackton kids experienced time as a *flow*—they usually got to finish what they started; they were not accustomed to people saying, "Time's up!" In school, the phrase simply confused them, and when they continued to play they were scolded and punished.

Schools ask lots of questions of their students. But the types of questions children become accustomed to in early childhood vary in different settings and point to different kinds of answers, different kinds of normal. We have seen that the most common questions asked of very young children in the middle class were "what?" questions in which the parent already knew the answer, and increasingly, so did the child: "What does a doggie do?" "Bark!" As children aged, these questions quickly progressed to "what *if*?" questions, and kids were expected to elaborate. But the most common types of questions asked of young children by adults in Trackton were analogy questions that called for a "non-specific comparison" of one thing, event, or person with another: "What's that like?" (pointing to a flat tire on a neighbor's car). The Trackton child answered correctly, "Doug's car. Never fixed." Questions where the asker already knew the answer were the *least* common kinds of questions asked of children in Trackton (1996, 104).

Another common type of question put to young children in Trackton were "accusation questions": "What's that on your face?" Trackton kids' responses differed from both white working class and white and black middle class children. The child would respond in one of two ways, either nonverbally with a lowered head or verbally with something creative enough to take the questioner's attention away from the original infraction, "You know about that big mud puddle . . ." Taking charge of the ongoing narrative and being entertaining, while valued at home, is considered sassy and disruptive in school. Needless to say, creativity is not rewarded in school when a teacher asks a question that, for her or him, has only one right answer.

What I find particularly significant is that the children of Trackton learned a highly complex language without any of the concerted cultivation or one-on-one coaching that middle class kids received. This is important because, as we will see later, there are problems that come with concerted cultivation that are now calling it into question (Rosenfeld and Wise 2000; Levine 2006). So it is not simply a matter of teaching these same techniques to working class parents, as many professionals would advise. The children of Trackton also learned essential rules of human interaction within their community, which were embedded in their young minds and that conflicted mightily with the middle class rules of school. How does a six- or seven-year-old child feel in an environment that discourages, even punishes, what is his or her normal and natural way with words? How about when it also misreads and punishes everyone else from your community? How would these kids ever get the idea that school was actually there to help them and/or their people?

Doin' It Right in Roadville

The third community Heath studied was "Roadville," a white rural working class community. Their culture's ways with words and lifestyle lay somewhere between the middle class townspeople of Laurenceville and the working class African Americans of Trackton, with some features from each of these, and some elements all its own. Superficial similarities to middle class methods actually made the real differences more invisible and confusing for both students and their teachers.

I offer Roadville as only an example of a white working class culture, not as a universal model. The differences between Trackton and Roadville are offered as examples of differences *within* working class communities. While some may see these differences as reflections of race or ethnicity alone, all the middle class parents in this study, black and white, used the same techniques with their children (as did both black and white middle class parents in Lareau's 2003 and 2008 studies).

White working class communities, based largely on ethnicity and local traditions, can vary wildly one from another. My own white working class upbringing in Mounds View, Minnesota, was pretty different from that in Heath's Roadville. Still, Heath's description of Roadville children's relationships with kin could have been written about my extended rural and suburban Jensen family.

In Heath's study, middle class teachers commonly complained that these children were losing the manners they had when they first came to school. The children were docile and obedient in the early grades of primary school, and teachers found them cooperative and able. In the later grades of elementary school, teachers complained that Roadville children showed "no imagination, answers are always minimal" and "neither boys nor girls want to step out and take the initiative on anything." But, even a quick look at the rules and roles of their culture shows that these children, like the children of Trackton (but differently), were simply behaving normally, as they learned in their families and community.

In Roadville, respecting elders meant not talking back, or being mouthy, as my family would call it. In their close-knit community, Roadville children were taught traditions, not innovations. They were raised to say it "right," meaning the way it has always been done. White kids in Roadville were instructed and coached to tell memorized stories verbatim, and adults would correct them midway, "But what happened before that?" They were taught to stick to the right facts and to use the particular language of the community. Roadville parents were concerned about doing things the "right" way. They wanted to bring their children up to work hard, do right, be good, and get ahead in life.

Not surprisingly, they imitated the middle class in certain ways. In Roadville, as in middle class homes, there were spaces for certain things and routine times for certain events. Also, as in middle class homes, both mother and father were active in parenting, and on weekends and holidays there were frequent nuclear family outings, often to go visit extended family.

By the late 1970s and early '80s, the time of Heath's study, Roadville's white working class mothers also read books to their small children and gave them instructions on when to pay attention, listen, and "behave." Babies initially received lots of talk and attention from their mothers. Women believed this was part of "bringin' 'em up right"—to coach them and introduce them to books, to attend to their coos and noises as if they were attempts on the part of the child to say something in particular. In Roadville, moms also asked their toddlers "what?" questions in back and forth exchanges, for example by pointing to the dog and asking, "Who's that?" "Nuffie!" But these surface similarities to middle class families only served to make Roadville children's customs more incomprehensible to teachers.

Babies in Roadville also received special status, and they were shared within extended family, but quite differently than in both Trackton and Laurenceville. Here the emphasis was on the role of *blood* kin. When mothers went back to work, they left their babies with relatives, or close friends, and sometimes in a church preschool, rather than with professional child-care centers. Family connections were "carefully drawn and much talked about." Relatives and family friends made special efforts to interact with babies, especially to touch, hold, and cuddle them, in direct contrast to the middle class families of Laurenceville, who frowned on too much handling of their babies. Cousins were encouraged to interact with babies and include them early on in their sense of "us." Parents in Roadville told cousins, "You will be like brothers and sisters." Children were introduced to others by their position in the family, for example, "This is your Uncle Donnie," "your cousin Debbie," and so on. A big-family atmosphere was still valued highly, though parents no longer had more than a few children themselves.

As I grew up in the 1950s and '60s in my large extended family, I felt connected to lots of people and often stayed with relatives. We spoke (and still speak) in a dialect similar to Roadville's: "I don't got it no more," "It just ain't important," "I seen Ant Shirley, she come up here just last week." People in Roadville, as in my family, relied on one another for help with "bringin' up" kids in countless ways, including passing on cribs, throwing baby showers (for each and every child) where mothers get things they will need for the baby, plus plenty of advice and babysitting. People in my family still count on one another for help with many things: figuring out what's wrong with a car, where to buy something cheaper, what to do about Nick's cough. This type of behavior creates a powerful psychological sense of community (Sarason 1988). Babies were treated similarly in Mounds View, too, as most parents there were originally from rural Minnesota.

But, again, Roadville's surface similarities to middle class families only served to obscure much deeper differences. For example, though sometimes asked "what?" questions during book-reading with their mothers, the most common questions directed at small children were "question statements" that required no verbal response from the child, for example, "Momma's got to get some softer bed sheets, don't she? Bobby's getting a rash." These comments are said to the child but are actually directed at other adults such as Dad or Grandma to let them know that mother needs some help. Accusation questions, "Now what are you doing there!" call for only one answer on the part of the child: "I'm sorry." As Roadville children grew there were innumerable occasions where parents ask "question-directives" such as: "What do you say?" ("Thank you"); "Can you say, 'Come again?'" Often, all that was needed was a particular look from parent to child to prompt the right response. When this failed, parents asked, "Don't you have anything to say?"

A fundamentalist church and a literal interpretation of the Bible were the foundation from which all else followed in Roadville: learning the right things, saying the right words, with the Bible as the final authority. Roadville folks' belief in strict adherence to a literal interpretation of the Bible both reflected and reinforced a cultural tendency toward concrete black-and-white thinking in general. Absolute truths were sought, with little room for shades of gray: "Both church and home activities called for *bounded knowledge* which is exhibited in the repetition of memorized words exactly as they have been taught" (Heath 1996, 140–41; emphasis mine).

In the black church of Trackton, the particulars were very different. A model of creative interpretation and spontaneous audience participation mirrored a cultural tendency that favored creativity and spontaneous expression of feelings, in words or other sounds, such as "A-men," "That's right," or "Mmm-hmmm." Likewise, the preacher made up much of his sermon as he went along, joining with and building on the murmurs and words the congregation gave him. Very little of the actual service was predetermined; the vocally spontaneous congregation was as important in creating the sermon as the preacher. Each service was different and somewhat unpredictable.[3]

Unlike the stories told in both Laurenceville and Trackton, Roadville stories generally had a "moral" at the end. I hear this in my counseling practice, too, from white working class Midwesterners. At the end of telling the story of an event in their lives, working class clients may say, "So, I guess that just goes to show you can't fight City Hall" or "Best to let sleeping dogs alone, right?" Often they repeat some advice I have given them previously and then look at me with a question in their eyes, as if to say, "Is that right?" Since I first wrote about this I have noticed how often I also close a story with something similar. This is akin to Bernstein's working class group saying, "you know?" and "isn't it?" at the ends of their sentences. The cultural command is that the speaker reconnect with the listener(s) and also to bring the story back home to something familiar, something connected to the worldview of the listeners.

In my life and in my counseling and teaching experience, I find two groups that working class white people gravitate toward in their communities: religious people, whose faith in God and His Word is the primary foundation for knowledge and interpretations of the world around them; and people who delight in being "bad," at least a little. In my white extended family, all of us believed in God and were confirmed Lutherans. The more religiously inclined in my family share many Roadville characteristics, but there are other folks, too, who do not. They like to tell dirty jokes, swear, outwit authorities, smoke cigarettes, drink beer, and sometimes whiskey. Some call this the "outlaw" part of working class culture, as exemplified by

the white working class hero Johnny Cash. There are, of course, less roman-
tic descriptions as well. White people in this group, like Trackton blacks,
often tell stories of resilience and triumph over authorities, and drama,
creativity, and exaggeration are encouraged. Listeners laugh and shout out
mouthy comments. In my experience, as in black Trackton, it is not unusual
for white folks to give a big talker some amount of shit.

Others have described similar dynamics in working class communities. Herbert Gans studied a working class Italian neighborhood and saw
four major behavior styles: "The maladapted, the middle-class mobiles,
and—the two most important ones—the routine-seekers and action-
seekers" (1962, 28–32). Joseph Howell's terms "settled living" and "hard
living," popularized by Lillian Rubin, also roughly translate into "routine-
seeking" versus "action-seeking" (Howell 1973; Rubin 1976). My mother
and my hard-core greaser brother Eddie tended toward action-seeking,
as did I and my young wannabe greaser friends in the neighborhood. We
grew up with irreverence toward tradition and started smoking cigarettes
by age eleven. I learned and told jokes well enough to get a whole classroom laughing in grade school and occasionally delighted in outwitting
people who had power over me (later on, frequently).

Eventually my big brother, like his action-seeking hero Johnny Cash,
turned from "raising hell" to the Bible. In the 1980s he became a member
of Jerry Falwell's Silent Majority, and he is still a born-again Republican
who champions Christianity in government. Our parents were dedicated
New Deal Democrats and believed strongly in the separation of government and religion. Once he had a wife and child to care for, Eddie simply
gravitated toward the opposite pole in our binary political system.

In Mounds View, we all traipsed obediently to Pinewood Elementary
each day. Putting in our time. I was a very good student at first because
I adored my first grade teacher, Mrs. Johnson, with her white finger curls
and sweet-smelling grandma cheeks. She gave out hugs every day as we
left. Roadville kids had manners the middle class teachers could relate
to—they were obedient, quiet, and said what the teachers expected them
to say. Again, Roadville kids started out well in school, as the early grades
focus on rote learning quite a bit. But cultural differences still ran deep in
Roadville as in Mounds View.

Teachers could not get these kids to elaborate, to be more creative
within a structured, supervised context, to move beyond basic skills. They

answered "what?" questions easily. But by the time they reached fifth grade they started to fall behind, as elaboration and "what if" questions became more common. By junior high and high school, when education shifts even more toward interpretive knowledge, it is likely that these students, much like my friends and I, would have already given up on school and been mainly looking for nonacademic adventures. By that time, most of us were eager to get to work and make money; I started my first job with a payroll check at fourteen (I lied and said I was fifteen) at a bakery in Spring Lake Park.

Patrick Finn's 1999 *Literacy with an Attitude* also summarizes Heath's white working class Roadville, and, from his description, the culture of Roadville looks mighty constricting and bleak for the children in it. But in my experience, both personally and as a counselor, white working class children rarely display all aspects of themselves when around adults. Peer, not power-negotiated, relationships are the norm in working class cultures. What we cannot know is how the children in Heath's study spoke and behaved when she was not with them. She mentions at one point that when kids visit from other places, Roadville kids "tell tales" to them. In my neighborhood, and in my rural extended family, we did a whole lot adults did not know about. Still, we knew how to behave, which meant how to act with adults around. After hugging my aunties and uncles at reunions, my cousins whisked me off for fun on adventures the adults never knew about. This dichotomy (behaving with adults versus having wilder fun among ourselves) was much more the case with kids in my suburban neighborhood. I identify much more with working class studies scholar David Greene's description of his working class childhood in Brooklyn, and his view of himself and his friends in relation to the middle class, than with Finn's bleak portrayal of Heath's Roadville:

> Early on, I developed the idea that the world was divided up into the real people and the fake people. And somehow, the fake people were the ones who got to run things; they were the ones who had all of the official power. They got to make up and enforce the rules. The fake people actually got to tell the real people what to do. And the things that they told them to do— how to talk, how to dress, how to eat, how to act, how to think and what to value were, just like they were, phony, lifeless and without real substance. Their goal seemed to be to prevent the real people from living their lives and to force them to become just like they were. (Greene 2003, 6–7)

Voices: Public versus Private

I struggle to avoid middle class–biased "deficit" models of describing working class people when I explain differences between the ways working class and middle class people learn to speak and think. But working class pride can also get in the way of understanding the relative strengths and weaknesses of class-related cultures. I believe there are damaging holes in the education of working class kids in America. These educational holes are based in the use of private, but not public, language.

In the contemporary world, working class habits of speech and thinking within a specific context impose limits on what folks can communicate to people outside their communities. For example, while I was first writing this chapter and the last one, I talked with my older brother Eddie on the telephone and arranged to spend the evening with him and his new girlfriend. I had just spent my writing day championing the intimacy and subtlety of working class communication, and, ironically, I found myself wishing fervently that he could just give me wholly abstract, objective directions to where I should meet him. Our conversation was a perfect example of the limits of contextual thinking. He gave me instructions to get to the Eagles Club in Elk River so that we could enjoy beer and karaoke.

"Well, you take a right there, and you'll go by the railroad tracks. There's a gas station, Beaudry's, yeah, you take a right and then—"

"*Another* right?"

"Yeah, yeah, a right offa Highway 10."

"Okay, I got that right. Is there another one?"

"Well, then, you see, you'll go by the strip mall, and the Wendy's there and there's Beaudry's. If you go to the park you've gone too far."

"Eddie, it will be dark, I can't see those things! How many rights do I take?" I was getting annoyed.

"Well, I'm tryin' to tell ya!" He was also getting annoyed. "Take a right off 10, and then when you get to Beaudry's gas station take a right—"

"Okay, two rights! The second right turn is at . . . Beaudry's? Will I see that on a sign?"

"Well, I think so. Maybe not. I'm not sure, I guess. It's owned by the Beaudry family right here in Elk River. Everyone calls it Beaudry's. Yeah, the Beaudry's are—"

"Is it a chain, like Holiday?"

"Yeah, it is. Oh, what is it now? Damn, I, I think . . ."

I heard his girlfriend in the background saying, "It's a Shell station."

"Okay!" I said. "I take my second right at the Shell station . . ."

And so on. When I drove down to interview my aunt Lu and uncle Bob Sharpe, my aunt Nancy Houg and uncle Rick Jensen, I overshot Glenville and went quite a way into Iowa, because the Short Stop, where Lu said I was supposed to turn, hadn't had a sign that said that for over twenty years. Now, if I were a better relative, in working class terms, I would know all these places, and what people call them, because I would visit more often.

Researcher James Meltzer (1978) used the following example from Schatzman and Strauss (1955, 337) to illustrate different language systems and the different social meanings these kinds of speech imply. When asked where chewing gum is usually purchased, the response from a "middle-class" person was "at a cashier's counter or in a grocery store." The "lower-middle" [working] class person said "at the National." And the "lower-class" [poverty] person said "from Tony."

It is not, as classism would declare it, that working class people are so ignorant that they think the interviewer knows where "the National" is located or who "Tony" might be. Nor is it necessarily the case that they are *unable* to produce abstractions. It is that doing so does not "feel natural" (or "come naturally" in elaborated code) to them; it is not how they learned to speak. Habits of speech are just that, habits that are assimilated at young ages. Residents of both Trackton and Roadville used a primarily private, or restricted, language.

I didn't know how to tell my brother or Auntie Lu what kind of directions I wanted. As I became middle class, I learned how to translate both speech and music into what I then called "the grid." I meant formal abstract language and other symbol systems. That is, I learned to translate my particular way of thinking into a manner of speech based on abstractions generally known in the middle class. In early adulthood, around some middle class people, I went from proud to ashamed of my own colorful metaphoric speech, because it was imprecise. In time abstractions became automatic, and now I sound like an egghead half of the time and I miss the grid with people who don't know it.

Nonstandard Lives

All three ways with words I have described in this chapter are "grids" of a kind—meaning coherent, entwined systems of language and culture. It's just that formally designated, so-called universal ones, have written counterparts that allow people that master them to communicate across many cultures and contexts. That is certainly not to say that all middle class children, or people, use this language well. Some fail miserably, and suffer their failures deeply in a culture where these skills are seen as normal behavior. But, culturally, they were far more prepared for school than either Trackton or Roadville children could be.

In terms of school readiness and success, working class children— white, black, brown, red, and yellow—are not typically prepared. On this everyone seems to agree. Neither working class community taught their kids all of the skills they would need for school, but what they did teach varied. In Trackton, black children were encouraged in creative interpretation and spontaneous expression (stories for boys and rhyme songs for girls). In Roadville, white children were raised with language that provided an ongoing test of their ability to grasp and commit themselves to traditional customs and ways with words. Speech both reflected and recreated long-standing community traditions. Both communities' ways with words stood in sharp contrast to those of the middle class families of Laurenceville. Though the middle class children also learned to memorize and repeat language verbatim, they learned that it is only one possible option along with verbal elaborations and creative interpretations. They also knew when to use each kind of speech and how to signal which kind of answer the listener was about to hear.

In both Roadville and Trackton, storytelling, not printed text, was the coin of the realm: children grew up hearing stories, not reading them. In both working class communities, language was specifically aimed at members of the community and was laden with buzzwords, local abbreviations, and references understood only by them. In both communities the meanings of speech could be hard for outsiders to understand, but, again, the shared *ways* within them created intimacy and a powerful sense of "us."

Though both Roadville and Trackton parents hoped their children would have "a better life" than they did working in the mills, they did not know the skills their children would need in school, beyond the ability to memorize and repeat. Roadville and Trackton parents did not put much stock in books themselves, nor did they give books to their children after they were toddlers. Beyond their early training and the gradual learning of the community's stories and rules of speech, these kids were left alone to play with other kids, often from their large extended families. By the time kids were school age, their parents simply turned them over, trusting school would take care of the rest. They believed, or hoped, they had prepared their children for school. No one told them anything different. At work, working class people are forced to submit to authority if they want to keep their jobs, and this attitude is passed to children: pay your dues and enjoy your free time.

The Latino class-crossover Richard Rodriquez described what he learned in school as gaining access to a public language, and a public self, in his autobiography *Hunger of Memory* (1982). In an interview in 2003, Rodriguez described having to give up his former self and never being able to embrace both of his worlds at the same time (Lubrano 2004). I want working class children in America to learn and use formal language and other aspects of public, or general knowledge, but not at the expense of connection with their former lives. And certainly not at the expense of losing respect for their working class families, the other people and places they came from, and ultimately, their working class selves.

I also wish they would not wholly abandon their working class dialects, which often have a pith and musical quality that Standard English does not. Rather, I want them to *also* learn other ways with words and when to use which ones. Indeed, most working class kids in American cities, and perhaps all teenagers, are "bilingual" this way already, switching language codes in different settings. It would be nice if all those years in school could effectively help them learn not only how to switch codes, but when and why.

I think of all these systems of language as pointing to different *frames* of awareness, like different lenses on a fancy camera. Pop on this lens, and suddenly things far away appear up close, down to the tiniest details. Pop it off again and put on another one, you get a very wide and faraway view. Still another lens and you see a green tint to everything, and contrast is enhanced. And so on. Different cultures put different lenses on people's view of things. We have seen that it is a mistake to assume that where Standard English is missing nothing else exists. We have seen there are many different ways of seeing or feeling the world, born of other cultures and language systems. But I wouldn't wish my own children to be limited to either middle class or working class ways of thinking, talking, or seeing the world and the people in it.

Bernstein challenged schools to bridge this gap for working class students by attending to their different cultural orientations; Heath's work reads like a case study for his theory, adding the dimension of race to the puzzle of language, class, and culture. We have seen that middle class children learn that books and print offer knowledge of things outside of personal context: stories and ideas that exist independently of one's personal life. In other words, they learn to interpret and use both public and private voices, both elaborated and restricted language. We have seen that working class children and adults live very community-oriented lives and see the world in the context of that community. But serious problems, and false assumptions, can arise when working class people need to use formal public speech in order to negotiate with authorities and other middle class people.

In my opinion, the problem and the responsibility lie with the teachers, professional helpers, and officials who assume their middle class lifestyle is in all ways superior and should be adopted by everyone. As Lareau noted, at the end of her initial study of twenty-six families and eighty-eight children, "I see it as a mistake to accept, carte blanche, the views of officials in dominant institutions (e.g., schools or social service agencies) regarding how children should be raised" (2003, 13). As one of those social service professionals, and after working with children all my life, I couldn't agree more.

Starting with Success

Fortunately, it is entirely possible to teach Standard English and other school skills while also respecting working class children's learned language and cultures. Through adult education classes at a local college, Heath eventually taught teachers and administrators to become ethnographers to help them better understand working class children. She had them dissect and describe the habits and values of their own middle class culture to make them more aware of unconscious biases and assumptions they were using with their students. Through the process of researching and studying their students' communities and cultures they came to know *how to know* the internal rules and logic of other forms of language use and the cultures they come from. Heath taught teachers to become ethnographers, and the teachers in turn figured out how to teach their grade school students to become ethnographers of their own and one another's lives. They studied and came to understand language and culture systems from all three of Heath's populations. One white middle class teacher wrote in her journal for Heath:

> I've been here [in the school district] during the transition period [of racial integration], so I know what frustrations we all felt. The thing that none of us realized was that these children were almost like foreigners to us. True, they lived within our communities; we have all associated with and talked with blacks in our homes all our lives, so we thought we understood them. We knew that their spoken language was different, but we assumed those differences were from ignorance and lack of education.

And another wrote:

> The fact that communication is so important to learning points out the need for learning the child's language and also for allowing children to interact and communicate with each other. The very pictures we put on the walls of the schoolroom show our ethnocentric leanings. Boy, was that a slap in my face. (Heath 1996, 270–71)

These teachers and administrators delighted Heath with the effective applications they created for students in their classrooms. All three groups of children—middle class whites and blacks from Laurenceville, working class blacks from Trackton, and working class whites from Roadville—were supported in their current ways with words. Teachers learned and came to use familiar aspects of Trackton and Roadville speech and cultures to build bridges to Standard English and other school skills. All children were also taught to recognize and understand all three communities' ways with words and how to recognize when each one was appropriate.

Teachers asked working class elementary school students to interview people in their communities and convert oral traditions into written form and showed them familiar language in unfamiliar text form. They used

newspapers and other familiar kinds of text in English; and they trained
the children to teach these different language systems to younger children.
Teachers wrote new science and math curricula that used familiar terms
and situations from the textile mills. In home economics they collected
proverbs and advice about childbirth from the working class communities
and enabled students to compare and contrast these with scientific ideas
and research, while judging neither.

Teachers applied the following general principles: They began by establishing foundations of knowledge familiar to all three groups of children to
serve as a basis for later classroom information. Expanding from this base,
children were taught to link what they already knew with unfamiliar areas
of knowledge. Teachers coached students to collect and analyze familiar
ways of knowing (like watching someone else do it, or being told a story
that illustrates the point) and then taught them to translate these into scientific or school-accepted labels, concepts, and generalizations. The children
were then gently pushed to accommodate and practice new skills. They
helped students learn ways of talking about language use to both organize
and express information.

The results were remarkable. The students progressed rapidly. They
were enthusiastic about and proud of what they were learning in school.
Working class parents became more involved, and students scored better on standardized tests. "Leaders on the playground" who were self-
acknowledged "failures in the classroom" built more versatile concepts
of themselves. Learning all three systems of language use weakened the
boundaries between the systems. Fifth graders then were enlisted to teach
these ways with words to second graders. Further, the teachers were ener-
gized and excited about their newfound abilities to understand and teach
all of their students. These methods can and should be translated and adopted to fit different regions all across the United States.

In 1991, Heath replicated her techniques and published *Children of
Promise*. Again, three types of language systems and cultural backgrounds
were taught to elementary school children, this time in Los Angeles (with
working class whites and Latinos, and white middle class children).
Heath and her collaborator, Leslie Mangiola, then had the students teach
these differences to younger children. Again, all three groups of children
learned all three language uses and were able to teach them to younger
students.

Land of Opportunity?

Though my concern is primarily with differences between people in the working class and middle class (together over 90% of our population), the picture of social class and culture is much larger than the one painted so far in this book. A quick glimpse through a wider-angle lens lets us see working class and middle class folks within the larger framework of class, culture, and education in America. With property taxes being a prime source of school funding, our education system is structured to give significant advantages to children from higher classes—the higher the class, the greater the educational advantage automatically received. Thus, in the "land of opportunity," children who already receive much out-of-school training in school skills, and whose parents can afford extra tutoring, music lessons, and other educational opportunities, are also given much more from public schools.

The education scholar Jean Anyon's (1980, 1981, 1997) work on class, culture, and education offers a big-picture view of how America hands out significant structural, or built-in, inequality to its children. It also illustrates dramatic differences between the schooling of lower middle class and middle middle class children from those of the upper middle class. She studied fifth and second graders in five public schools chosen by socioeconomic class of students attending: two working class schools, a middle class school, an upper middle class school, and one serving the upper class. She found that schools and curriculum were designed for the class of students who would attend them, and that this led students seamlessly into the occupational lives expected of them.

In the two working class schools, *work* for the fifth-grade students consisted of copying a teacher's notes off the chalkboard, checking the one right answer to textbook questions, and minor craft projects. *Knowledge* consisted of disconnected, memorized facts, without teachers offering any sense of overall context or application to the lives of students. Meaning was not addressed, and interpretation, or the making of meaning by students, was thoroughly discouraged. Very few, if any, "what if?" questions were asked of students. Learning was about rote repetition, obedience, and submission, and children never received any knowledge or skills that might challenge their current worldview. There were no requests to answer anything "in your own words"; indeed, children were punished for trying to do anything other than copy the teachers' notes from the board, exactly as they had been written.

In these schools, knowledge was received or, more often, resisted but never explained. For example, a teacher told students to make a grid, but would not tell them what it was for until they were finished following her exact directions. When a girl initiated a different faster way to make the very same grid, the teacher scolded and stopped her, then made her do it all over again, exactly the way she had been told (Anyon 1980, 74). Control seemed to be the primary concern for teachers: students could not leave their desks without permission, they were frequently held after class ended for reprimand, and they were often ordered to "shut up" (1980, 76).

A second-grade teacher, asked by Anyon what was important knowledge for her students, said, "Well, we try to keep them busy." Teachers and administrators spoke poorly of the students. Another teacher said, "I hate to categorize them but they're *lazy.*" A principal told a new teacher who was worried about teaching in a tough school, "Just do your best. If they learn to add and subtract, that's a bonus. If not, don't worry about it." Yet another teacher referred to the students as "animals" (Anyon 1981, 10).

In one working class school, the fifth-grade students, whose combined average IQ was above average (and a few way above average), were given assignments from a social studies text designed for "low ability" sixth and seventh graders, a total of sixteen lessons for an entire school year. In the other working class school, one social studies assignment for fifth graders was to cut out and make a stand-up figure of a cowboy roping a steer to represent the southwestern United States (Anyon 1981, 10).

Perhaps not surprisingly, *resistance* emerged as the dominant theme among these students. Anyon noted that these children were often resentful in school, pulled stunts to amuse themselves, and were pleased to see the teacher get upset or angry (1981, 11).

The first level of "middle class" schools that Anyon studied were also attended by working class children whose skilled-labor parents could afford to buy homes in a middle class neighborhood. *Work* also consisted of giving the one correct answer, but the directions allowed the student to make choices, to figure out things. The teachers explained the purpose of assignments and why the directions would lead to the right answer. Students could do steps "in their heads" rather than write it all down. They then had to say how they did the problem, not just give the answer. Teachers were concerned that children "understand what they read." As one teacher put it, "I think that's more important than skills, although they're important, too. But if they don't understand what they read, they won't know anything" (Anyon 1981, 13). Obedience and being polite were also highly valued.

Social studies was "discipline centered," with emphasis on understanding a variety of "fundamental concepts" from various disciplines in social science and developing the ability to generalize. For example, one "understanding" in economics was "Stockholders are the real owners of a company that is operated by a board of directors who acts in the stockholder's name." But controversial topics like why workers strike were routinely avoided for fear parents would complain (1981, 14). Social studies for these kids involved reading and answering comprehension questions: who, what, when, where, and, sometimes, why.

The students worried about grades and viewed knowledge as valuable, something that could bring good grades, good colleges, and a good job. The dominant theme among these students was a sense of promise, of *possibility.*

What Anyon called the "affluent professional," or upper middle class, school had teachers from middle class or upper class backgrounds, often wives of successful, powerful men. *Work* was creative activity, carried out independently, and it included individual expression and ideas, as well as choices about methods and materials of presentation. Creativity and personal development mattered. Students were expected to think for themselves and to make sense of their own experiences. *Knowledge* in this school was about discovery and making sense of many issues and events. Students' personal experiences were applied to the things they studied, and societal strife, like racism—and even class—were acknowledged and discussed. Students were encouraged to care about social issues.

Social studies revolved around higher-order concepts such as "the roles of savings, capital, trade, education, skilled labor, skilled managers, and cultural factors in the process of economic development" (Anyon 1981, 19). In social studies, these fifth graders wrote editorials about matters before the school board! Also, they were expected to understand that the assumptions of modern Western culture come from two preceding cultures, Judaic and Greco-Roman.

Students were encouraged in a variety of activities that included writing plays, painting murals showing "the division of labor in ancient societies," and frequent discussions of current events, including bringing in clippings from newspapers. Teachers' questions elicited connections between current events and what the students were learning in school, making these students' "context" the whole world. They were learning to manipulate *symbolic capital*, or how to use established grids or symbol systems (language, mathematics, musical notation, and more) for their own purposes.

Control in this upper middle class school was negotiated between teachers and students, and teachers rarely gave orders. Students could leave the classroom to go to the library at any time by merely signing their names on a chalkboard. When students asked how to do something, teachers replied, "What makes sense to you?" or "You decide." Students learned to go to various sources for "verification." The principal in this school said "students should not just 'regurgitate' facts, but should 'immerse themselves in ideas'" (Anyon 1981, 18). *Individualism* was the dominant theme and, to a lesser extent, a complementary *humanitarianism*.

Finally, in Anyon's "executive elite" school for children of wealthy parents, knowledge was focused on academics, intellectual ability, understanding and using the vocabulary of a variety of *systems*, mathematical, grammatical, and others. The students were expected to work harder, faster, and to produce more than those in any of the other schools. Social studies were more sophisticated, complex, and analytic than in the other schools, but the status quo was rarely challenged. Our nation's current way of distributing wealth and power was presented as "natural" and eternal.

Questions for discussion in social studies were, "What are the good and bad effects of imperialism?" Socioeconomic classes were explicitly named and discussed: upper classes, middle classes, and lower classes. An example: "Rule by the ignorant and easily swayed lower classes led to grave errors in judgment like the Syracusan expedition . . . when 'common men' became leaders of Athens: the rationality, direction, and sensible restraint that had characterized policy in Pericles' day suddenly evaporated, leaving a splintered, chaotic, and impulsive Assembly in charge of formulating policy" (Anyon 1981, 27). The kids discussed conflict between social classes.

How is it possible to compare working class fifth graders cutting out pictures of cowboys or pasting tissue paper onto paper turkeys, under strict, swift, and disdainful supervision, with these children? Children in what Anyon called executive elite schools didn't have bells to tell them to go to the next class; they went directly into the classroom whenever they got to school. They did not need passes to move freely about the school; they could go into the teacher's desk for materials, and they were in charge of the school's office during lunch. They were required to teach lessons to the entire class and were graded, in part, on how well they kept control of their classmates. The students worked very hard, as the material was demanding and moved swiftly; they stayed in class voluntarily just to keep pace. Teachers were polite to students, whom they knew held a higher social position than they themselves held.

When students acted up teachers did not punish or admonish them; they left the responsibility squarely on students, saying something like, "It's up to you" (1980, 86).

The focus in this school was on preparing to be the very best, to perform at maximum in school and in life. *Excellence* was the dominant theme Anyon found in this school.

Anyon concluded that schools are powerfully influential, though not necessarily consciously, in reproducing institutional or structural advantage, readying children to take on the occupational lives, and social classes, of their parents. Finn (1999) summarized Anyon's work well:

> The working class children were learning to follow directions and do me-
> chanical, low-paying work, but at the same time they were learning to resist
> authority in ways sanctioned by their community. The middle class chil-
> dren were learning to follow orders and do the mental work that keeps
> society producing and running smoothly. They were learning that if they
> cooperated they would have the rewards that well-paid, middle class work
> makes possible outside the workplace. The affluent professional children
> were learning to create products and art, "symbolic capital," and at the same
> time they were learning to find rewards in work itself and to negotiate from
> a powerful position with those (the executive elite) who make the final de-
> cisions on how real capital is allocated. The executive elite children? They
> were learning to be masters of the universe. (20)

Equality of opportunity is perhaps our most cherished American value, and the heart of our belief in freedom. We may not all start out in the same place, but—we like to believe—if one works hard enough one can be anything one wants. A top dog/underdog battle of cultures is perhaps no-where more acute, and ironic, than in public education. Acute because U.S. schools are biased against, even punitive toward, working class dialects, styles, attitudes, and values—in effect, against working-class kids. The irony is that public education is also likely to be the only chance for those kids to learn the skills they would need to "get ahead," to work in the better-paid middle class.

Increased federal and state funds in the 1970s made it possible for Heath and the teachers and administrators in her study to try new ways of teaching, after a previous decade of education reform efforts, including race and class integration. But by 1983, when Heath wrote her first epilogue, teachers were already losing both the funds and freedom to design inclusive curriculum. In 2011, schools in Minnesota are closing, skipping days, shortening days, and more in order to simply survive, while our nation's upper class increased its net worth by more than 70 percent between 1970 and 1995 (and more since that time). In Minnesota, as across the nation, we've been watching funding for public schools sink for decades now, like a setting sun, leaving the majority of our nation's children in gathering darkness.

Different cultures tune people to different ways of thinking and learning. These differences become deficits for children only when schools routinely apply middle class cultural expectations without offering bridges for working class kids. Schools give serious and automatic advantages to some students, while ignoring and even punishing others. This is accomplished through the medium of culture, but we have seen it is entirely possible to build necessary bridges for both students and teachers across those cultural divides.

By including all of America's social classes in her work, Anyon provides a vivid illustration of educational inequality. When an idealistic institution like public education is set up to benefit some classes of people more than others, we are looking at structural inequality, alongside cultural prejudice and discrimination. This is not equality of opportunity. Indeed, U.S. schools reproduce economic inequality, and the voices within them most often reflect society's dominant groups and their values (Bowles and Gintis 1976; Willis 1977; MacLeod 1995; Heath 1996). The social studies education of American fifth graders runs the gamut from making cowboy cut-outs and gluing them to a map to debating the pros and cons of imperialism! America structures advantage and disadvantage by not providing similar school experiences, both in skills building and content, for all children. Since this is a societywide problem, individual teachers and schools can do only so much to counterbalance inequality of opportunity.

Sadly, many Americans have come to believe that educational privilege is normal. The richer you are, they think, the harder you have worked and the more you, and your children, deserve. As we can see from both Heath's and Anyon's studies, this is simply not the case. Even middle class children do not all receive the same level of academic instruction, understanding, knowledge, or training in self-assertiveness and creative expression. Class-based schools train children to enter different classes as adults. This sets up a vicious circle in which those already more privileged, due to wealth, continue to get the best resources available.

American education does not need to be this way, and I don't believe it is what most of us really want. In better times—the 1960s, '70s, and '80s—education activists and research scholars helped foment the educational reforms that allowed Heath's school system to experiment with new ways of knowing and teaching. Understanding cultural differences is a good place to start. But without equality of actual resources—that is, funding—respecting and addressing cultural differences can only do so much.

Other wealthy nations offer much greater equality of educational opportunity, and wealthier citizens feel a moral responsibility to pay the national taxes that will supply extra funds to schools—to kids—that need it (Lamont 1992).[4] All parents, in this wealthiest of nations, should expect that their children will receive excellent educations from schools that respect them and their families, regardless of their class, color, or culture of origin. All school skills and symbol systems should be available to all children in America, both for personal enrichment, and because all Americans should have a real opportunity to chose their work as adults.

But school is just one part of life. Working class children have multifaceted lives—some difficult, some happy, some desperate, some bustling with energy and industry—all of them challenged by economic pressures. They develop plenty of resilience—initiative, independence, humor, and deeply bonded relationships, among other things. In school, these assets are rarely noticed, let alone appreciated or used to help them assimilate new ways of talking and thinking, effectively blocking access in adulthood to the crucial arenas (government, law, education) in our society that require exactly those *ways*.

Because the real lives of working class children are so often invisible to middle class people, I offer a story from my elementary school years, and return to a subject I raised in the last chapter: roller-skating. This time I will fill it in with one of my own experiences from fifth grade.

Saturday Night in Spring Lake Park

Saturday night was a holiday in Mounds View, Minnesota, but there wasn't much to do. I was lucky and I knew it. Marie Butler and I started going to the Spring Lake Park Roller Rink and Bowling Alley on Saturday nights when we were only in grade school. Marie's dad, a trucker with a jaw-dropping gorgeous new Indianhead semi, dropped us off and picked us up every weekend he was in town. The rink was connected to a bowling alley with a three-two (meaning they served 3.2% alcohol beer) bar right next door. We were the only little kids there; the rest were teenagers, whom Marie and I regarded with awe and flattered with every imitation we could manage at ages nine and ten.

Every part of going to the roller rink was fun. The knowledge we were going lit the whole day.

Walking into the rink—the music, the lights—we threaded through the much taller teens as cool as cucumbers, already knowing how to look tough. How to look people right in the eye and let them know you're watching every move they make. Marie and I dressed in stretch pants with stirrups and a seam down the front. I remember carrying my black patent leather purse with a shoulder strap that made me feel grown up.

We liked going into the can. There were lots of girls smoking cigarettes and adjusting their considerable hairdos. They were often tipsy and, to my delight, talked freely with me about boys, hair, parents, and their best girlfriends. I always listened, entranced, while trying to look matter-of-fact. Sometimes they offered us makeup, and Marie and I drew black lines above our eyes to make them darker and more almond shaped, then wiped it off before we went home. These older girls ratted up their hair into great masses, curling the ends up or down into a flawless flip or bob. The boys wore varying sizes of pompadours that made Elvis look quite conservative. The cooler the kids, the bigger the hair. Other people called them greasers. We just called them cool.

We always teetered a bit at first, as we pushed our wobbly legs on wobbly ankles into the circle of skaters, trusting we would catch our balance. The dim, flickering lights and rock 'n' roll music pulsated into our bodies. I loved the feeling of rolling on and on and on for hours, one small part of the great wheel of skaters. It was exhilarating. I remember the smell of sweat and the blessed blast of breeze when you skated by the big fans. It seemed to me then that we were one big creature with many parts. All of us one thing: skating round and round to the whirling lights, the thumping music, one mind with many bodies.

Junior Robinson had one of the biggest pompadours of anyone and was known to be one of the toughest guys around. He was also a roller-skating hot shot: skating backwards effortlessly, spinning around, doing tricks in the middle, zipping in and out of the group. Hot shots were cool but not separate better-than-you types—they often kept the rest of us, especially Marie and me, from falling on our butts. When we did fall, they spun around and raced back to help us up again.

Junior always greeted Marie and me like long-lost friends. He was almost courtly as he asked each of us to skate with him on couples' songs, a couple of times each Saturday night. We adored him. He, in turn, watched after and protected us. Several of the teenage guys and girls always made a point to smile and say hello to us; the guys asked us to skate now and then. They made us feel special and wanted, protected and safe. It only occurs to me now that these people we worshipped would have looked like criminals to some other parents, people who lived somewhere else and looked like Wally Cleaver or the Kingston Trio. They would never have left their children with these "hoodlum juvenile delinquents." In all the time we spent there, not one of these teenagers did anything but be nice to us or ignore us.

It was one of these nights at the roller rink that I suddenly realized that I would die someday and that life would go on without me. I don't know what line of thinking led me to this conclusion, but I was listening to Skeeter Davis singing "The End of the World": "Why does the sun go on shining? / Why does the sea rush to shore? / Don't they know it's the end of the world / 'Cause you don't love me anymore." I remember I paused at the side of the rink by myself after hours of skating. I suddenly realized there was no way around it, I would die someday and the world would just go on without me and I would miss the rest. I stood there shocked and paralyzed by my terrible thought. The lights went 'round the rink, the wind of skaters going by blew my hair back. I didn't even think about whether my bangs would get frizzy from sweat and wind. A glob of dread thickened in my stomach and I felt almost sick. I couldn't stand to know someday all this would be gone. I watched the skaters fly by. I felt lost and afraid.

I went into the can. A few of my favorite teen girls were there, and one of them offered to fix my hair. I would have been thrilled any other Saturday night, but I just stood there as she braided my frizzy hair, numb with my horrible knowledge. That night I looked at the girls I adored as if listening when they talked, but didn't hear what they said. I only knew I would have to leave this pulsing, fascinating life someday, and everyone would just go on without me. It wasn't that I didn't believe in God or heaven, but it broke my heart to know I would lose this magic and music and movement someday. I had no idea that, even while still alive, this world would be lost to me in a few short years.

After hours of skating, taking skates off and putting on shoes feels weirdly steady and very short. We walked out to the black, star-filled night in Spring Lake Park, into the gaggle of teenagers smoking cigarettes. We always hoped Marie's dad wasn't in the parking lot yet. When he wasn't, we got to go into the bowling alley/bar and watch the bowlers shoot the balls down shiny, slippery lanes and listen to the wooden pins falling down: *ka-blonk-a-blonk, ba-lonk, ba-lonk*. The old guy who gave out bowling shoes and beers waved when he saw us come in, as usual. We sat up at the bar on stools and he gave us free Cokes and winked when he said, "So, what are you gorgeous girls up to tonight?"

By 1982, by the time Lem and Auntie Mae's grandson Teegie from Trackton had reached the higher grades of elementary school, the special funds for the programs described in this chapter had been cut, and things went back to a dismal normal. By fifth grade they had already given up on school as a place to learn and begun to solidify their identities as disrupters. Lem and Teegie, unable to make it within school, found more self-esteem and entertainment in refining their identities as excellent resisters. Resistance became their resilience, protecting them from a system that punishes them simply for being from their own, non-mainstream, community.

Like Lem and Teegie, my best friends and I were getting tough by the time we were in fifth grade. In our neighborhood, and my immediate family, being cool was emphatically not about *school*.

5

IDENTITY AND RESISTANCE

In the battlefield of Edgewood Junior High, in long hallways clogged with children bursting into puberty, class warfare was as common as cashmere and cotton. All the children in my elementary school came from the same working class suburban neighborhood. It wasn't until grades seven to nine that we even saw kids from middle class neighborhoods. It was then that a division between working class kids fully emerged: the cool kids who were powerfully bound together—in part *against* school—and the working class kids who did well in academic subjects. In Edgewood, our working class pond of Mounds View kids was stirred into a much larger sea that included many middle class kids for whom it was actually "cool" to get good grades. It was immediately clear that many of these kids were already leaders in the parts of school that we avoided like the plague: extracurricular activities (stay *after* school?), holding office in school (when and where did students even vote?), writing for the school newspaper, attending and being crowned at school events such "homecoming" and other ones we never attended.

The Art and Science of Seventh Grade

It was hard enough to stay awake for fifth hour, but in sixth hour, that first year in junior high, I had nine long months of *science*. I was struggling to stay awake. Where I came from, just mentioning *science* (or *math*) was enough to make people look at you like you were short a marble. None of my friends were in science class with me so that we could pass notes—my second favorite way to stay awake, after talking. I loved writing. But not for *school*. The science teacher, Mr. O'Neill, talked endlessly without change in inflection. About science. He was also a coach. Some sport. Our half of the school didn't go for that goody-goody extracurricular stuff.

School was prison for us, but that's not saying we didn't enjoy going there. My best buds, Terrie, Marie, Maureen, and I finally entered the teen years we had rehearsed with Barbie dolls for years. We weren't playing dress up anymore, we were dressing—finally using our own bodies, not paper dolls—for fun with fashion. After our parents left for work, we joined Rene and Colleen McDonough in their girls-only, no-boy-germs attic bedroom. We smoked cigarettes we'd swiped from our parents' packs and helped each other get the last hair in place, each eye lined just so. With no big sisters of our own, Terrie, Marie, and I all held Colleen in the highest regard. She, in turn, gathered us like ducklings under her generous wing. Two years older and an actual *dating* teenager, she helped us backcomb our hair on top, cigarette dangling from the corner of her mouth, eye squinted against a gray swirl of smoke. As we plotted our movements and missions for the school day, she dispensed her wisdom and we listened.

Long-legged in miniskirts beneath our navy peacoats, we waited for the school bus. Winter bit through our nylons, sending short, sharp weather reports. At school, we dashed to the smoke-filled can where we lit up again and crowded together in front of one of a long line of mirrors, wisecracking to our images. Alongside us posed dozens of other girls from neighborhoods we had only heard about before. Every girl was dressed to kill and feeling cocky about what she saw in the mirrors. We eagerly traded notes and clothes with these new girls. They taught us to use code names and to fold notes into a neat, little package, easy to throw and catch when a teacher wasn't looking.

We had passed from grade school, where there were two or three twenty-five-kid classrooms per grade, into a gathering of many neighborhoods and hundreds of new kids. There were dozens of tough-kid tribes like ours, recognized immediately by clothes, straightened hair (we ironed ours), and mouthy attitudes. Other kinds of kids crowded the halls, too, from neighborhoods far fancier than our modest tract houses with their endless unfinished additions. These aloof middle class kids dressed in pastels and didn't appear to smoke, drink, swear, or fight. I don't remember one of them: we went to different schools in the same building.

Our time was the half-hour strut through clogged hallways in the morning before classes started. Through the teeming social sea, Terrie, Marie, Rene, and I, in maroon, navy, and loden green strutted down one long hallway to the next. Nylon stockings made our thighs slide sexily together as we wound our way through the waves of new kids swirling round us. We glided past the goody-goodys, talked tough with the cool kids, spotted and savored our delirious crushes. We saw our first rich kids and saw them *not seeing us.* Later we made a hobby of making sure they did. After hitting the can for one last smoke and a quick check on hair and makeup, we finally went to class. It was a kind of silence, a shutting down.

To stay awake in sixth-hour science, where Mr. O'Neill's monotone monologues were an irresistible lullaby, I taught myself to inhale and exhale as slowly as possible. I counted ticks on the big black-rimmed, white-faced clock. I moved from a few seconds per breath, to thirty seconds, to a minute and more. I learned to put myself in a trance with my long, slow breathing. It was from just such a trance that Mr. O'Neill abruptly awakened me that day. He was droning on about—well, I had no idea. Suddenly he stopped and addressed me, "Barbara Jensen?" Stunned out of my stupor, I looked up and saw he was expecting me to answer a question. He stared at me in his rumpled white shirt and tie; there were big wet spots under his arms and his glasses were crooked. The next twenty seconds turned into slow-motion, like a surprise turn in the plot of a movie. I looked into Mr. O'Neill's eyes and tried to read his confrontation. What kind of challenge was this? We were learning there were many kinds of challenges, and it was a matter of survival to see the ones made of malice. I saw no malice in Mr. O'Neill's face, just weariness and insult.

I looked around the classroom, while other kids waited to see what I'd do. There were a few unimportant kids from my neighborhood; a number of aloof goody-goodys from who-knew-where; a couple kids from the gated, wealthy North Oaks, and one or two cool new kids who made it feel important for me to not come out of this looking stupid or weak.

Mr. O'Neill's beady eyes bored into me, his lips tightened. He had me and he knew it. I knew it. The class knew it. We were learning there was always one safe way out, one that would not damage our dignity or let our jailers win. "Who cares?" I could say, or even, "Who gives a shit?" and make him kick me out—a partial win, showing I'd gotten to him, making him look either incompetent or like a bully. I liked the part where I got to prance alone down the empty hallways, peeking into classrooms and waving at my friends—at least until I got to the vice principal's office—dignity intact, detention certain. But by March, I was sick of the vice principal's office and staying after school for detention that kept me from precious hours with my friends. Those hours were all ours, after the school bus dropped us off and before our parents came home from their jobs, tired, dirty, cranky, and not needing any lip from us.

I saw a softening in Mr. O'Neill's eyes. Did he feel sorry for me? Two years later this would have been enough to make me *have* to fight him. At twelve, I saw it as an opportunity. "Well?" he said, looking at me and holding out two open hands, as if I might drop the answer into them. Without missing a beat I matched his tone, "Well . . ." then, with bravado, "it depends!"

He looked away. His eyes narrowed; my heart sank. But wait . . . wait . . . his eyes collapsed into friendly crinkles. His whole face broke into a *smile*. "No-o-o-o-o-o," he said, his face red with amusement, "it doesn't *depend*!" And he laughed right out loud, to my surprise. The classroom, still as detention just moments before, burst into laughter. I burst into laughter, too, giddy with relief, reveling in the alchemy of humor, in my newfound talent to turn a leaden classroom into gold.

Mr. O'Neill wiped his eyes, gave the *only* answer, and let me off the hook. In science, it turns out, as in math, very little *depends*. I relaxed and leaned back in my seat. In my mind, I was already telling Terrie, Marie, and Rene about my adventure in science class. Mr. O'Neill must have needed that laugh because when the bell rang and our class spilled into the hallway, he smiled at me on my way out, as if to say, "You're alright, kid." I rushed out to Terrie, standing against the lockers across from Mr. O' Neill's room, her brown eyes big and bright.

It has not always been the case in American history that working class kids have felt threatened by school and built identities based on resisting it. Reflecting on their school years, my aunts and uncles reported no such thing. But the mid-twentieth century, with its massive post–World War II baby boom, gave rise to "tracked" oversized schools and multitiered mass education that invited such divisions in a way the smaller schools attended by the aspiring children of immigrants in the 1920s, '30s, and '40s did not.

In secondary education we find the later results of communication failures between teachers and students in elementary school. We also find more obvious conflict between the middle class institution of education and working class community values. In this chapter I look into both sides of working class teens' experience. What fuels the young people who resist the American achievement ideology, scorning eggheads and academic study? On the other hand, how *do* working class children fare when they follow the American Dream, and their parents' wishes, by working hard to get good grades and other school skills to get to "the good life," or clean, well-paid employment in the middle class.

As a high school counselor today, I still hear the same anger, yearning, and blaming on both sides from upwardly mobile and resisting working class students. Working class kids who are into academics get shunned and teased by other kids because they care about impressing the teachers. Or, as likely as not, they did their individual tricks for the teacher because they already didn't feel welcome with the other kids (Labov 1969). We called them goody-goodys or goody two-shoes, brownnosers, and creeps. They called us hoods, greasers, losers, and white trash, but rarely dared say it to our faces.

The working class geeks and goody-goodys sometimes found a new kind of welcome at Edgewood and, if they could fake the right manners and dress, slid into the middle class. When the teacher wasn't looking we threw spitballs and crumpled paper wads at their obedient, ass-kissing heads from the back of the class. The rest of us enjoyed a different kind of developmental leap, a social one, with cool kids pouring in from dozens of new working class neighborhoods, converging to refine skills of resistance, humor, and fashion. For us, the great confluence of kids from all over was the rhyme and reason of junior high.

Together We Stand

Some working class people make no apologies for what they are; they do not try to parrot or enter the middle class. From white bikers in black leather on Harleys to the African American gangstas that once decorated my neighborhood with dueling tags of red and blue to the Latino and Southeast Asian gangs that have taken up where the black gangs of the 80s and early 90s left off to the white kids on my block who sag their pants and talk street. Recently, from my front porch on Columbus Avenue, I overheard one white teenage boy chastise another, as they slouched down the street, "Dude, you sound so white!" Some working class people define themselves by resistance to the established order. Like the white, Latino, and even African American greasers (what would you call Chuck Berry?) of the mid-twentieth century, these members of the working class upset the middle class the most, and they also disturbed the orderly, settled-living, routine-seeking people in the working class. These are people who don't waste much time or effort on a race where, they believe, their starting point is miles behind where "rich kids" (who are usually really middle class) start.

My friends and I came to excel at rebelling—not as solitary rebels, like actor James Dean in the movie *Rebel without a Cause*, but as a community of resistance to the authority of school. Report cards and teachers may have said we were bad kids, but "Who died and made them God?" My friends and I were losers and nobodies to the teachers but a very big Somebody all together, a Somebody that was strengthened by acts of resistance. Together resisters reinforce their knowledge that real smarts are measured by things other than what the classroom offers.

Working class children know the teachers and school have favorites, and they know they are not among them. In the small alternative high school where I counsel young people, we can tell when new working class kids come from public schools because they still hang together and resist, even when their new teachers are on their side. Like my friends and me back in the 1960s, they share an intuitive grasp that the scholastic cards are stacked against them, and they resist making themselves vulnerable by trying to select their successes from that particular deck.

If I found a reflection of my rural and more religious relatives in Heath's white working class community of Roadville, I found the action-seeking part of my family—my mother, my uncle Rick, my brother Eddie, his many friends, and most of my own friends—in the "Hallway Hangers" of Jay McLeod's *Ain't No Makin' It* (1995). McLeod studied two groups of teenage boys from a low-income housing project in an unidentified Northeastern city. The Hallway Hangers were the tough kids who thought school was bullshit, expected little out of life, and weren't about to "kiss anyone's ass." They were the kinds of boys my girlfriends and I were watching.

They excelled at being cool. "The subculture of the Hallway Hangers is at odds with the dominant culture," McLeod observed. "The path to conventional success leads in one direction; the path to a redefined success lies another. A boy cannot tread both paths simultaneously; orthodox success demands achievement in school, a feat that only can be accomplished by respecting the authority of teachers, which is inconsistent with the Hallway Hangers' alternative value scheme. . . . These communitarian values act to restrain individual Hallway Hangers from breaking away from the group and trying to 'make it' conventionally" (1995, 118–19).

The other group in MacLeod's study, the self-named "Brothers," subscribed wholly to the American Dream, the achievement ideology. They believed that if they worked hard enough and gave school "everything you got," they would end up getting "good, clean jobs" and "making lots of money." The Brothers were told in school, and often at home, that hard work, school, and a good attitude leads to "makin' it" and living "the good life." They believed it.

But the Hallway Hangers saw school as worthless and insulting to their personal and collective dignity. They had a profound sense of loyalty to their group. "An important characteristic of the subculture of the Hallway Hangers is group solidarity. . . . This loyalty is the glue that holds the group together and honoring it is essential" (MacLeod 1995, 34). In contrast, the Brothers were much more loosely associated with one another, dedicated to individual achievement as they were, coming together for basketball games after homework was done. The Hallway Hangers did not believe that if they worked hard in school, got good grades, and graduated from high school that they would do any better in life. Rather, they believed deep human bonds within their tightly knit group would help them through life. Working class kids most often choose to stay connected with their friends, and their cultures, over the development of skills that would be useful in academic and professional settings.

I lost no sleep over the fact that I started getting Ds and worse in junior high school. I remember few details about my bad grades: what teachers said to me; what, if anything, I said to my parents. It really didn't matter. I do not remember feeling any sense of personal failure, and I didn't think I was stupid: I simply didn't care, and, as far as I knew, neither did my parents. I was devastated, however, when my best friends, Terrie, Rene, and Marie, briefly all turned against me, after I had abandoned them for a new best friend from Greenfield neighborhood.

When Sennett and Cobb (1972) named this choice fraternity versus ability, they were referring specifically to the choices available to working class children in school. They further pointed out that schools are a competitive environment, with only a few spots at the top, as such they are designed to create winners and losers, the "few" and the "many." They concluded that the losers in the school system forge a sense of self-respect by being nobodies together. But I suspect that highly educated people overconceive the immediate influence of schools on working class kids' self-esteem, certainly in secondary schools, and underestimate the power and pull of working class community. The immediate experience of being part of a very tight group that approaches school success by turning it on its head must also be factored into the education equation. Still, my friends and I certainly did, collectively, protect ourselves and one another from "teacher shit." Indeed, that is an understatement. Kids like us didn't compensate for bad grades and negative attention from teachers, we *reveled* in it. We cut up, acted up, acted out, and took delight in our ability to "turn this classroom into a circus!"

Slick, one of MacLeod's Hallway Hangers, was an extraordinary boy who scored very high on standardized tests and was given a scholarship to a prestigious private elementary school, where he learned skills of middle class speech and reasoning. In high school, during MacLeod's initial study, Slick still dreamed of becoming a lawyer, but not if it meant losing his friends:

> *Slick:* What it is, it's a brotherhood down here. We're all fucking brothers. There's a lot of backstabbing down here, down in the streets. But we're always there for each other. No shit. There's not a guy in here who wouldn't put out for the rest of us. If he needs something and I got it, I'll give it to him. Period. That's the way it works. It's a brotherhood.

Frankie: That's the fucking truth. If you don't have fucking buddies, where are you? You're fuckin' no one. Nuttin'.

Slick: *If I had the choice, and this isn't just me but probably everyone in here, if I had the choice between being a good person and makin' it, I'd be a good person. That's just the way I am. If I had my bar exam tomorrow and these guys needed me, I'd go with them. That's just the way it is down here.*

Shorty: Yeah, you wanna be here with your family, with your friends, they're good people. You're comfortable with them. You don't feel right with these other people. (1995, 34–35; emphasis mine)

The detention room roster was a who's who of cool kids in my school, in our multiethnic Midwestern community. From our point of view, challenging teachers and skipping or sleeping through classes were acts of daring that brought admiration. They were rebellions against authorities we disliked. It was heroism to fight the system. We regarded school as jail, and, indeed, that is just how it functioned for us. If heroism in middle class terms means breaking away from the crowd and creating an outstanding individual accomplishment, in working class terms it is staying solidly within one's community and bravely resisting invaders who threaten it.

Getting poor grades and not being on the "A list" at school, for kids in middle class families with a lifetime of training and an expectation of excellence, can be devastating. The assumption that it must mean the very same thing to working class kids is classism. In my experience, protecting ourselves from the teachers' judgments was not a major psychological preoccupation since the teachers meant very little to us. For me, going to school was like my parents having to go to work. If I didn't like it, well, nobody said life was easy. Going to school was my job.

Still, there was no doubt about it, for kids like us school was about submission, not personal advancement. The more battles I went through with school authorities, the more I was reinforced in my belief that school was jail. Being tough, and taking it, was a working class motive to go to school, but not enough to make me want to do anything but the bare minimum. Certainly, my friends and I did not see school as a stage upon which we could rise and shine, a place where we could *actualize* our abilities. But middle class kids, as we have seen, develop a sense of entitlement before and within schools that allow them to later blossom in academics, sports, music, mathematics, art, and much more. This attitude will also follow them into adulthood, where they will expect and seek personally meaningful and publicly recognized work. As I wrote this, I asked my old friend Terrie if she saw school as a place she could "actualize her abilities," and we both began to laugh out loud.

The rejection was mutual. The teachers rarely believed we did anything right. We didn't have to wear anything but our class-coded clothes, hair, and makeup for the teachers to know who we were and to mistrust us. I had given up on trying much in school even before seventh grade science, but it was eighth grade that really cemented my sense of resistance to all things school. I loved writing stories, so English was one class in which I always managed to do well, in spite of hating school. I so loved writing stories that I didn't mind that the teachers liked them, too.

My eighth-grade English teacher pillaged that small vestige of scholastic pleasure when she refused to give me credit for my short story "Tornadoes Headed." I wrote about the tornadoes that wracked my town, Mounds View, in 1965 and demolished entire trailer parks in Fridley. I stayed awake in the basement that long night in sixth grade, fearing we would all die, and wrote careful notes by candlelight. My English teacher was convinced I had copied it from a magazine. There was nothing I could do to convince her. She got even more upset when I refused to admit I had stolen it!

They sent me to a school counselor. She asked if there was anyone who could prove I wrote the story. Talking to my parents, who knew I was good at writing stories, never occurred to me. I finally admitted to the counselor that I had actually first written it in sixth grade, and I had just rewritten it for eighth-grade English. I was wholly prepared for punishment for presenting the same story in two different grades, but by then I just wanted to prove I wrote it. To my surprise, the counselor told me you could turn in the same story in a later grade if you had rewritten it. She then suggested I contact my sixth grade teacher and get him to confirm that I had written it. I tried, but by then he had left Pinewood Elementary. My English teacher didn't believe an eighth grader had written it, let alone a sixth grader, and so I got my first D in English for "cheating." After that, I excelled at only one thing in junior high school: not taking shit from teachers, English or otherwise. I'm not saying she created the culture of resistance I was part of, but her own classism sure didn't help build any bridges from her world to mine.

I also remember, with some sadness, how I chose between the joy of singing and being cool in eighth grade. I found out that if you joined the school choir you got out of a class every week. Being musical, I easily passed the exam to join the choir and found myself really enjoying the singing, even if the music was dopey and old-fashioned. I could hardly believe I was getting school credit for doing something I *enjoyed*. On the other hand, getting onstage and singing before cool kids was a humiliation I could not have lived down. The first concerts were at Christmas time: I sang in the evening concert, the one for parents, knowing nobody cool would ever attend a school event that wasn't required. The next day the choir gave a concert for the student body. I stayed home "sick" so no one who mattered would see me stand up on the stage like a dork. I would have done this again for the midwinter concert, but the music teacher must have known what I was doing: he told me outright if I didn't attend the in-school concert, I was out of the choir. No question about it, I left the choir.

So ended my six-month music career in school, and with it the only formal chance I ever got in childhood to learn to sing harmony, train my singing voice, or learn to read music. Even piddly little Pinewood Elementary had sent a note telling my parents that, in a battery of mass testing, I had scored exceptionally high in musical ability. They said I should have an instrument. I had already spent much of my childhood pining and begging for a piano. Though I loved music and singing more than almost anything—and though I actually enjoyed singing stupid songs in the dorky choir—I never even considered going up on that stage to save my spot in it. To do so would have been social suicide and I knew it. Not only would bullies tease and harass me, I might even be avoided by my own friends for fear they would not considered cool if they hung out with me. Excelling in any way in school was like putting on a sandwich board saying, "I'm not one of you anymore!" The price was too great and the choice was obvious. Music never even had a chance when it was pitted against my social worth.

I suspect it was no coincidence that eighth grade was also when I was first physically injured by a teacher. By injured I mean not merely hit— they did that all through grade school back then—but that the violence produced something you could show to your friends after school. Some-time after my so-called cheating in English class and my expulsion from the choir, my eighth-grade science teacher physically dragged me out into the hallway, where no one could see, and slammed me up against the lockers, for whispering in the back of the classroom (for the zillionth time, I'm sure). This happened to cool kids a lot. I don't doubt that I was annoying, but what stands out to me now is that not one of my friends ever told our parents, or the vice principal, or any school counselors. We only told one another. And then we bragged about it as a badge of courage.

MacLeod found that the Hallway Hangers knew that schools demand respect be paid to teachers, but it was hard for these boys to give respect to people who they believed did not deserve it. Certainly they did not believe they should defer to the teachers, not when their own dignity and social worth was at stake. He also pointed out the costs of submission: loss of self-esteem, loss of—or at least a lot of shit from—their friends, and, importantly, the giving up of their earned positions in the hierarchy of cool. And it wasn't all teachers they hated; there were a couple of formerly working class teachers the Hallway Hangers liked a lot. That was true at my school, too. I think now Mr. O'Neill must have been one of them.

Sennett and Cobb suggested the boundary between the worlds of individual achievers and the cool kids is relatively intact until one of us crosses over into their world and gets rewarded for it. When one of us chooses to enter into their contest, and wins, we abandon and betray the rest of us. When they make one of us a somebody it reinforces the achievement ideology that says it *can* be done. Maybe it isn't all bullshit, and maybe we really *are* losers.

Teachers point to the traitor and try to inspire other kids, for example, "Look what Nicole did. You could do that, too!" The kids do not feel inspired, they feel shamed. They are simply reinforced in their conviction that the teachers are bent on making them feel bad. And they are expert at converting shame into protective anger. Most likely, this anger will be aimed at Nicole for siding with the enemy.

Some parents, eager for their kids to have a better life than their own, will say, "See what Nicole did? Why can't you get your nose out of that comic book and accomplish something?" Nicole's "success" is a betrayal. The other young people may feel that to follow Nicole's path would cost more than they want to pay. They not only risk the ridicule of their friends, their sense of self may suffer. "Oh right!" exclaimed a working class teen to her mother in family therapy. "Like I'm going to become this total geek and lose all my friends just to make you happy!"

For Nicole, the choosing is unfair at best. She can continue to be part of her group or she can actualize her scholastic abilities. If she chooses the latter she will discover many new parts within her, and she may well pave a different path into the world of work, with satisfying work and good pay. With a lot more schooling, she may end up well rewarded as an adult. But along with social rejection, she faces the guilt of making her own people look bad. Indeed, education, and higher education in particular, will most likely encourage Nicole to resolve this tension by learning to respect and care about her own people less. A culture based on connectedness combines with dynamics of resistance and betrayal to close her within, or shut her out of, that community.

MacLeod did not find his Hallway Hangers lacking in confidence or suffering from "low self-esteem." Nonetheless, they expected very little out of life. Like Sennett and Cobb and Bernstein (1971, 1972, 1990) MacLeod criticized "the system," especially our class-based economy, as "a race by the many for relatively few positions of wealth and prestige" and concluded that the low aspirations of the Hallway Hangers "seem to be a decision, conscious or unconscious, to withdraw from the running. The competition, they reason, is not a fair one when some people have an unobstructed lane." The Hallway Hangers feel that "only a sucker would compete seriously under such conditions" (1995, 74).

I have seen the same things over thirty years of working with teenagers; I see it still in 2011. Working class kids think being a sucker is one of the worst things that could happen to them. Being smart, for these kids, is not about doing well in school, it is being savvy, clever, about street smarts. Street skills are about survival, both literally and psychologically, but also about resilience. For the Hallway Hangers, kids I counsel just out of inner-city schools, and my own best friends as a young teenager, being a resister is a worthier identity than being an ass-kisser, doormat, or pet. As I heard an upwardly mobile student being taunted not long ago, "You're nothing more than a stray dog to that teacher!" Anger is a more forward-moving emotion than despair or helplessness, which may seem the only other options on a bad day. Anger, especially anger against an obvious target, bonds people and give them energy. Bad kids develop cunning acts and strategies of resistance that help them maintain a sense of personal dignity as well as building community, like slow-downs and strikes in the world of work. Where loyalty, indeed *solidarity*, is value number one.

From the street orphans of the turn of the twentieth century to the anonymous masses of the oversized "tracked" classes of the mid-twentieth century to the pathologized DBD (disruptive behavior disorder) kids in special ed in the twenty-first century—the experience of working class children says, "Stick together." As long as they do, they maintain the prize and pride of belonging. This is a very different kind of prize than the prize of individual achievement. Ignoring the dubious promise of "a better life," these kids choose belonging over becoming again and again.

If working class kids like Nicole were considered traitors, my friends and I were just plain puzzled by the real middle class kids. They got good grades and ran for office. They were neither geeks nor dorks, and they obviously already knew one another and had meaningful lives together. They didn't have any problem getting up in front of the school; they did so proudly. They were forever getting up on stages and parading their individual glories, while the rest of us were forced to watch.

A few years back, I went to my great-nephew's graduation ceremony in Elk River. I was struck with how the "good" students were more glorified than ever. Not only did they frequently parade up and down the stage, and not only were all those who won scholarships listed in large type in the program (along with the cash amounts). But the part of the program that listed every single graduate in smaller type also put asterisks and other signs, with a key, to highlight those who got certain grade-point averages, as well as whether or not they were admitted to the National Honor Society. That left everyone else standing out clearly as non-asterisked non-winners.

The keynote speaker made no apologies about speaking only to the "special" students, describing our education system accurately, if heartbreakingly: "For those of you have done well here, things will only get better!" What he didn't say was: "For the rest of you, the Marines, Army, Navy, Air Force, Coast Guard, and National Guard have had recruitment tables set up in our school all year long. Go fight for the country these people will inherit." Indeed, my non-asterisked, bright, creative, and extraordinarily sensitive nephew joined the Marines at one of those tables before he graduated, and was shipped off to boot camp before his nineteenth birthday. He completed his first tour in Afghanistan and has just been deployed for another.

Makin' It

"Behave yourself, work hard, earn good grades, get a good job, and make a lot of money [have a good life]." So said a guidance counselor at the high school attended by both the Hallway Hangers and the Brothers. Anyone could have said it; the achievement ideology is as common as number two lead pencils in American schools. It is what school officials, teachers, and counselors like me tell students all the time. It is the promise of American public education. Is it true? In sharp contrast to the Hallway Hangers, the Brothers in MacLeod's study believe that this recipe works and are determined to "make it."

Derek: If you put your mind to it, if you want to make a future for yourself, there's no reason why you can't. It's a question of attitude.

Super: It's easy to do anything, as long as you set your mind to it, if you wanna do it. If you don't want to do it . . . you ain't gonna make it. I gotta get that through my mind: I wanna do it. I wanna be somethin'. I don't wanna be living in the projects the rest of my life.

Mokey: It's not like if they're rich they get picked [for a job]; it's just mattered by the knowledge of their mind.

Craig: If you work hard, it'll pay off in the end.

Mike: If you work hard, really put your mind to it, you can do it. You can make it. (MacLeod 1995, 80)

The Brothers all believed that in America opportunities are equal and that their own intelligence, effort, and ingenuity will be rewarded. Their story is an important one, and one I have often seen in my counseling work with teens. MacLeod asked them if they thought their chances for good-paying work were as good as for an upper class kid from a rich neighborhood in the city. They all said yes. On the other hand, not one of the Hallway Hangers believed America is a land of equal opportunity (1995).

MacLeod describes the attitudes of two actual brothers, one a Brother and one a Hallway Hanger: Mike and Chris. Both told MacLeod about the school's philosophy of education, echoing the American achievement ideology. Mike (a Brother) believes what the school says is true. He spoke with great enthusiasm about going into computers since a teacher had recently told him about someone who made two thousand bucks a week.

The teacher had assured his students that there were more jobs where that one came from "for those who don't fool around and really learn the trade." His brother Chris, a Hallway Hanger, didn't buy it: "They tell you they'll get you a job when you're done. They say that to you right at the beginning. They say it to you all the time. . . . That's *bullshit*. They don't fucking give you shit" (MacLeod 1995, 98).

The Brothers don't do drugs or drink, they study hard, and they participate in extracurricular sports at school. The Brothers don't understand why the Hallway Hangers don't care about school, since, as MacLeod put it, "it's the only game in town." He asked Derek why the Hangers don't care about school: "I don't know. I really don't. I guess they just don't realize what they have to do. It just doesn't get through to them. I dunno. I don't think anyone has really told them straight out what it takes to make it, to be a winner" (1995, 81). But the Brothers have the drive and the dreams needed to do whatever it takes. MacLeod asked them why they work so hard in school.

> *Derek:* I know I want a good job when I get out. I know that I have to work hard in school. I mean, I want a good future. I don't wanna be doing nothing for the rest of my life.
> *Craig:* Because I know by working hard it'll all pay off in the end. I'll be getting a good job.
> *Mike:* Get ahead in life; get a good job." (1995, 98–99)

In spite of cultural difficulties similar to those of the working class children in Heath's study, McLeod's Brothers started out very well in elementary school. One of them tested so high he was sent on scholarship to a fancy private school in another part of town. Unlike the Hallway Hangers, in elementary school the Brothers started to build an identity based on being hard workers, A students, and going somewhere. One significant difference between them and the Hallway Hangers is that they are all African American except Mike. Their families moved to the North looking for new opportunities. Their parents believed that affirmative action could change things for their children and pushed them to work hard at school. The Hallway Hangers were mostly white, and they, like the Brothers, came from generational poverty, but their families had been in the same city, even the same housing projects, for generations. Not having any special circumstances, the Hallway Hangers saw too many relatives before them work hard and get nowhere and they had decided school was bullshit.

In secondary school the Brothers' grades started to sink. In a mixed-class high school with tracking, they were increasingly expected to compete with middle class teens who had been groomed for performance in school since they were little children. Their middle class friends at school already had cultural capital—school-type language and critical thinking skills—comparing, contrasting, and synthesizing ideas.

Working class people, like the Brothers and the poverty class inner-city kids I see in counseling, are often unaware of the many ways that middle class people network through middle class organizations. In their highly structured lives, middle class folks belong to a number of voluntary organizations that welcome people of their class: country clubs, tennis and racquetball clubs, Masonic lodges, Elks clubs, and work-related social activities. Indeed, joining these kinds of organizations is part of membership in the middle class. As Shirley Heath wrote: "[Middle class] children continue friendships initiated within their parents' network of friends. Hence both in-school and out-of-school activities, the [middle class] young choose as friends the children of those adults with whom their parents interact in specific clusters of voluntary associations" (1996, 241–42).

All of this contributes to middle class kids' sense that the world is theirs to inherit. Since they do not see the barriers working class teens face, they believe that their achievements are determined by nothing but their own individual efforts. This is cultural capital in action. We have seen that the skills, styles, and values of the middle classes are prized qualities in the world of school. They operate more effectively than money does to get people inside institutions that both select and reward them for those same cultural qualities (such as student government, band, and choir).

The Brothers certainly knew that their middle class friends had more money than they did. Nonetheless, they really believed they had an equal opportunity to make it. While this belief certainly motivated them to try harder, their lives had not groomed them in the ways it had groomed their middle class peers. Their middle class peers had been groomed to feel entitled to use school to advance themselves and their chances in life beyond school. They felt entitled to good grades; they felt entitled to lots of things. They and their parents routinely requested special accommodations when they needed them.

The Brothers hoped and dreamed of a much more vague success, the good life, but took nothing for granted. Over and over they picked huge and unrealistic goals (to be in the NFL) or smaller, sudden ones, like Mike who heard computer operators make two thousand dollars a week. They had little idea what subjects colleges offer, though most of them wanted to go. These kids were the ones who most needed teachers and counselors to make accommodations, and they were the least likely to get them. In my inner-city neighborhood, and at my school, I see this same dynamic with both boys and girls. They believe that in the future, if they just "believe in myself," they are going to be supermodels, famous athletes, or television stars, but they do not connect this to their present life, where they have a hard time even getting good grades or finding entry-level jobs. I tell them, "You'll need a Plan B, you know, just in case."

The Brothers lacked the sense of entitlement to request special help from the school when they needed it. They didn't have enough cultural knowledge of middle class life to know what things they were already supposed to know so that they *could* request remedial help. Nor did their parents run interference with the school; they too lacked both the cultural capital and sense of entitlement to do so. Middle class parents expect school officials to answer their phone calls and adjust things at school to suit their children's needs. In my school, these are the parents who demand to speak with me about their children's needs. The parents I really want to talk with will barely answer my calls. Working class parents dread school officials and other authorities, either feeling inadequate to address them or fearing that to do so might only invite trouble. I asked a frustrated high school teacher about his work and kids' middle class parents. He said, "Do they make any special requests? My God, they never *stop!*" I asked if the working class parents ever did the same, and he replied, "Never. I wish they would, because then I could justify giving those kids more attention to our principal."

Since we get students from all over the Twin Cities at my school, we have quite a spread of classes: from upper middle class kids from wealthy suburbs to inner-city kids who have to work as well as go to school—along with perhaps taking care of a disabled or alcoholic single parent, siblings, and their own accidental babies. I tell all the students they don't have to have a problem to come see me, to make it easier for those who don't feel ready to share their problems just yet. The middle and especially the upper middle class kids think nothing of signing up to see me week after week—though I have limited hours—even when they have little to discuss. But our poor and working class students generally need to be coaxed to come see me, even when they have severe problems that the other students could never imagine: "My family wants me go fight these guys in St. Paul that shot my brother." "My mom left my dad and he hasn't gotten out of bed for a week. I keep calling his work and telling them he is sick." They have no sense of entitlement, and little sense that asking for help might actually work. I have to convince them I really do have time for them. And then I have to convince them their problems are "enough" to take up that time.

In the higher grades, there is a sharp increase in interpretive knowledge and formal abstract reasoning. The Brothers' middle class peers drew on a lifetime of training in these skills. But Standard English is *not* what these inner-city African American boys grew up hearing, nor did the Brothers know how and where to "look up" things. They did not grow up knowing the middle class speech and skills I have described in previous chapters. Cultural barriers are profound and effective. The Brothers do not seem to realize that school regularly gives advantage to middle class children in specific and measurable ways. This is at *least* as true in secondary schools as in elementary school.

Poignantly, the Brothers did not do well in high school. MacLeod attributes the Brothers' academic failures in high school to the same kinds of social reproduction processes experienced by the younger working class children in Heath's study. A child's best efforts in his own language and culture do not translate easily—or sometimes at all—into the skills that schools require and reward. But these boys did very well in elementary school. Nonetheless, for all their hard work and inspiration, by high school the Brothers got clobbered by schoolwork that required the middle class cultural knowledge they did not have. Sadly, lack of this cultural capital translated into several of them being placed in "basics" and "occupational education" classes rather than in the college track, though all of them intended to go to college. In keeping with the American achievement ideology, the Brothers felt they had only themselves to blame for their failures.

Lareau (2003) found that while middle class kids generally flourished in school, working class kids had a gathering "sense of constraint" in school and other institutional settings. Far from blossoming or thriving in school, working class kids all too often merely *survive* school. I see the same thing today; for working class kids who want to "make it" in school, it is all about buckling down, not about blossoming or becoming. In this very different way, school does prepare working class kids for adulthood, but in their case it is to learn to dampen big dreams and get ready for a life of submitting to authority in the workplace in order to bring home the bacon.

Paul Dimaggio (1982) tested Bourdieu's theory of cultural capital with 2,900 eleventh-grade girls and boys (discussed in MacLeod 1995, 100). He included measures of cultural attitudes, information, and activities. He concluded the impact of cultural capital in high school was "very significant" and that his study "dramatically confirmed the utility" of Bourdieu's theory of cultural reproduction. Many others have also argued that the middle class bias of schools results in structural inequality (Bernstein 1971, 1972, 1977, 1990; Bowles and Gintis 1976; Willis 1977; Anyon 1980, 1981, 1997; Giroux 1983). But, of course, people experience their lives in intimate, personal terms, not in abstract statistics. People do not want to see themselves as "a pawn in a behavioral game of chess" because it violates and erases a dignified sense of self (Sennett and Cobb 1972).

In addition, working class people have learned that their own hard work, along with help from friends and family, have given them what little they have in life. As life brings its challenges, they are unlikely to see themselves as passive recipients, even in areas where they may be exactly that. For the Brothers, nothing they learned in school gave them a clue about the institutional biases they were working within and against. The Brothers brought all they had to their efforts in school, further feeding their hopes and dreams.

Nor did the Brothers fare well in life after school, though, again, they gave it all they had to give.

Only Derek, who had been sent to the exclusive elementary school on scholarship, graduated near the top of his class. When he got his girlfriend pregnant, his sense of responsibility kept him with her and their child, despite his dreams of college. They married just out of high school. So, Derek joined the Navy instead and began to study aviation electronics when he found he could be stationed near home and live with his wife and child. But when, inexplicably, his Navy pay was suddenly cut off for two months, and none of his superiors could, or would, make it come through, he went AWOL to get a different job to pay the rent and feed his family. "Thus, the promising thirteen-year-old pupil at a posh private school ended up festering in a military prison five years later" (MacLeod 1995, 200–201). He got out with a lawyer's help, and after three more months of unemployment got a job as a ramp worker at the local airport. When MacLeod interviewed him the second time, he had been there for seven years and was making $7.50 an hour.

A Brother named James must have heard the same teacher Mike did, who said that computer programmers make two thousand bucks a week. His story illustrates the way racism intertwines with classism to make things even harder for people of color. He went to a computer school in which the total costs were a staggering $7,000 (in early 1990 dollars), which he covered with grants and loans and the better part of $1,000 saved up for him by his parents. Still, when he went to register for school, they put him in the night class, which puzzled him, as he was available during the day. The night class was remedial and far below what he could do.

"Night school was all black people," he explained. He finally managed to get himself into the day classes (with all white people), where he did well: "That class was way more advanced than the night class. So we got a lot more out of it." Still, after school he was only able to find a job as a night operator, not a programmer. When that fell through, he was unemployed. He told MacLeod, "It's been over for a year now. Sending out resumes, going to different companies, filling out applications, I've been on interviews to banks out of state. . . . I've sent out an average of twenty letters a month. Nothing. So here I am sitting at home watching MTV" (1995, 204).

Craig is the only one who made it through college. He started well at a junior college only to find out, when he went to a large out-of-state university for his junior and senior years, that only one of his previous two years at community college would count. While carrying a full credit load, and taking out a fortune in student loans, he worked fifteen to twenty hours a week to make ends meet. During the summer he worked seventy hours a week. Still, in the fall he found he could not afford to buy the required books. "Man, some of those books were so expensive it was incredible. I remember one called *Structural Dynamics* went for a hundred and fifteen bucks." So he switched from a major in architecture to business and graduated in good standing. It took him a year to find a steady job, a clerical job in a large store's credit department. It required nothing he had studied. He had worked himself like a dog to finish five years of college, and his annual salary was "barely a third of the national median for a male worker" (Mac-Leod 1995, 204–5).

Mike enrolled in a residential college but dropped out after several weeks. "I picked the wrong school. Maybe I should've gone to a junior college to break myself in. The people were different, goddamn airheads. All they could do was go out drinking, come back puking. My roommates were scared of me, so I wasn't that friendly. I kept to myself. And the girls—they were snobby as hell, I couldn't stand 'em. Plus, y'know, I was used to city life and there I was all of a sudden in the middle of the fuck-ing woods, nowhere to go. . . . I just didn't like it. It wasn't me" (MacLeod 1995, 203–4).

Mike eventually got a full-time job in a bank and worked another twenty-four extra hours a week in security to bring home $550 a week. He finally quit them both for a job as a mail carrier at the post office. He still looks down on "losers," blaming individuals for their economic plight, but nonetheless sings the praises of the postal union because it means he gets regular raises and good benefits. He believes that he pulled himself up by his bootstraps. But MacLeod points out he only got that first bank job by forging a college diploma (using Craig's first one from community college). The only white Brother, Mike is also the only one who believes race is an issue in employment. His comments on his friend Craig's dismal situation show he believes race was an obstacle, though Craig does not.

Super, who said "I wanna do it. I wanna be somethin'. I don't wanna be living in the projects the rest of my life," has made more money than all of them, but his story is the saddest of all. First he got a job at Burger King for $4.50 an hour, then at a grocery store for $6 then $7 an hour. He finally achieved financial success by remaining in the projects and entering the street economy he would have no part of as a teenager.

Never one to drink or do drugs, Super didn't even smoke cigarettes. But he could not find a better paying job, and then he also ended up with a girlfriend and a son to care for. When he got into the booming crack cocaine business of the early 1990s, he was able to advance, get promotions, and eventually become his own boss. When MacLeod came back in 1995, Super lived with and supported his son and girlfriend, who was a crack user. The fact that he still did not use drugs was an asset in his new trade, but he worried all the time about getting busted and being forced to aban-don his son and girlfriend.

The ultimate result of the Brothers' faith in the American achievement ideology—of equal opportunity and individual initiative—was a sense of personal shame. All of the Brothers graduated from high school, but none "made it" in the sense they thought they could. With the exception of Craig, who graduated from college, most went to college, but not for long. MacLeod concluded that the way schools reproduce class inequality was far more important in determining how these boys fared in school, and in the world, than was their belief in the ideology of equal opportunity, hard work, and achievement. The Brothers belief in these things, along with the admirable characteristic of assuming personal responsibility for others in their lives, merely completed the invisible process of social reproduction, leading them to blame themselves rather than the society, or the school, that promised them so much.

In twenty-first century America, when working class teens I have counseled come back to check in with me in their twenties, some heart-breaking stories pour forth from proud people who worked very long and hard and graduated with such high hopes. They are often lucky if they can find entry-level jobs. They are now routinely given "tests" to "qualify" for entry-level work such as waiting tables. Another twenty years of job losses and a near national financial collapse (created by the upper and upper middle classes) mean there are even fewer jobs available now than when the Brothers went to school. At my school, I watch the middle class kids get jobs from their parent's friends (who own businesses), while the working class kids wander from mall to mall looking for work, trying to be responsible but unable to find jobs. Or, if they get one, they may be bitterly disappointed at how little responsibility they are allowed, and how little pay they receive.

"I'll kill myself if I have to do this for the rest of my life," Lucy threatened. Tears of despair and frustration ran down her cheeks, spilled onto her Nine Inch Nails T-shirt. She wiped them angrily away, disgusted with herself for giving in to her despair. At the high school where I work as a counselor, she became part of a group of young intellectuals. People respected her sensitivity, her creative writing, her piercing critiques of society. She came to replace shame with pride for the African American part of herself and to develop the beginnings of an original and courageous theory on the particulars of mixed-race Americans. Two years later she was spending her time applying her considerable intelligence to the creative task of how to commit suicide without hurting people who love her.

She spends her days ringing up items on a cash register in a drug store. At first she tried to engage her customers with witty conversation: "I don't even exist to them! I might as well be some idiot that can't do anything *but* run a stupid cash register!" Recently, she was put on job probation by the manager. She had quizzed and then debated with a man who had come in to buy film. Why had he had "Dr." printed on his checks, she wanted to know.

"I have a doctorate in American Studies," he said. "I'm proud of that."

"Don't you think other people work hard, too, even if they never get any degrees awarded to them? Don't you think that as an African American poor woman I know more than you about American experience?" Lucy retorted.

"As a matter of fact, I don't," he replied curtly. "And I'd like my film, please."

It degenerated from there.

Lucy is a remarkable young woman who survived sexual abuse as a child, the death of her mother at an early age, being raised by an angry older sister who regularly called her "fat" and "ugly." She survived poverty and a lifetime of taunting by white classmates for being of mixed race. She was tough and resilient, though struggling, when I counseled her in high school. She ended every meeting with something like, "I just won't let them get me down. No way!"

She came to see me in my private practice, two years after graduating from high school, because she was "losing it." She had dissolved into tears at work just that day when a customer yelled at her for grabbing the wrong pack of cigarettes from the shelf. Other workers, trying to comfort her, only incensed her. "They act like I'm *one* of them! This one woman lives in a *trailer court* and her husband used to *beat* her! And *she's* feeling sorry for *me*!" The tears began again and her voice got small and frightened. She repeated, "She thinks I'm *one of them*!" and dissolved into sobs. "Is this it?" she finally asked me, as I was remembering the night of her high school graduation, the inspired speech she gave to those assembled, the shining promise in her face of a meaningful and interesting life ahead. What should I tell her?

I was trained to look to parents and family as the source of children's failure to achieve. But, after many years of experience, I do not believe this is where the problem really lies. As a community psychologist, I have come to believe what MacLeod concludes:

Theories that give primacy to the family inhibit critical scrutiny of the nation's schools. The problem is not that lower-class children are inferior in some way; the problem is that by the definitions and standards of the school, they consistently are evaluated as deficient. The assumption of some mainstream sociologists that the problem must lay with the contestants, rather than with the judge, is simply unfounded. . . . Clearly, what is needed is a comprehensive analysis of how the educational system's curricula, pedagogy [manner and methods of teaching], and evaluation criteria favor the interests of the upper classes. (1995, 100)

A Lucky Landing

So how did I achieve an upper middle class job when my attitude was the same as that of Hallway Hanger Chris: "That's bullshit. They don't give you shit."? It wasn't through working hard in school while growing up, earning good grades, having a good attitude about school, or any other part of the American achievement ideology. Lucy and the Brothers had all the right attitudes but couldn't get to the vague good life that certainly would have included the kind of professional work and income that I eventually achieved. I did none of those things as a teenager, and I am a respected member of an elite profession with earning power that is obscene compared with theirs.

I got my great job through luck. Through the personal experience of having one middle class friend who happened to have an older sister attending the University of Minnesota and protesting the Vietnam War, I, almost accidentally, ended up interested in the world outside of my own. I was rebellious by nature and culture, and then I stumbled across a middle class mentor and the student movement against the Vietnam War. The antiwar movement was led by middle class college students rebelling against both the war and individualistic middle class values! I fit right in. An angry working class kid, I stumbled on a way to channel that anger at specific institutional problems.

I couldn't quickly figure out *what* my college friends knew, a significant factor in cultural capital, but I quickly learned how they spoke, how they put words together, the ways they argued. Having a highly verbal Jewish mother from New York City also didn't hurt, though college certainly was not among the things she valued. Eventually, through the counterculture that I moved into when I graduated from high school at seventeen, I learned new meanings of familiar words, and new words for familiar ideas and feelings, and, finally, I learned some new kinds of thinking. But I also learned and adopted—for a time—prejudice against my own people. Even in the "counterculture," I assimilated middle class attitudes and values, such as educated people are smarter, reading is better than television, and we only find life's meaning within our individual selves on our long individual journey or path in life, where it is our responsibility to keep growing, improving, and evolving.

In short—I made it through *accidental* cultural capital. Only much later did I decide to apply this learning to pursue and gain, through higher education, meaningful and well-paid work. Once I realized that my new friends believed they deserved a meaningful work life, I wanted one, too. Indeed, in the middle class, you are somewhat suspect if you have not achieved something considered valuable, suspected not of being working class but of having failed to achieve. Yes, I worked hard in higher education; I got that precious 4.0 grade point average, but it was not nearly as hard as I had worked as a waitress, or as a fry cook, or in a ceramics factory, or in bakeries for far less reward.

In my Minnesota family, it was a big deal to get a college degree, but not necessarily a good deal. After the first degree I stopped talking about it; I didn't want to feel any more *different* than I already did. Nor did I want to make anyone else feel badly. When I first told my cousin Mike that I was graduating from college, he hugged and congratulated me. Then he said, "I'm still just machining." Nobody in my family ever says they "just" work at this or that; they are proud of their work. And machining in particular is incredibly difficult. Seeing his shame was agony for me; he was the one that got "A"s all through school, not me. I did not feel proud of my degree, but shameful for getting something he did not.

Competition, Cooperation, and Human Development

Middle class psychologists and parents believe adolescence is the time in which people "naturally" develop their individual abilities and learn to compete. We have seen that only comes naturally to people whose culture(s) have taught them to focus on individuality and competitive achievements (and not all of them succeed, as any counselor can testify). In chapter 1, I challenged the assumption that individual achievement is the measure of the man for ignoring working class people and their cultural values of co-operation and connection.

In the now-classic 1982 book *In a Different Voice*, Carol Gilligan re-analyzed interview data on moral development in middle class boys and girls. While using the model psychologist Lawrence Kohlberg created, the boys scored higher in moral development than the girls did. Gilligan ana-lyzed the actual text of the initial researchers' questions and the student's responses and found that the girls' responses clearly indicated a different *kind* of thinking from that of the boys. Interpreted from a male model, the girls' responses led interviewers to believe they could hardly grasp the question. While the boys made the moral exercise a kind of "math problem with humans," the girls persisted in trying to meet the needs of all people involved in the story, rather than choosing decisively between one relation-ship and another. Gilligan demonstrated that, read differently, the girls' responses indicated a much *higher* stage in Kohlberg's theory than the boys' stage, and suggested girls often develop superior emotional and relational intelligence, or ability to form and tend to relationships with others.

I have described how a relationships versus achievement dynamic is at play for many working class kids in school. Like the middle class girls in Gilligan's study, working class students' speech and reasoning, both girls and boys, are frequently judged by outsiders as underdevelopment, lower intelligence, or outright disobedience. Gilligan concluded that women should not be evaluated by psychological systems based on the develop-ment of men. Working class people also violate the assumption that self-interest and individuality are universal human characteristics, and therefore a basis for testing human development. Since working class people learn to focus more on developing emotional and relational intelligence, they also demonstrate complex emotional equations and significant response-ability, replacing concern for number one with care and concern for "us."

At different times in American history, and in other cultures and coun-tries around the world, many of the characteristics that describe work-ing class children would be prized: emotional intelligence, loyalty, utility (helping with chores and younger children), the ability to build relation-ships and bond deeply with others, and considerable initiative to both solve problems (such as fixing a broken bicycle) and make their own fun. Indeed, as we have seen, Heath and Lareau both found the middle class children more exhausted, more demanding, and less able to make their own fun alone or with other children:

> In a society less dominated by individualism than the United States, with more of an emphasis on the group, the sense of constraint displayed by working-class and poor children might be interpreted as healthy and appropriate. But in this society, the strategies of the working class and poor families are generally denigrated and seen as unhelpful or even harmful to children's life chances. The benefits that accrue to middle-class children can be significant, but they are often invisible to them and to others. (Lareau 2003, 13)

Border Crossings

Whether parents went to college is still the most reliable indicator of whether or not their children will attend college. This is social reproduction in action. Nowhere are the cultural underpinnings of different ways with words more important than in schools, the very institutions that are supposed to equalize opportunity in our democratic republic. As a result of the social revolts of the 1960s and '70s, American education has become more conscious of issues of ethnicity, race, and gender. But the invisibility of class remains.

As poorly as MacLeod's Brothers ended up "makin' it," the Hallway Hangers, whom he had expected to become men with working class jobs, fared far worse in the new economy the 1980s ushered in. MacLeod emphasized the need for fundamental changes in secondary education and suggested that energetic anti-authority students could become activists for their own cause. Unfocused rebellion against "the powers that be" can be usefully harnessed into a focused critique of society and a determination to change it, to make it more equitable for all. Indeed, that is the American dream: liberty, justice, and opportunity for all, not only for the already privileged or number one.

I have said that I have been counseling young people at an alternative public school—for kids who have not been able, or willing, to make it at larger public high schools—for more than twenty years. Started by counterculture types some forty years ago, the school teaches about sexism, racism, and class in the United States, along with math, science, and other traditional subjects. I see many working class kids of all ethnicities and colors go through a reformation of generalized anger into anger at the specific societal structures that have made their parents' and their own lives needlessly difficult. Many go on to meaningful careers where they help still more working class kids. It is empowering to find out your anger isn't just "oppositional disorder" or "attention deficit disorder" or whatever other new "diseases" might be created to pathologize working class kids.[1]

At the end of the day, as parents, grandparents, aunts and uncles, as teachers, counselors, clergy, and social workers, we want to help young people we care about make good meaning of their lives: to earn enough to live a comfortable life, to find work that does not harm them physically or mentally, to develop their talents and intelligence, and to have loving family and friends. Whatever the odds for their success may be, we care deeply about them and we want the very best for them.

The trouble is where do working class kids like Lucy, the Brothers, the Hallway Hangers, and the others in this chapter belong? And what do we do with the reality that there are not, and never were, enough spaces for everyone to *make it* in America, as the middle class is only about 36 percent of the population (Zweig 2012)? And what happens when they do succeed in college? How do we help them keep the resilient qualities of working class life: cooperation, loyalty, strength, and standing up for, rather than competing against, one another?

I will continue to tell teenagers to get a college education because the line between the college educated and the noncollege educated is an important one in terms of power and control over one's work in this country. I will also continue to help young people see the real situations and limitations they face, along with engaging and enlarging their considerable resilience. But most of all, I will continue to remind them what they already know in their bones to be true: people like us, raised on heart, sweat, and hardship, should be anything but shameful; our ways with words, and one another, are *not* wrong. People like us have faced down the powers-that-be all through American history.

We can do it again, if we stand together.

6

ACROSS THE GREAT DIVIDE

The blonde curls of Shelley's home permanent stuck to the tears on her face as she dashed from the classroom. "Oh God, I'm so sorry," she cried out. Just ten minutes earlier she was in the midst of an animated discussion in a college course she likes—the psychology of women. Shelley had never thought much about being a woman before; she finds it exciting and comforting to do so. She sees now, as she put it the week before, "the shit my family gives me about school is all about my 'duties' as a woman. It's just prejudice." On this night, we were having a classroom discussion about relationships between women and men. The subject was "intimacy," and the class was discussing some of the different ways men and women understand and express it. She felt she was starting to understand some of the problems in her marriage. Maybe she could make things better between herself and husband. She was eager and animated in the discussion.

But something went wrong. She was talking about the declining intimacy in her marriage. She started talking about how college "made things really weird" between her and her husband. It wasn't just his complaining about the time she was gone; he was starting to make fun of her study-ing, saying she was turning into a "geek" and an "egghead." She surprised herself when she suddenly teared up. She blurted out, "He even threw my math book against the wall! He smashed the spine of a sixty-five dollar book! Then he hollered, 'This shit means more to you than me and the kids!' and stomped out of the house." She said that later, when they talked it out, he said she wasn't any fun anymore, she wasn't interested in any-thing! The class laughed out loud, because in class Shelley was interested in everything. Encouraged, she exclaimed, "I couldn't believe it! That's just what I think about him! He's the one . . . I'm interested in things now that I never even *thought* of before, you know what I mean? I asked him 'What am I not interested in?' and he said, 'Bowling with Georgie and Bill and watching TV'! Like I have time for that now! Like *he* has shown any interest at all in all the things I've been studying."

Shelley's eyes blurred with tears again, and she fell silent, her pale skin flushed. A couple of older women in the class started to talk, gently and with warmth, about their marriages. Each said they had to leave their hus-bands because they needed to "find myself" and "get away from the con-stant expectations." Another woman, in her early forties, offered that her spouse really wanted her to go to school and Shelley deserves to have that kind of support. A male student, on the board of a battered women's shel-ter, emphasized that she has a *right* to expect that support, that men have to learn to give women the things they have always had. He went on to mention "offender psychology" and how "they can't stand for their women to be independent, that's how they keep control." The other women from blue-collar backgrounds were uncharacteristically quiet.

"But that's not it!" Shelley insisted, frustrated. "You don't under-stand . . . ," she trailed off, struggling for words and understanding. "He, he's a good husband, you know? He was my *only* support at first . . . when my family was lecturing me about my duty to him and the kids. He was great, he—"

At this point, a woman who had identified herself as a former battered woman and the man who works for the women's shelter exchanged mean-ingful glances. Shelley saw this and stopped midsentence, then scrambled to undo the impression she had given. "That's not it! He really doesn't mind me going to school. I know how it must sound. . . . He doesn't nor-mally yell, and he'd never hit me or anything! He's never even thrown anything like that before, you know? My girlfriends always envy me because he's so sweet and he's great with the kids and he's *so* handsome, I mean. . . . He always knows what to say to people, I mean, not *college* people, but, you know, regular people. And it never really got stale, I mean, I was still crazy about him until . . . until . . . I don't know. . . ."

Shelley stumbled to a halt and fell silent. Just when someone else was about to speak she blurted out, "I love him! When I think of losing him [starts shaking her head] it's like the whole world is turned upside down." She looked around quickly, hopelessly, like she was trapped. She realized that her new people don't understand either. As the tears steamed down her red-hot face, she ran from the classroom to the lavatory down the hall.

Shelley is a college student at a small urban university that often serves "returning" older and first-generation college students. She is close with her extended Scandinavian and German American farm family. Her family, husband, and friends are all working class. She never thought about going to college before her boss said that they would pay for it and she could lose her job if she didn't accept. To her surprise she loves college. She eagerly reads class materials; she finds it surprisingly easy to talk in class, and other people often seem to appreciate what she has to say. She fears she talks way too much, but as she says, "I just get so excited." How could she not know before that she "loved ideas," as another woman in class had put it? She is thirty-two and has had two children. "Where was I all those years?" she asked once in class.

After the others in the class left, Shelley came back to apologize to me. She assured me that in more than two years of college, she had never behaved like this before—acting so "unprofessional." She apologized a few more times. Her shoulders sank, deflated. "Maybe he's right, maybe I don't belong here." She was embarrassed, and afraid.

Classism Goes to College

In higher education, as in primary and secondary education, classism hurts working class people in unseen ways. Shelley is experiencing an exciting, confusing, and debilitating situation in both her outer life and within her. She is by turns excited, lost, elated, angry, bewildered, shameful, grateful, and numb. All of a sudden, her past doesn't cohere with her present. Her future has become uncertain. "Nothing fits right anymore," she told me that night after class. Shelley feels that no one she knew before college understands what she is going through now, and some resent it. Shelley expected to go to school to get "my piece of paper" so she could keep her job as a legal secretary. But now she is in the midst of crossing over to a new social class, something she hadn't expected. She had no idea she would find and fall in love with a new world. She certainly didn't know that she might actually begin to become someone else. Though she is delighted with all the new ideas she is learning, nothing she has learned so far in this new world helps explain her family conflict to her. With no language, no concepts to explain the psychological contradictions in her situation, she is falling prey to them, resulting in confusion and suffering for both Shelley and her family.

Like Brothers Mike and Craig from chapter 5, Shelley is the first in her family to go to college. Unlike them, she is from a stable working class family, and she has had a complex office job for years after working her way up from the typing pool. Also, unlike Mike and Craig, she is attending an urban university for adult learners that aims to reach a largely working class student body. All this gave Shelley a decided advantage over the Brothers in college, both financially and psychologically. Nonetheless, she silently suffered this passage, unaware what the problem might be. Unvoiced and unseen, in the midst of unexpected success at school, hers was a painfully confused suffering.

This struggle to figure out "who I am anymore," as Shelley once put it, is the subject of this chapter. There are striking psychological similarities among upwardly mobile working class people: the collection of contradictory emotions, beliefs, and loyalties, as well as the invisible and presumed individual nature of this often-painful process. I have come to believe Shelley's struggle constitutes a particular psychological and sociological—inner and outer—constellation of problems that plague many working class people who enter the middle class. I call it a *class-crossover* constellation. Common psychological reactions are anger, shame, grief, elation, a shining sense of promise, cognitive dissonance, dissociation, imposter syndrome, survivor guilt, and more. No public voice addresses these issues, and these feelings are often so muffled as to be invisible to *crossovers* themselves.[1]

Visibility and voice are the first practical antidotes to Shelley's invisible identity crisis. "To people from the working class who find themselves on the manicured lawns or inside the vine-covered brick buildings of a pretty college campus: our advice remains the same," Jake Ryan and Charles Sackrey warned in the introduction to *Strangers in Paradise,* their collection of essays by college teachers originally from the working class: "Make sure you wear a helmet" (1996, xvii). As we have seen with primary and secondary students, college students from the middle class generally find in higher education the cultural rules, values, language, and community mores that are familiar to them. Working class students, again, face a maze of new rules, values, language, and a world of indecipherable references.

The less cultural capital they have gathered from previous schooling, the more they face a tangle of extracurricular psychological, sociological, and cultural confusion. Also, the closer middle class students are to their parents' working class backgrounds, or the "lower" they are in the middle class (as in Anyon's first middle class school), the more they may be mystified by traditional higher education, which is largely designed by and for the upper class and upper middle class. An awareness of the role of class-related cultures is crucial because when these cultures clash the result is alienation and suffering. Nowhere do working class lives and cultures clash more than in higher education.

Central to the crossover's experience is an *existential* dilemma, problems and decisions about how to best live one's life (literally problems of existence). Existential issues most often surface at times of change in our lives: having a child, choosing a life partner, dealing with the death of a loved one or the decline of an aging parent. An existential dilemma can stem from anything that alters one's usual life so much that previous assumptions are no longer enough to explain the present. In crossing classes, previous assumptions can include one's entire former worldview, the basement upon which the house of personal psychology is built. For working class people who travel across the class divide, there are stories and sacrifices that have precious little voice and find no ear to listen.

For example, the fierce competition among students in Ivy League colleges may lead to having to choose between friendship bonds and personal success. In most working class communities there is no question about this choice, as loyalty is much more important than being "a show-off." In Ivy League colleges there is no question that making it requires the courage to stand out, to be an impressive individual. Only through this achievement can one earn the right to belong in the professional middle class. For the first-generation college student, it probably means straddling and balancing family of origin and school, where different value systems clash regularly in an ongoing existential struggle.

People in the middle class will likely be the vehicles of change for the "upwardly mobile" working class person: in higher education, in job promotions, marriage, psychotherapy, and other crossover experiences. They can show Shelley how to write and speak in Standard English, how to keep her cool with difficult clients, and even to put her napkin in her lap instead of on the table. But they can't tell her where she's been, how it has made her who she is, or where it is she might be going. Her experience of crossing classes is likely to be completely invisible to people from the middle class because they were raised to assume their inner and outer lives are normal. Little that they learn in higher education, or see in television or movies, contradicts that. If you have learned to walk and talk middle class well enough to pass, middle class people will assume you have always been one of them, especially if you have white skin. Successful crossovers can't necessarily help you either. As likely as not, they have already been "made safe," as Bernstein pointed out in 1990. To get where they are, they have most likely thoroughly assimilated the styles and values of the middle class.

The invisibility and unconsciousness of crossing classes is what can make it painful, debilitating, and for some even devastating. The dilemma of conflicting cultures manifests in a multitude of personal problems. Unless there is awareness of the cross-class experience, the problems it creates hide behind many individual perspectives, particularly in the United States where individuality is currently prized above community and mutual aid. For Shelley, her problem appears to be in her marriage. For someone else it is a problem with her "backward" parents. For yet another it is a "chemical imbalance." For many it is an impulse to ditch class and get loaded, or to suddenly blow off an important exam. Maybe it is simply having the blues too much. For marriage or family-of-origin problems, depression, substance abuse, and fear of success there is some amount of collective wisdom about coping and treating, changing or managing.

But not for Shelley's problem. Part of her dilemma is that there is value in each culture, as well as drawbacks. For Shelley, previously happy with her family, life-long friends and working class life, there is a blazing new star on her horizon: a life of the mind. This complicates her psyche and her life because she wants to both keep her working class roots and develop her intellectual abilities. She loves her husband and kids, her family of origin, and her best girlfriends, she can barely stand the strain of not "doing it together." The upset in her relationships is a mirror of her own gathering ambivalence, her own feeling of being torn—torn not between success and failure in college, but between *two different notions of what it means to succeed in life*.

When I was a young adult a friend recommended the movie *Breaking Away* to me because she saw me struggling with the tension between my two worlds. It is about a working class teenager who sings operas in Italian and races his bicycle, eventually gets involved with a girl in college, and leaves home. The clear implication was that he was leaving a know-nothing, crude culture for the finer things in life. I could not keep from weeping through it. At the age of twenty-two, I felt like the boy in the movie, so different from the rest of my family that I felt I would never fit in again. It was very painful at the time. As a psychologist, I can now see I may have needed that single-minded and—I now see—distorted view of both cultures to make the developmental leap I wanted to make. After an adult life amid those finer things, which comes with the uglier parts of that life as well—the competitiveness, the pressure for continued achievement in public arenas, the lack of loyalty and directness, the obsession with me and mine, the ever-striving for self-improvement—I see both cultures differently.

Escape is a recurring theme in autobiographical crossover literature. For young people, breaking away from a life of hard, lower-paid labor for a life of promise and possibility is a formidable task. Doing it requires a great deal of courage and inspires big dreams. But if young people assimilate into the middle class so thoroughly they never again find value in their former life and former self, the change may result in lifelong problems. They may suffer unnecessary losses that plague them and hurt or alienate members of their family for life. In middle age, I have found my balance and have long ago come back to treasuring my loyal and generous working class family. I have also been able to persist in doing things out of the working class ordinary, and I also realize that much of the discomfort came from within me. It turns out, for me at least, that as long as I show up, my extended family will always hug and welcome me.

Unexpected Cultural Collisions

Most working class students start college because they want better work, not a change of culture. But cultural clashes abound in higher education and prepare students as much for life in middle class culture as for professional work: "The real function of the Bachelor's degree in our society is certification, all right, but it is class certification, not professional certification. The B.A. stamps a [person] as a candidate in good standing for the middle class. It is the great social divider that distinguishes the working class from the middle class." (Dahrendorf, quoted in Ryan and Sackrey 1996, 104). That was true when Dahrendorf wrote it in 1979, and it is still true, though a bachelor of arts or science degree had greater value then.

What happens to the few who overcome the odds, give up their working class identities and reach away from everything that is familiar? In *This Fine Place So Far from Home*, a 1995 collection of essays by graduate students and college teachers from the working class, Stephen Garger describes how a colleague interrupted his presentation three times to argue against it in the same way:

> Where I came from, the immediate and practically the only response to a fellow ignoring or contradicting an explanation three times is to yell and go for the throat—literally and figuratively. Early in my college career silence was the only way to override that response, and this is exactly what happened. . . . All the verbal cues I was receiving indicated the questioner was insulting me and pushing for a fight. However, his physical demeanor most certainly contradicted that impression. The mixed message I was getting was further clouded by the fact that we were violating the unwritten [working class] rule that you don't fight with the people you hang with. (Dews and Law 1995, 41–53)

After a friend of his explained that intellectual arguing was something of a recreational sport among academics, Garger mused, "John, the questioner, just may have been opening the door for fun. When I did not respond to the protocol, he tried again and again. Undoubtedly, *he* was receiving mixed messages, too." He concluded: "It was as if we were engaged in different and separate rituals in which neither of us understood the rules the other was playing by" (Dews and Law 1995, 41–53).

As rules start to change for the crossover, family problems arise. Many parents, like those of the Brothers, push their children toward middle class work, "good, clean jobs," asking life to "pay them forward" for their own difficult work lives. But their reward for this sacrifice is sometimes very sad. As Sennett and Cobb (1972) pointed out, if their children succeed through higher education, more likely than not they will adopt the culture, style, and classism of the middle class. How many parents shrink back in shame or lash out with anger and accusation as the children they worked so hard to send to school become cultural strangers to them.

"Working-class families," Carol Leste Law, coeditor of *This Fine Place*, observes in her introduction, "whether they are able to articulate it or not, know that a college degree has everything to do with class, unlike professional or managerial-class families, who believe it has to do with merit and entitlement. They know that somehow the very existence of a college degree undermines and actually threatens their children's and consequently their own working-class identity" (Dews and Law 1995, 5).

Though many working class parents devote themselves to sending their children to college, "in the end, they do not want what they would wish for" (Dews and Law 1995, 5). They fear what too often is true—that their child has become someone else, someone who has become embarrassed of their so-called low-class, backward family. To survive and achieve in their new environment, many working class people in higher education begin to adopt the classism of their peers and mentors. Classism confronts them as soon as they enter the halls of higher education, as Julie Charlip reports: "I vividly remember visiting Bates College with my mother. It was winter, and it was cold in Maine. She wore her good wool coat, the one to which she had sewn a small mink collar, the one she had had all my life. The dean of students greeted us in his plush office and looked my mother up and down with a sniff of disdain. Clearly he thought we were so far beneath him that he didn't need to mask his scorn. I felt small and inadequate and terribly sorry for Mom" (Dews and Law 1995, 34).

Too often, these students escape the dissonance of clashing cultures while they are in school, and later in middle class careers, by distancing themselves from their family. This is not only a tragedy for the parents but, as we will see, it disconnects the crossover from his or her own history.

Other families are frightened or insulted if their children get "too big for their britches," and try to knock them back down to earth. "You'd think with all your education you could use an electric can opener!" my mother snapped at me, after I got my bachelor's degree. She seemed to resent me for going to college. Perhaps, contrary to middle class opinion, this latter group is in the less tragic situation; at least these parents remain *engaged* with their children. The shit given by family members to "Miss High and Mighty College Student," often reported by working class college students, may be the family trying to bring this member back into the fold for the good of everyone involved.

My parents seemed genuinely disturbed when I first decided to go to the university. "Why don't you do something useful and get a nice civil service job? You're smart," my father argued. "You could pass the exam easy!" He spoke with real concern. He thought I was "wasting" my intelligence, throwing myself away. My mother, when I asked for a bit of financial help, asked me what the point of this "college deal" was. I said, "I don't know yet, I just want to learn." She was aghast, "We're not gonna pay for anything if you are just going there to *learn*!" She said "learn" like I had said I was going there to do heroin. Clearly, and culturally, they thought it was a waste of time and money. I think it is fair to say they were also afraid it would take me further away from them. It was out of their frame of reference, and it conflicted with their values. And there I was at seventeen, with all the enthusiasm of a religious convert, already correcting my mother's English.

My mother resisted my evangelical efforts to improve her perfectly good and colorful working class English. She was a fighter, and a talker, and she knew it was not merely a matter of *different* cultures but of one dominating the other. Anyone who knew my mother could tell you she wasn't about to be bullied by anyone, leastwise by eggheads. And, indeed, I dropped out of college after my first year of "just learning." I went back years later, with exactly a new work-life in mind. Is it any wonder that working class families do not easily surrender their children to the people they know help make their own lives difficult, or worse? In the world of work, the middle class is employed by the upper (or capitalist) class to inflict severe control, and sometimes appalling abuse and neglect, on so-called lower class workers.[2]

Internal Conflicts and Cognitive Dissonance

Analyzing the experiences of college teachers originally from the working class, Ryan and Sackrey declared,

> It must be recognized that moving from one social class to another involves more than simply improving one's lot, which is, indeed, the most obvious and celebrated feature of the mobility experience. It is also a matter of moving from one cultural network to another. Central to this movement is not only that social promotion involves engaging new circumstances and new cultural networks, but that the old and new ones are antagonistic and conflictual. (1996, 103)

Cultural capital is the invisible curriculum in colleges, much more than in high school; but there are no classes in it. People who have the cultural currency of the upper classes routinely use it for entrance into, and access to power within, higher education, as they later will in business and government. Working class college students, like the Brother Mike in chapter 5, are left on their own to figure out what it all means, one by one. They do this while routinely being ridiculed for what they don't understand. As the Brothers were eliminated from the running for their lack of middle class and upper class cultural assumptions and knowledge, those working class people who "make it" into and through college report the lack of cultural capital as an ongoing source of difficulty.

This cultural barrier is at least as effective in shutting out working class people as the significant economic barriers to college education. To succeed in higher education one must learn to adopt and represent middle class culture as one's own. This culture does not grant dual citizenship. You must leave behind your low-class ways, your "bad" English, your values of humility and inclusion (don't "show off" and be a big shot because it might make someone else feel bad) and much more—not least of which are the people you love most deeply.

In early adulthood there are developmental tasks at play that probably help fuel the leap young working class students are trying to make. They are leaving home, letting go of childhood, developing parts of themselves that their parents and family may not approve of, and needing space to do so. They are eager for the freedom and adventure of adulthood. But it is a cruel and unsuspected consequence to have that process set up a chasm that may never be bridged again. In her introduction to *This Fine Place*, Carol Leste Law went on to say:

> My success in academia has been possible only through years of silence . . . the effort to defend my family in what I knew was a hostile environment was just too great. . . . As an undergraduate, I wanted only to be accepted into the club, the university. . . . So you better believe I kept my mouth shut. . . . [At home] to talk about my studies seemed ridiculous or stuck up at best in a context that appeared to be as mistrustful of academia as academia was condescending to it. No one in my family ever wrote a college paper, no one ever tried to enroll in classes that were closed, no one ever put together a degree program and, more to the point, no one ever cared about such things. So you better believe I kept my mouth shut there, too. (Dews and Law 1995, 4–5)

As these consequences start to impinge on the student, confusion and ambivalence can threaten not only school success but the sense of self and identity one needs to feel comfortable in one's own skin. This clashing of cultures is not only invisible to others but, most poignantly, to those who bear it: "By Thanksgiving of my first year of college, I wanted to go home and stay there. What was I doing at this place for rich kids? What was I accomplishing? How was I helping my family? I was a mute, a heavy drinker, a class skipper" (Black, in Dews and Law 1995, 21). A middle class counselor might see this in terms of success and failure in school, surviving or not surviving your own history. The middle class observer not only misses the pull of a working class culture they can't see, but also doesn't see the contempt for that culture that working class students encounter almost daily. William Pelz proposed that "most college teachers are proudly and boastfully anti-working class. If the civil rights movement, the black empowerment movement, and the women's movement have created more self-consciousness about open expressions of racism and sexism, the typical professor still thinks nothing is wrong with being anti-working class. The same person who would never use the word *girl* to refer to an adult female openly rails against 'blue-collar slobs' " (Dews and Law 1995, 281).

The assimilation of a new culture that is hostile to the one that feels like home threatens psychological *integration*, the internal process of layering new experiences on top of old ones. Linking old and new experiences creates an ongoing evolution of personal meaning—where I've been, who I am, what I can expect, or hope for, in the future—of one's own story in life. If you take the basic differences between these cultures, stir in the unchallenged assumption that the "new" culture is far superior, and fold in our cherished national myth of equality of opportunity, you have an excellent recipe for personal *dis*-integration. In chapter 4 I discussed working class children's need to link old and new experiences to make sense of school. Linking the old and the new is at least as important for young adults, who are attempting to make sense, not only of school, but of life itself. For too many, college cooks up profound cognitive dissonance.

Those attempting to cross over the class divide are likely to either *re*ject the new culture—there is a much higher dropout rate among working class students—or try to *e*ject their former culture from their current sense of self. As we saw in the last two chapters, the painful distance between the ideal and the real is absorbed, and suffered, by those who fall between the cracks. Higher education provides plenty of cracks in the facade of equal opportunity in America. Cognitive dissonance comes from trying to balance conflicting parts of the self with two opposing worldviews. The clashing worldviews that create cognitive dissonance creates an inner instability, an anxiety that pushes one to come up with something more or new in one's personal psychology to accommodate conflicting values. This is not necessarily a bad thing, since a resolution of the conflict can result in a new point of view that may be larger and more accurate than either of the original views. Indeed, cognitive dissonance often requires and inspires necessary psychological development.

But, in the case of invisible class differences, lack of awareness of where the conflict lies, and the invisibility of one whole side of the conflict, makes it much more difficult to resolve. The deeper the conflict and the more powerless one feels, the greater the need to escape the pain and confusion. Michael Schwalbe reported a telling example of this:

> Once when I was talking to a professor in his office, another professor leaned in the doorway and said, "I just heard a new excuse for missing an exam. A student said he couldn't come in today because he had to move a trailer house." The professor to whom I was talking laughed and replied, "That's one I never heard before. I guess it tells you you're really at a blue-collar college." Part of me liked being privy to this exchange. I took it to mean I was

being treated as an insider. But I also sympathized with the student. It made sense to me that you might have to miss an exam to move a trailer house. What was funny about that? (Dews and Law 1995, 312)

Rosa Maria Pegueros answered his question. "Being working class," she observed, "means never knowing with certainty why someone is laughing at you" (Dews and Law 1995, 96). "All the awards and honors cannot convince you you're in," Mary Cappello reflected on her cultural struggle in higher education. "You still think analogically in a profession that welcomed you into its precincts for your clarity and logic" (130).

For all but one of the Brothers, this mental dissonance was so great that they left college quickly, after dreaming about and desiring it all their lives. "Nothing will ever be enough to stitch together the before and after of this life," despaired Renny Christopher as a graduate student (Dews and Law, 1995, 141). Later in her career, as a full professor, she realized, "What I have lost is irreplaceable, and, I have belatedly realized, was much more worthwhile that I ever believed before I crossed a bridge that took me forever away from it" (2009, xii).

bell hooks is a once-working class black woman who went through the process of elite higher education with her eyes wide open:

Throughout my [Stanford University] graduate student years, I was told again and again that I lacked the proper decorum of a graduate student, that I did not understand my place. Slowly I began to understand fully that there was no place in academe for folks from working class backgrounds who did not wish to leave the past behind. That was the price of the ticket. Poor students would be welcome at the best institutions of higher learning only if they were willing to surrender memory, to forget the past and claim the assimilated present as the only worthwhile and meaningful reality. (2000, 36–37)

Those class straddlers who court or are courted by the "classiest" schools, that is, Ivy League and tier 1 colleges and universities, appear to suffer the most dissonance and personal dis-integration. The conflict increases because elite schools require more cultural capital than community, state, and other colleges, which more commonly serve first- and second-generation college goers. Ivy League colleges are the intended reward for Jean Anyon's top two groups of elementary school kids, the children of affluent professionals, or the upper middle class, and the children of the executive elite, or the upper class. Second-generation middle class college kids, from Anyon's first middle class school, also have trouble when set to compete against those who have been groomed all their lives, not just for college, but for an Ivy League education.

Of course, among elite schools in the United States, reaching out to working class people has never been the goal. In fact, if you subtract the legacy admissions of children of wealthy alumni (who donate money) and also annual designated scholarships, only 40 percent of all college slots are left for all the middle class and working class folks who want to go (Golden 2006). These revered and exclusive institutions are the gatekeepers in the achievement race we call the American Dream. If colleges and universities really did want to reach all our citizens, instead of weeding out so-called losers and selecting the best and brightest, they would have to change the dog-eat-dog competitive nature of education and achievement ideology in America.

The more that schools raise awareness of and validate class-related cultural assumptions and skills, the more they allow young students to have a coherent sense of the development of personal meaning in their lives. The more students can integrate all of their personal experience, the less class mobility will confuse and punish them. Heath said this about elementary schools; MacLeod said it about secondary education; and it is even more the case in college: if schools want to reach working class children and adults, they need to understand and validate working class cultures.

Ongoing Psychological Hurdles

There is a growing body of work by higher education's successful "discontents." To take a more systematic look at the invisible obstacles working class students face in higher education, I combine and contrast that work with the experiences of my counseling clients, students in my college classes, workshop participants from a range of education-related settings, and my own experiences. As a psychologist, I am concerned with how people *internalize* these conflicts and the suffering that creates within them. I offer here some commonly reported difficulties for working class people who climb the class ladder. Not all upwardly mobile working class people suffer from these, as there are many other factors in a person's life. Some folks have more personal support, more resilience, more accessible colleges, and a host of other factors. At the heart of these hurdles, for those who stumble, is a process of trying to leave behind one's "old self" and the construction of a disconnected "new self." Classism drives this process. "For a very long time I saw [myself moving] into a different culture," Renny Christopher recalls, "as if 'learning' were a transcendent, universal and value-free condition. That's why I was so happy those two years at Mills [an elite school]—I thought I was 'just learning.' The process being worked on me was as subtle as brainwashing—alteration of my fundamental self in return for approval. . . . And without knowing what was really happening to me, I had no choice about how much I wanted to change, or not change" (2009, 58).

My list of working class difficulties in college includes any of the following: (1) serious mental health problems such as major depression (including suicide), dysthymia (a lower level, long-standing depression), post-traumatic stress disorder, and substance abuse; (2) a complicated and confused bereavement, or grief process—of leaving home forever; (3) internalized classism; (4) *anomie* or a sense of placelessness; (5) imposter syndrome; and (6) survivor guilt.

Trying to accomplish something so big and new as college while suffering major depression, post-traumatic stress disorder, substance abuse and/or other addictions can put students even further behind than lack of cultural capital does.

The *Diagnostic and Statistical Manual of Mental Disorders* IV includes a diagnosis for Complicated Bereavement. Grief and loss are normal parts of life, though they are difficult in the best of situations. In the case of these invisible losses, in the midst of an external success, a form of clinically complicated grief can beset the soon-to-be professional. Without access to information on what is happening to the student, this seemingly irrational grief may be disturbing, even disabling. Untreated or even acknowledged, it can easily lead to Major Depression or Dysthymia.

Internalized classism, with its accompanying cognitive dissonance and dissociation, can present formidable roadblocks to peace of mind and satisfaction with one's achievements or oneself. Seeing one's parents as an embarrassment and a liability is not only painful and confusing, it also can result in the worst kind of separation from family: a separation of *meaning* and a loss of respect for the family. Moreover, internalized classism can mean a loss of one's own self, at least all the parts that preceded the new, improved self. Psychologically, this is dangerous. Something inside resists the new successes: if "those people" are too stupid or lazy or whatever to do this, and I was—am—one of those people, sooner or later someone will find out. This may give rise to an internal hypervigilance, in which one constantly edits and corrects oneself. Some of the most contemptuous and hateful classism toward working class folks comes from people who long ago chose to side with the middle class part of themselves and to annihilate the working class part. Dissociation, a psychological defense that separates conflicting parts of the self and buries unwanted ones, results in a compartmentalized inner life that can backfire when least expected.

The three most commonly reported problems are anomie, imposter syndrome, and survivor guilt. I saved them for last as they often carry over into the new self's new life beyond school as a member of the middle class.

Anomie is a sense of "placelessness" with an attending absence of clear social norms and mental confusion. It can be overwhelming not only for those who face the things discussed above, but also for the fully assimilated. "Estrangement from the class of origin and from the class of destination refers to *the feeling of being nowhere at home*, at once disaffiliated in one direction and unassimilated in another. This oblivion is, in some part, a function of being perceived as no longer a full member by family, friends, and class cohorts in the class of origin or of one's own lack of affinity and identification with the class of origin" (Ryan and Sackrey 1996, 120; emphasis mine).

Mary Cappello, another working class college teacher, states: "The borderline state, the sense of being neither here nor there persists: the working class academic can never fully 'move in.' The people from your former life refuse to understand what you do; in your new one, what happens at the dinner table will always give you away" (Dews and Law 1995, 130). I hear some version of this over and over in my counseling practice and from my college students and workshop participants. I didn't have the experience of my people "refusing to understand" my life so much as I just assumed they would not. Also, because working class life is oriented toward tradition—staying *one-of-us*—and because working class schools do not generally attempt to train children to be scholars but to be docile and obedient, working class family members may not have a framework with which to understand it. Still, many crossovers report real animosity from family members about their chosen path (into the middle class). In any case, my sense of being neither here nor there, or anomie, lasted for years and years and is something I still hear reported by working class college students and formerly working class professionals.

Imposter syndrome is a key theme in *Strangers in Paradise* (1996). It is not a clinical diagnosis, but an existential one—the feeling that one has fooled people to be successful and the fear that one will be "found out." It is hard to find personal essays by formerly working class college teachers who do *not* make some mention of some form of imposter syndrome. In an essay named after the Ryan and Sackrey passage above, "Nowhere at Home," Christine Overall writes: "Like philosopher Robert Nozick, I am an 'immigrant to the realm of thought.' As a result I never felt that I knew the academic rules, especially the unwritten ones, well enough to participate as an equal with my supposed peers. I had to learn, slowly, painfully, to 'pass' as middle class" (Dews and Law 1995, 216). Ryan and Sackrey put it this way:

> This phenomenon is best described by the feelings expressed by those suffering from the experience. "I'm just not good enough." "I never feel I know enough." "I always knew I was going to be exposed." "If they only knew what a fool I was, then—." In its most basic form, it is a combination of feeling one is an intellectual fraud and a fear of being found out. What has been discovered about the nagging sense of inadequacy and vulnerability is that for some who suffer, it does not abate over time. For others it does. . . .
>
> Yet for a subset of individuals, the fear does not abate; in fact, the more successful one becomes, the more positive the response to one's performance, the more acute becomes the anxiety. The sufferer imagines each success to be further evidence of his or her capacity to fool "them." As the incidence of success accumulates, there is just more and more about which to feel fraudulent. (1996, 120–21)

In "Survivor Guilt in a University Setting" Geraldine Piorkowski (1983) described psychological barriers for upwardly mobile poverty class and working class students. She developed the concept of *survivor guilt* as director of a counseling center for students at Roosevelt University in Chicago: "For low income, urban, first-generation college students, survivor guilt has emerged as a significant explanatory concept for academic difficulty." She drew on community psychiatrist Robert Lifton's work on survivors of human and natural disasters. The survivor's haunting and disabling dilemma, "Why should I live when they died?" was recast by Piorkowski, "Why should I succeed when they failed?" Piorkowski and her colleagues found the concept of survivor guilt to be a helpful explanation for "higher attrition rates, lower GPA's, significant conflict with less affection toward parents, problems organizing time, lower self-esteem, and more psychosomatic problems than their [dorm-staying, middle class] peers" (1983, 620).

Though we have seen that working class cultures can offer a richness of community and other human qualities that tend to be overlooked by the larger society, crossovers also know working class *work* can be hard, even brutal. Inequality is at the heart of survivor guilt. Heading toward professions that provide long vacations and never endanger their fingers, eyes, or lives, crossovers may have few illusions about deserving this better life. The working class survivor suffers from "makin' it" into a new class that provides far greater pay, creativity, and control, while important others—family and friends—do not have these things. While their middle class mentors pat them on the back for their courage and hard work, these people know their working class families are no less smart, hard-working, or courageous than they are.

Robert Lifton (1967) said any form of "symbolic breakdown," where the world and people that once felt like home are lost in a way one can neither grieve nor retrieve, can be a source of survivor guilt. For those who enter the middle class through acquired cultural capital (like education) there may be a loss of ability to deny this injustice. With advanced study in economics, political science, sociology, and more, the mystification of class is penetrated and there you are—rediscovering with fancy procedures what your family always told you. All that stuff about equal opportunity really is bullshit. Anger and guilt about the difficulties one's family faces can build up within crossovers, and, without recognition or voice, they can subconsciously reroute into a host of other problems.

Lifton (1967) suggested that psychic numbing, a feature of survivor guilt, also suppresses anger and, more broadly, any resistance to the source of injustice. Often there is a general numbing, a fear of feeling, as if feeling emotions might disturb a delicate psychological balance that may never be regained. We may rush forward to stay ahead of the cluster of feelings that we fear would drag us down. Again, the antidote to social silence is speech. Piorkowski found that explaining the concept of survivor guilt in counseling sessions and in workshops helped students and evoked powerful testimony:

> One minority woman reported that her most stressful experience was being the only one in her south-side [Chicago] neighborhood going to college. Another student described her frustration in trying to persuade family members to take positive steps on their own behalf (e.g. to continue their education or get jobs) with no success. Other first generation college students who work at improving their English grammar find that their manner of speaking becomes the object of ridicule by family members who feel threatened by such differences from family norms. "So you think you're too good for us" is a taunt frequently directed at the family member who is trying to escape the family socio-economic level. (1983, 620)

When I found Piorkowski's work while I was writing my thesis on working class people and psychotherapy, I actually wept with sorrow and relief. Someone was bearing witness to what I thought were my private difficulties. Especially in youth, starry-eyed and excited about how big my world was becoming, I wanted desperately to take my family *with* me on my journey. Reading Piorkowski made my own struggle visible to me, eased my struggle and helped me go easier on myself, and her work has helped me to help my college students and counseling clients over the years. As with imposter syndrome and anomie, some form of survivor guilt is reported over and over by those who cross from poverty class and working class into the professional and managerial upper middle class.

Although they may not suffer from major psychological problems, many class-crossovers report chronic anxiety and fear. Many report a sudden drop in self-esteem that results from having always been the "smart kid" and then suddenly finding oneself completely out of one's depth, unable to compete with classmates who have been groomed for college all their lives. It can be overwhelming. Also, as colleges encourage these students to reject their low-class ways, they help students internalize classism and create a punitive self-censor that harangues them. As any counselor can tell you, negative messages about oneself, repeated internally to protect oneself from doing something wrong, is an excellent recipe for anxiety, depression, and other mental health problems. As bell hooks reports,

"Students from non-privileged backgrounds who did not want to forget often had nervous breakdowns. They could not bear the weight of all the contradictions they had to confront. They were crushed. More often than not they dropped out with no trace of their inner anguish recorded, no institutional record of the myriad ways their take on the world was assaulted by an elite vision of class and privilege" (2000, 36–37).

My aim is not to reduce the rich and varied experience of crossing classes through higher education to a psychosocial syndrome. Not every working class student suffers all or any of this. Still, these factors, and the confusing combination of them, present invisible costs for the working class college student that middle class students, for the most part, do not even have to consider. My wish is to provide a context that can help illuminate the social nature of these too frequently presumed private and personal problems. If working class students, as well as their teachers and other (middle class) students, can see these common problems, they may be able to avoid having to bear the personal sense of inadequacy and shame that many suffer quietly (Dews and Law 1995; Ryan and Sackrey 1995; Register 2000; Lubrano 2003; Jensen 2004; Christopher 2009).

These reactions to higher education are *not* a result of personal failings but of cultural clash and domination. I am not just describing individual problems or psychopathology that may occur for working class students. I am describing a pathology in American social and educational systems that *shows up* in people who go against the grain that can punish people in college from working class backgrounds, to varying degrees, and that spares people from middle class backgrounds, but not completely.

Furthermore, not all commonly reported psychological factors are negative. People often report an inspiring sense of hope and promise, even elation, at the exciting pursuit of an ever-evolving intellectual life. Another significant benefit, which begins in higher education and increases over time spent in one's new social class or career, is personal and political power—what Bernstein called access to "meta-change," access to the social policies and institutions that can create material changes for the betterment of all citizens.

There is much that is enriching and exciting about crossing classes, but the psychological obstacles I have described make it harder to enjoy the benefits. The joys of finding new parts of oneself and the world, to be immersed in a world of ideas, are satisfying, even exhilarating, for someone whose education previously denied these things. To say nothing of avoiding sometimes back-breaking or mind-numbing manual labor. Gaining access to and the ability to change the very institutions that serve to exclude people like us can be liberating. Still, the confluence of all the above factors can make for a confusing, even debilitating, experience in college. As the sociologist Julie Withers said to me in 2007, when she was a graduate student, "It's confusing to experience elation and imposter syndrome at the same!"

Coping Strategies

The three psychological coping strategies I see most commonly practiced by college students attempting to resolve the conflict between new and old worlds are distancing, resisting, and building bridges. Many of the hurdles I have described appear to plague people who have already crossed the class divide, particularly if they still feel loyalty to their roots. These coping strategies easily become lifestyles, built to deal with ongoing mental dissonance, and are not limited to college years, though they generally start there.

Distancing

Throughout the autobiographical literature of academics from the working class, the most common coping strategy is distancing oneself from one's family and former life. This is the way most working class academics resolve the dissonance of "the before and after of this life" (Christopher, from Dews and Law, 1995, 141). For the ones who distance themselves there is loss, unstated and often misunderstood. "A few of us manage to break with our origins, denying our 'incorrectness' or the 'incorrect' class into which we were born," Irv Peckham writes. "I do not know how others manage the break but I erased my incorrectness by infrequently going home. In time, I more or less forgot who my parents and siblings were. Although I hesitate to admit it, I have to tell you that the only time my parents and I and my brother and my sister have all been together since I left home was for my parents' silver wedding anniversary. I suspect the next occasion will be a funeral. That's called erasure" (Dews and Law 1995, 274).

For people who distance themselves from their backgrounds, geographically and/or psychologically, life may be simpler. Distance makes the transition easier, as the choice has been made and one is not so torn between worlds. Distancing oneself from one's origins is something professional life encourages, with its expected promotions and geographical moves. Some distance themselves more profoundly than others. One woman in the world of business, interviewed by Alfred Lubrano in his 2004 book *Limbo: Blue Collar Roots, White Collar Dreams*, routinely lies about where she was raised to other executives. She feels people will dismiss her if she tells the truth. "I'm embarrassed by the blue-collar origin of [the town where she grew up]. I don't want to feel inferior. I'm dealing with coworkers and bosses that grew up on the East Coast. Some of them make millions, put their kids in exclusive schools. I don't want them to know what my origins were. We're not classless in this society. My mother said education would raise us up, but I'm still blue collar. It doesn't go away" (Lubrano 2004, 199–200). Class background doesn't go away, but a person can go away from their background. Some run like hell to do so.

In middle class families, it is not unusual for grown siblings to be strewn across the country, pursuing their careers (or their husbands' careers). But in the working class, family comes first. Every one of the relatives with whom I recorded oral histories counted family as their most important value. All but seven (two couples and their kids) of my 140 plus Jensen relatives still live in Minnesota, and most still crisscross the state regularly to attend family reunions, weddings, graduations, and baby showers. My cousin Cindy [Jensen] Koslowski was the second person in my family to go to college. Ten years my junior, she has pale blond hair, blue eyes, ruddy skin, and a ready smile.

"My kind of people? Family," Cindy articulated the importance of family in working class culture. "I notice my family ties are a lot stronger than a lot of people's, and I think that's cause my dad always emphasized that— gotta get to the Christmas party. You gotta get to the picnic; you gotta meet your family; some day I'm gonna die and this is all you're gonna have. I'm thinking maybe Grampa instilled that in him 'cause all those boys and girls show up [our fathers and their siblings]. It's just amazing. 'Cause I'm sure some days, I'm sure they're like, 'Drive to Albert Lea? No thanks.' But they all come, by golly, and all their kids come, and it's amazing."

Students who distance themselves from a working class family, with its emphasis on maintaining lifelong connections, may find their new world cold and emotionally empty by comparison. Alice Trent, a coal miner's daughter turned college professor, said, "The most important thing to me was to get out of that small town. So even though I come from a working class background, in reality I have never really identified with the working class. In fact, I have felt detached from it and oppressed by it. . . . The most important thing about my being working class is that I identified with no group" (Ryan and Sackrey 1996, 218).

Alice Trent is not alone; the majority of academics in two of my primary sources for this chapter felt similarly, perhaps in part because the life of an academic usually requires moving to the state of the school that hires you. Physical distance from family of origin means little straddling of cultures is necessary most of the time—except within one's own head. But it does not bring an internal sense of belonging in one's new social location.

Resisting

Resistance to the dominant middle class culture is harder to track than distancing because it often manifests in the act of *not* going to college, *not* writing papers, and so on. As we saw last chapter, many people do just give up on college. There is a high college drop-out rate among working class students. They are then punished, with the rest of the working class, with much lower wages, less control, and so forth.

Others, like my big brother Eddie, manage to *not* change cultures, just work and income. Eddie and I both ended up working in professional jobs for most of our adult lives. But I went to college and graduate school, and he was a mail carrier who gradually worked his way up to postmaster of several large post offices in Minneapolis. I became a left-wing type who did community organizing and then focused my later counseling work on poor and working class kids and adults. I also developed a love of abstract, atonal music with multiple time signatures, international travel, and gourmet food. I became, ironically, both politically committed to working class people and increasingly embarrassed to bring my new educated activist friends home to my redneck family. My brother became a right-wing type who nonetheless worked very hard to bring an "employee involvement" management style into the post offices he managed. He still plays rockabilly guitar and sings karaoke, wears a cowboy hat, and can't imagine paying as much money for an entire meal as I do on a tip. He never stopped enjoying the company of and connection with the many members of our extended family. Who is the more advantaged and who the disadvantaged one of us? If the answer seems easy, it shouldn't.

My cousin Cindy, daughter of Uncle Gene and Auntie Pete from my Fridley story, is an example of someone who stayed within her working class life while also getting an education—a BS in nursing, an MS in nursing, a nurse practitioner's licensure, and a masters in business administration—and achieving significant success in her work. She had to fight hard for it. Although among the top ten students in her high school—taking double the normal load and no electives so she could graduate a year early and start college—she was forced to quit high school when she got pregnant at sixteen. She had to go to a different school, where she was told it didn't matter anymore what courses she took or didn't take. I interviewed her.

> *Barb:* Can you remember any other instances where you felt hurt and discriminated against?
>
> *Cindy:* Well, I remember going to, you know, when I was in high school there at [her new school] it was like, what classes can I register for? And they were, like, you can register for anything. Why don't you take this one, it's easy. And I was like, well, I don't want to take it 'cause it's easy! And then they wanted to register me for classes I'd already taken, like it doesn't matter 'cause you're just going to get enough credits and have your baby anyway.

She married her high school sweetheart, Nick Koslowski, who worked as a lineman, had her baby, and hustled to get a GED, feeling it was a "waste of taxpayers' money" to learn things she already knew how to do, like knitting and cooking. Then she began to apply to local community colleges.

> *Cindy:* I tried to get into colleges, you know, and they discouraged me from going.
>
> *Barb:* Because you had a GED?
>
> *Cindy:* Yeah, I called the colleges and applied and they discouraged me from going.

Barb: What'd they say?

Cindy: They said they really . . . I was probably too young. They said I hadn't had a high school education yet. They told me that I hadn't had college classes yet.

Barb: How do you have college classes before you go to college?

Cindy: Well, exactly!

Barb: Did you feel discriminated against?

Cindy: Very much so.

Cindy was told to take college classes before she was accepted to prove she could do it (though her high school record showed stellar grades). With baby in tow, she did take college classes to prove herself in chemistry and other formidable subjects, some of which she had already taken in high school.

Cindy: I actually applied at [a local community college] and they were the ones that told me not to bother applying.

Barb: Okay, so that's one of the places that said . . .

Cindy: That counselor actually said to me, "Don't bother applying."

Barb: Really?

Cindy: Very true.

Barb: Oh, my God. Did you go home in tears?

Cindy: I cried, yeah. I cried afterwards. It was kind of hurtful. I'm like, "You don't even know me."

With college courses taken she finally was accepted to a junior college, earned her RN, and then her BS at a local Christian college that was mostly middle and upper middle class kids, and where she found someone else from a working class background. Together they got their nursing degrees and went on to graduate school. She found a working class way to face college, with a best friend at her side.

Cindy's story demonstrates a kind of "resistance from within" to the domination of middle class culture that spared her most of the difficulties I have described. She is still happily married to her high school boyfriend, who still works as a lineman. She has had three children, and her eldest daughter also just graduated from college. Cindy lives just a few miles from her parents in a small town north of the Twin Cities.

Many crossovers create their own forms of resistance-from-within during college. Alfred Lubrano, author of *Limbo,* lived at home in Bensonhurst,

Brooklyn, while attending prestigious Columbia University and working part-time in the law library. He reports that "Budding Baileys [law students] would read assigned material from books, then razor-blade the pages out, so that no one else in their class could see them. The vast majority were spoiled, entitled, competitive middle and upper class kids. . . . I got a few of them back though—part of my ongoing campaign of class warfare." There was a strict rule in the library that students could keep research books for only twenty-four hours in their study carrels. Lubrano continued:

> The librarian—a prickly Straddler herself who despised law students more than I did—would send me to collect books. . . . I did it with glee, taking special delight in first removing the bookmarks the students had placed in the hoarded volumes. Then I'd shelve them. When the students found out, they'd be livid and would run to the front desk of the library to complain. I especially liked fielding the "How dare you's?" and the "Do you know who I am's?" I'd simply get all six foot three and Brooklyn on them. They backed down fast, and I got the impression that they weren't used to anyone saying no to them. Ever. (2004, 77)

Others develop their forms of resistance to upper class and middle class dominance within their new professional world and use their new status to facilitate their resistance to the status quo. Many crossovers not only resist being shamed for their backgrounds, they manage to take a strong sense of self and history with them to counter the negative messages; may even feel their backgrounds give them advantage. Louis Potter said:

> Growing up . . . must have established some basic values that have been with me since. Sharing physical things along with mutual psychological and emotional support were necessities for survival in a tough outside world. The idea of equity became equality. Survival of the fittest wouldn't wash. You didn't win and you were not better just because you were bigger, stronger, or smarter—that just wasn't fair! So we were taught to root for the underdog and do battle with the powerful. "I may not be better than anybody, but I'm just as good," was my mother's admonition. (Ryan and Sackrey 1996, 188)

A "good person" in the professional middle class is, too often, a "brilliant" individual who achieves something mighty for "the good of [an abstracted] humanity"; such a person may get prizes and awards. A "good person" in the working class has time to hang out, wants to keep the circle of connection intact, and offers many small generosities to personal and particular others. In a society where virtually everything, and particularly education, is "classed," might not some decide to opt for a culture that emphasizes cooperation over competition? To choose "hanging out" over pushing oneself to achieve (and achieve and achieve)? Christmas cards that simply say "love, Aunt Mary" versus Christmas letters that compile the year's achievements, evidence of one's worth—or brilliance or ambition or travel budget—for the past year?

In middle age, after decades of living the successful professional's work-aholic lifestyle, this is not hard for me to imagine at all. Working class people choose to live in their cooperative cultures, despite economic penalties. Many even prefer working class work (Torlina 2011). They choose to remain with the people and places that feel like home. But, in a society dominated by the very wealthy and largely run by the professional middle class, the privileges and economic rewards are far from equal. "We also learned a healthy suspicion of slick arguments," Potter continued, "and were taught to trust our gut in values of right and wrong and also to appreciate simple common sense. It made us more argumentative and hard-headed, but much less likely to be bamboozled by selfishness masquerading as intelligent analysis" (Ryan and Sackrey 1996, 188).

Sociology instructor Julie Withers is quite intentional about resisting the status quo. She explains to her community college students that she, too, was a working class student, and that she didn't think she was smart or lucky enough for higher education: "Certainly, I didn't look like 'the good kids.'" She added, "I see awareness flash in students' eyes every semester, the look of connection when I talk about growing up poor, being a first-generation college graduate and what it's like, growing up in a household like mine filled with smart people that discourage and disdain higher education because of what happened to them in school" (Withers 2010).

Building Bridges

This chapter started with Shelley hiding and crying in a bathroom stall at college. It would be wrong-headed to try to tell her what her own solutions might be. What we *can* do for her is clarify what those decision points are by seeing her dilemma more clearly. We can start by illuminating and validating both her past and her present. If she can see the problem she shares with her husband as a clash of cultures—rather than a battle of good and bad, better and worse, normal and abnormal—she may be able to avoid choosing decisively between the cultures. If she had someone to talk with about how she might reconcile them in her own life, she and her family might move forward in a way right for her and them.

Withers also wrote a three-page manual she gives to her students that she calls Survival Skills 101: Negotiating Class Dynamics. I wish I had had it to give to Shelley. Wither's list includes: (1) Family and friends matter; (2) Know yourself and trust your gut; (3) It's okay to be wary, you do not have to trust people you do not know; (4) Use what you know; and (5) Learn to pass.

Under the heading "Learn to pass," Withers encourages students to not disclose their background unless they feel genuinely comfortable doing so, and also not to share the nitty-gritty details of their life and struggles in school unless you know the person you are talking to well. Because "they will repeat this information in meetings, usually in a way that shows they feel sorry for you but 'boy, are you a mess.'" She states, "What you need to know is that many of [your teachers] think that you are flawed, They feel sorry for you and are determined that what you need is a better attitude."

I do not intend to romanticize working class life, which can also be a difficult life with limited options, but it is easy for me to remember, and enjoy to this day, many positive aspects of working class life. Again, working class cultures have humane, healthy, and life-giving qualities that people from the middle class pine and search for, often at no small consequence to their bank accounts. Like most counseling psychologists, I too have spent a good deal of my career helping both "failures" and "successes" from the middle class improve their mental health. We help them, often, to embrace a kind of humanity that values warmth over brilliance and emotional connection over intellectual competition. We try to help them to find an inner self that endures in spite of outer-world achievements and failures.

A college teacher, Donna Burns Phillips, had this to say about teaching crossovers, "I believe that academics have to be just as clear and deliberate about the attitudes towards the students they teach as they are about the theories they teach" (Dews and Law 1995, 230). I think it is exactly the job of college teachers, and other perhaps unwitting gatekeepers to the middle class, to help people remember, even see more clearly, where they came from and what value it has. Phillips suggests that "education sets up a dialogue between past, present and possible selves." I want it to do just that for Shelley.

I call this choice building bridges, a third response to the clashing of cultures, classism, and the resulting confusion. College should give Shelley what it gives her middle class peers: *additions* to herself, not, as Phillips points out, subtractions from herself or a "transformation" into a new self. What she needs is integration of new abilities and awareness, not a rejection and loss of all that has come before.

If helping working class students integrate the old with the new is difficult, if it seems contradictory to people who long for a classless society, we nonetheless need to apply ourselves to this task. We need to experiment and figure out how to help Shelley and others like her to make meaning of their rich and complex lives, not to saw half of it off. There is much she can teach us, if we listen. In this area, our role must be as much about facilitating as teaching. Helping her see and define her own cross-class experience is important. Indeed, after a section on class and culture in my community psychology course (a couple years after the story that started this chapter), Shelley was the first to list positive things about working class life when asked.

Working class people do not see their lives as something to survive. I do not see working with one's hands as inherently inferior. Yes, working class people have a hard time getting respect and decent pay for their work. The conditions of work can be truly awful, as my father's widow, Lillian Jensen, testified vividly in her oral work history, after twenty-one years working in poultry plants. But only in the middle class is work your life. It is middle class solipsism, and arrogance, that takes the institutional injustices working class people face and reduces their lives and cultures to nothing *but* that. Among the qualities that Shelley listed were several that I help middle class therapy clients strive to achieve: being real or "emotionally honest," pitching in when there is work to be done, being loyal to others above personal advancement, and having that unselfconscious humor that makes people laugh out loud.

Working Class Studies

In colleges and universities across the country, the newly emerging field of Working Class Studies is pulling professionals like me and students like Shelley together to counteract the negative messages of higher education and to mine our personal understanding of class for instruction on life and humanity. As in Women's and African American studies, the personal and the political are viewed as intimately related. Working class people headed into the middle class, or already there, talk, listen, write, and read about social class and start to notice the similarities between their stories and feelings and those of others. A shaft of sunlight illuminates a darkened room and we realize we are not alone. People who have felt a personal sense of failure, or fraudulence, begin to recognize they are not alone in their alternative intentions, their blurred double vision, their divided hearts. Middle class people in higher education seek out and listen to these voices, adding real-life and cultural experiences to their economic understanding of class in America. Though working class cultures are diverse, the foundations of belonging and being are generally held in common. It is the Western, white middle class and upper class cultures that are relatively unique in the world in their focus on individuality, competition, and personal achievement.

At the beginning of this chapter Shelley was not only seeing her husband with newly judgmental eyes, she was also beginning to distance her new self from her old self. Before she had a conscious appreciation of the complex journey she was making, or an appreciation for the working class woman she was and is, she could have lost that woman, as well as her husband and family. College is a dubious success, at best, if one must relinquish that much to achieve it. But Shelley went to a school where there are many first-generation college students, with many teachers who think hard about who and how they teach, and she did come to a reasonable integration of her "two selves." I know this was due in part to her husband wanting her to succeed in school, even after his temper tantrum, and that he repeatedly told her so. Many crossovers tell of the spouse or partner who helped them through, and without that cooperation it would be much more difficult.

I saw Shelley and her husband at graduation ceremonies one spring a couple years after she took my Psychology of Women class. When I asked if she might like to go to graduate school to continue her "life of the mind" and perhaps even find work she would enjoy more, she replied, "No way! This has been hard enough on my life!" Shelley's concern is not primarily that this is hard on *her* but on "her life"—on others in her life, on her connection to them, and also to her sense of meaning. She graduated with her bachelor's degree and a 4.0 grade average, and she not only kept her job, she won a promotion at work. Smiling beside her after the ceremony, her husband was full of pride, and he thanked me for believing in Shelley. She told me she was looking forward to "just living!" Then she winked at me, looked at her husband and said, "Tell her!" He blushed and hesitated. "Tell her!" she demanded. Then he told me they had gone together to a lecture on dream interpretation. "And he loved it!" Shelley cried, too excited to wait. He nodded. "Some interesting stuff, I gotta admit," he said shyly, and then he finally looked me in the eye and gave me a crooked smile.

7

Pain in the Promised Land

Several years ago I shared a taxi ride from a Working Class Studies conference to an airport with a young woman. She was working on her PhD in English literature. We were leaving Youngstown, Ohio, the site of the early conferences that spawned Working Class Studies. We had not met previously, and as we chatted in the taxi I told her I had been there to talk about the differences between working class and middle class cultures, the prejudice against working class people, and the difficulties of people from blue-collar backgrounds who try to get ahead by moving into the professional class. To my surprise, her eyes filled with tears.

She told me her father had taken out a new mortgage on the home that he had finally paid off to finance her education. He had been about to retire, having worked many long and hard years as a plumber. He postponed his retirement for her. She and her father had thought that meant she would learn to do easier work than his or her mother's in a factory. But she was learning a lot more than that.

She heard educated people putting down people just like her father all the time; she knew how to handle that. But for the first time she was afraid she was becoming one of them. At the conference she heard certain long-time professors dissecting and attacking higher education with sarcasm and razor-edge, rapid-fire, reference-laden, and hope-numbing analyses. They spoke of their long struggle to make changes in what they saw as a hopelessly entrenched education system that only reproduced social and economic injustice and privilege. She wondered if she had made a terrible mistake by choosing a career as a college teacher of English. She felt she was betraying her father: with his money she was joining a system that held him in contempt; she was moving further and further away from anything like common ground with him. She was learning how *not* to be him; and she was getting really good at it. She was also learning how hard it would ever be to make a difference.

She felt guilty, confused, and some measure of real despair. She said her family called her Miss Fancy Pants when she used words like "discourse"; she was angry with herself for using "those words" with her family. She was afraid she was going to become someone she did not want to be. She was considering dropping out of school. Her eyes filled up again with tears. What would that mean to reject the education her father had put himself in debt to give her? How could she ever explain it to him? And if she went on, where would she go? Who would she be when she got there?

In chapter 6 we saw Shelley near the beginning of developing her middle class self, and reclaiming her working class life as well. The young woman in the taxi had almost completed her PhD at a prestigious university, and she was falling prey to the contradictions inherent in her new life. What are the experiences of people like these women once they have lodged fairly firmly in the middle class? In my personal history and in the histories of many of my counseling clients, I have seen that continued confusion and pain often accompanies the gains realized by crossing over classes. Prejudice against working class people, classism, is just the beginning of what crossovers have to contend with in their new life. They also face many unhealthy features of middle class life that hurt people raised there as well.

In this chapter I explore the privileges and problems that come with the territory of middle class life, of achieving and becoming. I will examine both positive and negative effects of middle class values that direct people toward individual achievements, look at different ways of becoming, return briefly to child rearing, and come to rest with class crossovers who have built lives of belonging *and* becoming. We have seen that class location can inspire different worldviews; it also gives different vantage points from which to view middle class culture in particular and American society as a whole.

Becoming Somebody

In the middle class, a cultural emphasis on *becoming* through individual achievement is central. Whether one is climbing a corporate ladder, attending morning yoga classes, practicing violin eight hours a day, or plumbing the depths of one's own psychology, there is a premium on self-improvement and, especially, on publicly recognized individual accomplishments.

Becoming is called self-actualization by psychologists. And self-actualization, whether it is called that or not, is admired and expected in middle class life. Self-actualization is the development of one's individual talents on one's journey through life, what some career-assessment tests call "using your abilities." Middle class culture sees this process as one of proper parental preparation and encouragement, opportunity, individual will and self-discipline, along with the proper setting of long-term goals, followed by the steps necessary to reach those goals. We do these things to find ourselves, to create meaning, and to try to become the best and brightest individual we can.

I know full well that if I were not middle class, I would never have written this book. It wasn't that I got money or institutional help, as I am not employed as a full-time academic. But I had accumulated the required cultural capital to write the papers that brought academic people to me, including my editor, and to have two author friends reading every chapter as I wrote the first draft and giving me comments. I know still more people who have written books and heard them say, "You can do this, it's not that hard." I choose to live a middle class life, and I am glad I landed here. I love having work that directly helps other people, pays a more than decent wage, and I like that I can expect I will remain physically able to do it the rest of my life.

In the middle class, emphasis on becoming "somebody" through competitive achievement means that each person also has some responsibility to create his or her own particular meaning in life. In my personal and professional experience, for better or worse, working class people don't think too much about this. The norms of community tell people where to find meaning—marriage, children, family, unions, churches, personal hobbies—and people apply themselves in their own particular ways. The psychologist Robert Kegan (1995) has pointed out that in traditional communities meaning is often collectively prescribed.

In contemporary middle class life, much more is up for grabs: who, even whether, we will marry; whether or not to have children; whether we stay near family or move away; and whether we will follow the educational and occupational paths expected by our families or embark on some less-traveled road. Individuality is expected in the middle class, and as long as one is "growing," actualizing oneself, the ways of doing it can vary, though some are culturally preferred.

In working class settings, the same behaviors can be seen as selfishness and may indicate a character problem. Or self-actualization may seem just to be self-aggrandizement. It may be incomprehensible. My Jensen cousins have never said—would never say—anything critical about me not raising kids, but sometimes awkward silences speak for them. How can they not have wondered why I didn't bear and raise children and felt sorry for me, when each of their lives are filled with the deep fulfillment and meaning that comes with raising children and building a family. Meanwhile, in my middle class life bursting with events, activities, and avocations, I bought a T-shirt that says, "I can't believe I forgot to have kids!" It is not unusual in my world for women to not have children, and many of us have very demanding and rewarding careers.

Being in the middle class makes an individual search for meaning in life easier, as there are more options to explore and the search itself is valued and respected. But the road can be a lonely one, especially for those who have grown up with a cultural sense of *us* rather than *I*.

Despite the shady psychological underside of American class mobility, the benefits of middle class life are considerable. Amounts of money and power over others vary, but almost everyone makes way more than people who work in entry-level service jobs, where more and more members of the working class are expected to find employment. In addition, there are greater choices, access, and advantages in almost all areas of life. Worldliness and travel, learning other languages, opportunities to develop our abilities to excellence, both access and ability to compete in exclusive circles that bestow prestige and cultural power, access to other cultures all over the globe, developing and enjoying high levels of speaking and reading ability—to varying degrees, all of these are features of middle class life.

Also, without a deeply bonded community's expectations, one has more opportunity to find one's individual self. For one thing, extensive kin networks take a whole lot of time. My cousin Cindy could tell you more about this than I can. She has had both a professional career and three children and has attended many baby and bridal showers, confirmations, graduations, weddings, and anniversary celebrations in our family. I didn't go to most of these events as an adult, though I still couldn't imagine missing the Family Christmas or Aunt Mary's Summer Picnic. I couldn't see how to do all that and fit in the rest of my middle class life. And, unlike the other women in my family and neighborhood, I didn't want to get married after high school, maybe not at all. And, honestly, I didn't know how to deal with the contradiction, the tension, between my life and theirs, that is, between my chosen path and the one expected of me in my first world. When I did go to showers, I felt awkward and *different*. I felt suddenly embarrassed that I didn't have kids or a husband. At that time I was reacting against, and breaking away from, all those conditions of community membership and, surely, from the part of me that wanted that traditional life. Life in the middle class life can feel like an immense freedom to crossovers. It did to me at that time.

I never forgot where I came from, and I believed fervently in economic justice, workers' rights, unions, and working class pride. At the same time I was gobbling up every non–working class cultural experience I could find and afford. When I finally went back to college for my degrees, in my late twenties, I went expressly to secure a personally meaningful work life, where I could use my abilities and be paid well for my work. I went to join the real middle class. When I began visiting my New York family, my maternal aunt Flora and her husband Milt had a powerful influence in validating my new life. They joked that my interest in education, despite my parents' lack of enthusiasm, was proof that I was genetically Jewish. I had a sense that the whole world was opening up to me. I could go anywhere; I could become anyone.

This great sense of promise, of an ever-unfolding, new-improved life stood in contrast to my working class world in Minnesota. My first world seemed to say, "Stay the same, one of us. We remember you in diapers; we know you as no one else ever will." In middle age, I see benefits and draw-backs in each culture, and I try to keep parts of each of my different class worlds, but that's not how I first experienced middle class life.

Middle class work is more flexible and relies on mental abilities (with symbols) that can strengthen with age, more than on physical abilities that may wear out. I am writing my first book in my fifties, potentially starting a new branch of my career, while my cousin Mike was suddenly laid off at the age of fifty, after seventeen years of machining for the same company. He found another machining job, and he thinks that in about three years he will finally be making what he used to make per hour. Our younger cousin Cindy is finishing up her second master's degree and has gone from being employed as a nurse to managing a large health-care facility. Cindy and I would be the first to say we certainly don't deserve better-paid work than other people in our family. Everyone works really hard, but that's what middle class work gives us.

The money is significant, and while it is rude or déclassé to talk about earnings and assets in the middle class, that modesty also hides what I be-lieve is gross inequality in what working class and middle class people are paid for their labor. It wasn't rude to talk about money where I grew up. People talked about money all the time, especially bargains. As working class people lose health insurance, pensions, and some 20 percent of real wages, some middle class people now have a workplace where benefits include veterinary insurance for their pets! The difference in pay scale, between working class and middle class, is unbelievable. I went from a waitress job at $1.20 an hour (in 1971; it would now be $7.25), to the ability, as an upper middle class psychologist, to charge $150 an hour and three or four times that as a consultant.

Learning Loneliness

In spite of material reward and the psychological advantages of self-expression, life-long learning, and an emphasis on personal growth in the middle class, there is a down side as well. From my vantage point, doing and becoming—individuality versus community, the ongoing pressure for public achievement, the increasingly intense competition to win those awards, and living with hierarchy as a daily way of life with near-constant power negotiations with those "above" and "below"—can be really stressful. This is true for both people born and raised within the middle class and, certainly, for working class crossovers. Also, the requirements of middle class work often require moves across the country, as well as many trips and conferences that interfere with family life and social connections.

Social commentators within the middle class have long been concerned about America's increasing focus on individuality and competition, as opposed to community and cooperation. As early as 1970, the sociologist Phillip Slater was worried about the effects of declining community in the lives of middle class Americans. He did an extensive review of the sociological research and wrote about it in his *Pursuit of Loneliness.*

> We are so used to living in an individualistic society that we need to be reminded that collectivism has been the more usual lot of humans. Most people in most societies have lived and died in stable communities that took for granted the subordination of the individual to the welfare of the group. The aggrandizement of the individual at the expense of his neighbors was simply a crime. This is not to say that competition is an American invention—all societies involve some mixture of cooperative and competitive institutions. But our society lies near the competitive extreme, and although it contains cooperative institutions, we suffer from their weakness. . . . The competitive life is a lonely one and its satisfactions short-lived, for each race only leads to a new one. (1990, 8–9)

In any culture that is not forced to look outside itself, everything one learns comes to seem normal. Because middle class life is considered normal, as well as better, the personal pain that arises from personal failures (and successes) within that culture of competition is not seen as cultural strain or the product of an unnecessarily competitive education system. For people from the middle class, and also for assimilated working class crossovers, these failures and their emotional consequences are experienced simply as "life" or "me." This value on competitive winning, combined with the increasing isolation of the upper middle class, has effectively kept many people from any real awareness of classes below them in America's economic pyramid. In the forty years since Slater first asked us to worry about our hyperindividualism, the value of individual winning has only grown, and so have the consequences, as America saw a devastating decline in community ties and organizations of all kinds (Putnam 2000; Putnam and Feldstein 2003). Since 2008 we have seen the drastic economic consequences that Wall Street "winners" have inflicted on the rest of the United States.

On a societal scale, loneliness, life outside of a traditional community, is seen as endemic to modern (read middle class) life. The loneliness of the achieving individual who battles to the top of the heap is now assumed, at least in the middle class, to be a part of the human condition. The individualistic worldview currently popular in American society now insists on personal responsibility above all. Nonetheless, on a very concrete level, the facts of our economy, as well as our nation's priorities and policies, clearly affect what individuals can achieve. Winners are glorified beyond good sense, and everyone else is called a loser. From my vantage point as both a class-straddler and psychologist, I see a mounting host of societal pressures are too often simply seen as failures of the individual or as personal problems.

Certainly people do have personal problems for which they sometimes need professional help, but there is a tendency in individual psychotherapy, and especially in psychodynamic therapies, to miss glaring social deficits in people's lives. In my community psychology course a student once asked me about the use of antidepressants by "almost everyone I know." She wanted to know why they call it "abnormal psychology" if so many people are diagnosed with Major Depression. When we find depression widespread in a diverse population, something that *was* once abnormal, one really has to wonder what is happening in our larger society (Seligman 1992; Putnam 2000; Putnam and Feldstein 2003; Levine 2006; Christopher 2009). Are people alone because they are depressed, or are they depressed because they are too alone? I suspect the latter.

But we have seen that not all people want to live competitive, striving lifestyles. Al Gini, in *My Job, Myself* (2001), showed that we are working more hours, far more than forty hours a week, while stress continues to go up. This is true of both working class and middle class people, but for different reasons. Working class families have not been able to survive on one forty-hour-a-week paycheck for decades, and even with two full-time workers they can barely make ends meet (Rubin 1994; Eitzen and

Johnston 2007). But in the middle class, working long hours has become a sign of status in and of itself. Gini quotes Harvard economist Juliet Schor on the irony that technological advancements have produced more, not less, work, as well as "the unexpected decline of leisure" among managers and professionals (75).

Caring and Connection

One of the first college courses counseling and psychology majors take is called Counseling Theories and Techniques. The first theory I teach in this class is Carl Rogers's "client-centered therapy," because it is intuitive for my (mostly) first-generation college students to "tune in" to others. This theory and practice helped usher in all the expressive humanistic therapies (e.g., Gestalt and bioenergetics). With his middle class therapy clients, Rogers found a great need for what he called "unconditional positive regard." His clients needed to feel warmth and acceptance from another person without *doing* anything to get it. Becoming through outstanding individual achievement can be hard on people's inner lives, even, sometimes especially, for winners. People can feel like they always have to earn care and concern from others and, ultimately, from themselves.

Rogers said a context of care and connection is necessary for people to self-actualize, to *become* in a way that is in synch with their innermost feelings and needs. In my terms: his clients needed to feel they could *belong,* no matter what they did or did not *become.* My first- and second-generation college students have usually already developed their skills in empathy and expressing personal warmth. Rogers's unconditional empathy and understanding provided the necessary foundation for most types of contemporary counseling and psychotherapy in the second half of the twentieth century.

Of course, Rogers's ultimate goal was to build sturdier individuals, in line with his class and the class of his clients.[1] Individuality and competition can be healthy within certain bounds, but not without a larger cooperative context that helps keep achievements and failures in perspective. Excessive emphasis on individual achievement may involve underdevelopment of emotional intelligence, social ability, and, occasionally, it can create overweening egos in emotionally disconnected people.

Psychotherapy in the mid-twentieth century was developed, in my view, to help middle class and upper middle class people alleviate problems that come with achieving and becoming: investing too much self-worth in work, losing personal connections and intimacy as a result of neglect, anxiety about the meaning of life, and simply driving too hard, doing too much. The drive to achieve publicly recognized prizes leads to competition, which leads to hierarchy or pecking orders of power—someone has to decide who wins, which leads to a loss of *horizontal* or peer connection to others, which can lead to a variety of mental health problems.

The notion of the individual path is the very basis of psychotherapy. In other words, psychotherapy helps people with the art of becoming. I was trained to help people find an "internal locus of control." This means I am supposed to help people weigh the demands of their life in the world or at home against an internal sense, to find that "small still voice" that tells us our own truth. I have worked with both middle class and working class people, and especially women in the middle class who are given a lot less permission to actualize themselves than men, to find this inner voice and balance it with outer-world demands. And I will continue to do so. But I do not think it needs to be at the expense of community.

Many aspects of popular psychology that stress development of the self were developed during the 1940s, '50s, and '60s when community ties and pressures were stronger in the middle class and Americans in general were embedded within much stronger communities (Putnam 2000; Putnam and Feldstein 2003). People took belonging with others for granted, in relatively cooperative, mutually dependent lives. In the middle classes, in particular, individuals showing independence and initiative, who dared to "stand out" within a larger more conformist culture, were admired, as movies like *The Man in the Gray Flannel Suit* and *There's Always Tomorrow* demonstrated. But only because, in those years hyperindividualism was *not* the norm, certainly not the way it is now. Since the early 1980s, in my counseling work I have emphasized the art of connecting, and I have often helped clients to scour their lives for opportunities to find new people to connect with or to rebuild lost connections.

It was easy to see that many of my private-counseling clients needed the simple comfort of other people in their lives; but how to arrange this was another matter. After difficult but important therapy sessions my clients had no community to return to—nowhere for them to practice new behaviors, new roles, or new rules of dealing with conflict, no one to support them emotionally as they made changes in their lives. For far too many people there was no social backdrop at all.

Over the last twenty years of private practice, I have seen many people who have no trouble meeting their material needs, yet loneliness, addictions, workaholism, and marital problems bring them to my office. From high-achieving middle class clients I hear about emptiness, depression, and anxiety that comes "when I finally stop." Middle class people who did everything right, according to the values of achieving and becoming, still come to therapy because, as one client, a surgeon, said to me, "I made it, so what's wrong? Why can't I enjoy it?"

Like Rogers, I have often seen the negative effects of striving to be outstanding by earning worth and recognition through school, work, or, for some, absolutely everywhere. Heart attacks are very real; so are other physical and emotional effects of too much work and work-related stress—ulcers, high blood pressure, depression, chronic anxiety, workaholism, obsessions, and addictions. For some, a preoccupation and pressure to always move on to the next achievement can consume all of one's time and energy at the expense of simple pleasures like walking a dog, relaxing on a porch, or enjoying meals with family or friends. In some cases, cultural and personal tendencies combine to create self-absorbed individuals focused on their own goals and on an ever-improving self. This excludes the development of empathy and intimate connections, creating a side effect of lonely lives for these high achievers.

Excessive personal reserve is another problem middle class people come to psychotherapy to overcome. They want to connect, to express themselves, to find out "what I feel" as well as to figure out how to tell these feelings to others. Middle class people often come to therapy because they long to get real and "just be myself."

And, of course, for every winner there are many losers. In a culture that defines self through success and winning, losing can be devastating—loss of confidence, loss of work, loss of friends, or even family, and certainly a loss of meaning. Losers populate therapists' offices to find value in themselves, and direction in their lives, after they have failed to achieve what their families and culture asked of them. For many, the sense of personal shame and worthlessness can be completely overwhelming.

Ways of Becoming

In chapter 1, I introduced Michèle Lamont's (1992) book about the values and boundaries of upper middle class men in the United States and France to illustrate and refute biases against the working class, or classism, on the presumption that these powerful winners set standards for the rest of the middle class. I return to it now to uncover differences within middle class life. I also want to revisit Anyon's four types of schools, to parse life in the middle class.

Lamont's work yielded three relatively distinct groups of "somebodies," in both the United States and France, sorted according to how they defined their "kind of people": cultural becomers, moral becomers, and socioeconomic becomers. Each group in the American sample displayed differences in worldview, styles, attitudes, and values, as well as three ways to achieve and compete, to become somebody.

All presumed a high level of individualism. They were likely to believe they earned their superior positions in America's economic pyramid through their own hard work and superior intelligence, taste, determination, and tenacity—as individuals. But they earned their spots in different ways: culturally, through their command of "high culture"; "morally," by virtue of their commitment to help others, and their belief that hard work itself is a sign of good moral character; and socioeconomically, through plain hard work and the fact of their economic winning. These differences map alternative ways to live and strive within the American middle class. All of these people valued self-actualization and viewed their lives as a journey that they hoped was leading to an ever-evolving self and life.

Cultural Becomers

Because the cultural capital *becomers*, for example, authors, professors, psychologists, have the kinds of jobs that allow them to write about their lives, they are overrepresented in the crossover literature and in cultural "production" in general. They are more likely than the other two groups to have contact with the upper class, the executive elite of Anyon's four social class positions. Or at least they identify with the cultural elite and want to be educated in their schools.

This group, along with the upper class they emulate, sets the standards for what is considered having knowledge and being cultured in the United States. But this was the prominent value system for less than a *third* of upper middle class American men, behind the other two in popularity. By contrast, among the French men, cultural capital was the most likely choice of the three. Lamont offers this character study:

> Julien Lafitte is a young scientist, born in Nice, who is studying the volcanos in Clermont-Ferrand [France]. . . . He is vaguely punk looking but carries himself with style. . . . Julien highly values the aesthetic dimension of life. He expresses great contempt for his culturally narrow scientific colleagues. He is easily bored and has no patience for people with poor taste. He selects his friends with great care, he wants to share intellectual experiences and political discussions with them. He cannot fathom being friends with a right-winger. . . . Julien feels superior to people who "watch television everyday, everyday, everyday, everyday," and to conformists "who would never take a position in politics, who always talk about money, who would take their vacation in August at the beach, who would change their car every two years . . . who have no personal ideas, who would never say what they think of a movie, a record, a play, an exposition. They never express an idea, they are afraid to say what they think." (Lamont 1992, 88)

While some might say the French have perfected snobbery to an art form, I hear plenty of Americans in the upper middle class say the very same things. Indeed, I have heard an embarrassing amount of it coming from my own mouth! High culture—including visual art, music, dance, and theater; established and esteemed literature, philosophy, humanities; highly elaborated language use in orating, writing, critiquing; and other complex intellectual activities—is the currency accumulated by those whose route to the upper middle class is Ivy League education. This includes most of the people who are paid to write and speak about their experiences.

Ironically, cultural becomers are the most politically liberal of Lamont's three groups, even about concrete on-the-job rights of workers, while at the same time being the most culturally classist. Most likely to be from upper middle class or upper class backgrounds, they also include working-class crossovers. Crossovers are drawn to this group because education was their route to the professional middle class, and, having so little cultural capital already, they had to work extra hard to master it.

While they may champion working class people politically, these folks' radar for class-based correctness is tuned to the highest frequencies of disturbance. Too many of these people (I admit I have been one) may jump at the chance to correct someone's bad grammar or a misspelled or mispronounced word. They are likely to snicker or roll eyes about the person who blundered. In other words, cultural becomers habitually display their cultural capital and enjoy besting others in a game of competing cultural capital. Think of the frequency with which those who have recently become liberal Democrats sarcastically mock the speech and fact-challenged details of certain right-wing Republicans. They also mock, perhaps by accident, everyone else who doesn't have, or act like they have, an Ivy League education. No wonder many working class folks don't want to vote for these folks when they run for office, even when they actually are trying to help the working class keep its hard-won rights. People in this group tend to automatically judge those with little cultural capital as stupid, or worse.

As we saw in Lamont's research on upper middle class men and in chapter 6, intellectual competition is a sport in the middle class, among men at least (1992; also Belinky et al. 1986; Garger 1995). Competitiveness is common to each of Lamont's groups, but this group's specific method of competition is verbal argument, verbal acuity, sarcastic wit, word play, and clever "repartee," seasoned with frequent references to the specific cultural cachet of the initiated. They may care deeply about economic justice, but they habitually drop high-culture references when they speak with a hyperelaborated verbal style that signals "not us" to anyone *not* in the upper class or their third of the upper middle class.

Among the now-middle-aged (even once-countercultural) baby boomers, the same thing happens with a twist. Both left and right politically, these people make up nonprofit organizations, college faculties, and helping professions, for example, lawyers and doctors, promoting causes from women's rights to free-market economics. For left-leaning cultural becomers, with training in economics, philosophy, and politics, the game of competing cultural capital simply continues with changed key words, concepts, and references, a style learned in high-status schools that teach the art of cultural one-upsmanship. Despite the best of intentions by many, cultural capital is still used to argue, and win, the right to change the world *my* way.

Cultural becomers may be less than a third of America's upper middle class, but they command respect from the rest of the upper middle class, as well as the upper class, for their command of language, education, and high culture. Cultural becomers have a strong influence in society as they tend to be educated in highly prestigious schools and groomed for careers in higher education, government, or professions like psychology, media, politics, and other "makers of culture." They are more likely to share the cultural tastes—food, art, fashion, music, travel destinations—of the upper class, Anyon's executive elite.

For cultural becomers, other people's styles, attitudes, values, and behavior are seen as good or poor individual "taste" (Bourdieu 1984). Taste is seen as some inner wisdom that is reflected in individual preference. When taste is perceived and judged by the standards of a cultural (or countercultural) elite, class-related cultural divisions are invisible. Working class crossovers can be among the worst offenders in this game of cultural competition, as we often have to become hyperfluent in this hyperelaborated language to earn and continually prove our membership among the privileged.[2]

Working class crossovers who have *not* developed what I call "the amnesia of cultural capital," often complain that other people in this group are too segregated and self-absorbed to see outside themselves. As Dwight Lang, a class crossover, pointed out:

> The desire to be unique, to be on the cutting edge, is central to academic culture. It is, in part, linked to the strong sense of individualism that is first and foremost middle class in origin. Competition, rather than cooperation, is the predominant mode of interaction. This runs counter to the stronger sense of community that organized my working-class world-view. My father had always stressed union and working class solidarity. I asked myself, how can everyone be the best? How can we truly be unique in a society where we are all asked to be individuals? (Dews and Law 1995, 172)

According to Lamont, the values of the upper middle class can vary significantly, though some things are the same for all three groups. For example, like cultural becomers, both "moral" and "socioeconomic" *becomers* also highly value education, intelligence, and self–actualization, mentioning it to Lamont often. Still, a full two-thirds of these epitomes of middle class success in America do not consider cultural capital all that important. On the contrary, they pride themselves that "I know people at all levels. Some are not educated, but they are very intelligent, and they bring you something" (1992, 24).

Moral and Socioeconomic Becomers

Lamont's moral and socioeconomic becomers have a lot in common. Like most working class people, they don't like snobs, social climbers, or phonies. Also, like many working class people, they place a very high value on honesty, trustworthiness, competence, and resilience. They also pride themselves on hard work. Unlike working class people within traditional communities, they have probably often felt the sting of cultural classism in their personal lives. They hold strong values of equal opportunity for all, a value that runs deep in America.

People in these two groups also share with many working class people an enjoyment of material success and are not embarrassed about displaying it. While many in the cultural capital crowd shy away from what they would call materialism or ostentation, and often make wisecracks about those who value it, these folks take pride in the fact that they have worked hard for what they have—and they are not embarrassed by their significant advantages. These people often worked past class prejudice themselves to get a leg up in life. Why can't everyone, they reason. As a New York chief financial officer, a socioeconomic becomer, put it, "I've always worked hard, I worked my way through college, through undergraduate school, and even through high school. My family didn't have much in the way of assets. So I was kind of motivated to work hard. . . . Everything was always hard work, and once I went to work for my present company twenty-three years ago, I was poised with an opportunity to succeed. If I failed, it was my own fault" (Lamont 1992, 43).

They believe in God and attend churches, though not usually fundamentalist churches. Religion is a crucial cultural difference between these people and those who define themselves with cultural capital. People with cultural capital tend toward a morality based on social justice and (secular) human rights for all. They are less likely to believe in God and may be quite critical of religion in general, which they may see as tricking people into accepting human injustice on earth.

In other words, in America, most middle class (and also many working class) people see success as something that one has "earned" as an individual, and "good morals" are demonstrated by personal purity. A social consequence of America's adulation of winners, and focus on individual purity, is that personal blame is cast on those who not only have a starting line far behind the middle class and who also value solidarity much more than winning and standing out. For many moral and socioeconomic becomers in the United States, simply not being successful financially or professionally may be seen as a sign, in and of itself, of "low morals."

Although moral and socioeconomic becomers often have more in common with working class people than they do with the cultural capital folks, they are nonetheless often eager to distance themselves from the working class, at least personally. They are more likely than cultural becomers to come from lower status backgrounds. Perhaps their own greater proximity to so-called lower-class people helps fuel their classism, as they define themselves by their separation from, and superiority to, working class folks. Eager to rationalize their claim to greater privilege, they may harshly judge poor and working class people, even though they are less likely than the cultural capital crowd to think of them as brainwashed "idiots." They may feel real revulsion toward poor folks that they call "lazy inner-city" people, a phrase that probably also signals black or brown skin color.[3]

The main difference between these two groups is that "moral" becomers share a strong sense that their privileges translate into a mission to give to others. Lamont called them "moral" because of (1) their commitment to use their advantages to help others, and (2) their tendency to believe that people who have failed to achieve just aren't hard enough workers, a sign of lower morals. Psychologists, social workers, attorneys, teachers, and many other professionals in helping occupations devote their working lives to trying to help less fortunate others get ahead in the achievement race to the top. In business, too, Lamont found men who strongly believed their superior positions—while earned and deserved—gave them a profound sense of personal responsibility to their employees. They believed that it was their responsibility to use their education and ambition to better the world in some way and find meaning in, and perhaps justification for, their greater privileges.

While for some this helping is motivated by the gut sense of belonging and sharing with others that working class cultures often emphasize, it can also be quite different from working class giving. Professionals generally believe their lifestyle is superior and attempt to help others to become more middle class. Though very often good-hearted and principled, they may still be classist solipsists who look at life from their own limited perspective, while disregarding the richness and complexity of the lives of working class people. But middle class folks should not blithely assume everyone lower on the class pyramid must want what they have. In my experience, working class people frequently see professionals as talking heads who are more or less clueless. They are *not* jealous of those in the middle class and are far less likely to believe that class power is earned. Working class people know that class power is about money, not morals (Lamont 1992). Helping professionals frequently see working class folks as not understanding the important stuff, stuff professionals value, as well as being too emotional, chaotic, or underdeveloped (Jones 1974; Meltzer 1978; Withers 2010). As we saw in chapter 2, mistaking cultural attitudes or behaviors for personal deficits is common in the middle class.

The middle class contains different *ways of becoming*, reflecting different points of view, different backgrounds, and a range of cultural characteristics within the middle class. Whatever their attitudes may be toward working class people, however, people in the middle class raise their children to compete for the top. One thing upper middle class—and more and more often *all* middle class—folks generally share is a devotion to having their children be "winners" (Brantlinger 2003). Two-thirds of them may be by turns intimidated by and dismissive of cultural capital, but they are still doing everything they can to make sure their children will get it. The pressure is mounting in the new middle class, as an ever-exploding market for stress relievers demonstrates. The pace keeps getting faster, and the number of material "necessities" for the good life also continues to climb. Nowhere is this pressure more obvious than in the raising of children for the "impossibly competitive new millennium" (Rosenfeld and Wise 2000; Levine 2006).

Early Life in the Fast—and First—Lane

As American society continues to speed up, so does the pace and extent of parenting within the middle class. I used Lareau's term "concerted cultivation" to describe middle class child rearing, the kind professionals have routinely recommended over the last several decades (2003; Lareau and Conley 2009). We have seen that kids from the middle class have access to language skills, cultural capital, and, crucially, an individual sense of entitlement that enables them to make requests and negotiate on their own behalf in all kinds of settings (school, sports, doctor's offices). The "power"

1980s and '90s brought with them "power-parenting." More recently, the phrase "helicopter parents" (those who continually hover over their children) has been gaining traction. I would like to look more closely at problems with middle class parenting in light of the rise of individualism and competition in America.

Since Shirley Heath's book was first published in the early 1980s, middle class parents have greatly stepped up their efforts to create "custom kids." Many middle class parents are not content to raise children who are merely able to compete; they desperately want them to win. In *The Over-Scheduled Child: Avoiding the Hyper-Parenting Trap*, authors Rosenfeld and Wise document the extremes to which today's parents will go.

> It is Tuesday at 6:45 AM. Belinda, at age seven, is still asleep. School doesn't start until nine and her mother usually lets her sleep until 7:30. But not on Tuesdays. That's the day Belinda has a 7:30 AM piano lesson. From it she goes directly to school, which lasts until three. Then the baby-sitter drives Belinda to gymnastics for the 4:00–6:30 class. While Tuesday is the busiest day, the rest of the week is filled up too, with religious school and choir practice, ballet, and (Belinda's favorite) horseback riding. "She's pretty worn out by the end of the day," her mother laments. "But you know, she's much more alert for the morning piano lesson than she was for the Friday afternoon time slot we had before." She pauses for a moment and then says, thoughtfully, "Kids today are so much busier than we used to be. I'm not really sure it is a good thing. But I want to give her the advantages I didn't have." Then she opens the door to Belinda's room and gently pats her daughter's back to awaken her. (Rosenfeld and Wise 2000, 1–2)

The authors make clear what class these hyperparents come from, as the authors introduce themselves and identify with their audience: "We Americans have grown accustomed to hiring help when we need it. We believe in education. We believe in Science. We believe in specialization. We hire experts to help us with our cars, computers, and careers. It's a good thing we can, because more often than not, we'd be clueless without them" (Wise and Rosenfeld 2000, 76–77).

Middle class parents appear *more* nervous about their parenting, even though the very fact of their greater wealth and social status give significant advantages to their children. In the last thirty years professionals have aimed innumerable how-to books, articles, and products at middle class parents to (supposedly) help them raise the best possible children. Like most parents, middle class parents love their children and want the best for them. Professionals guide parents authoritatively. Rosenfeld and Wise found that newspaper reports and magazine articles reinforce the sense that "normal" is no longer enough. Professionals and the media exhort parents with strong and active verbs to make their kids excel: "'*Make* your baby smarter,' *Parenting* magazine urges. '*Build* a better Boy' advises *Newsweek*. It is as though children were born mediocre and by tinkering with their valves and fine-tuning their design to help them function at the optimal level, parents could engineer them into superachievers" (xxi).

Rosenfeld and Wise provide many examples of just how silly hyperparenting can become. In one example, a successful couple visits an expensive psychiatrist to discuss their "sweet and studious" seventh-grade son. They feel he lacks "the drive, the 'killer instinct'" he will need to make his way to the top of today's fiercely competitive business world. They wonder, could the doctor work with their child to "help him toughen up, sharpen his ambition, hone his personality so he drives himself just a little harder" to increase his chances of success (2000, 137). Another set of parents micromanage the speech of their live-in babysitter, who has three grown children and four grandchildren. They instruct their live-in working class babysitter to speak like a middle class professional.

Middle class kids today do little that their parents don't know about and are often more comfortable with adults than with other children. Well-intentioned, loving parents intervene on their children's behalf with everything from school (teachers and assignments) to athletic directors to the language their children may speak or hear. But they also risk creating either super self-conscious or super selfish children with their intense focus on maneuvering the world and driving their children to get, and give, the very best.

As a counseling psychologist who works with families, teens, and adults, I can't help but wonder about the long-term mental and physical health effects of overwhelming schedules and stress on both middle class kids and parents. In 2006, the psychiatrist Madeline Levine published *The Price of Privilege: How Parental Pressure and Material Advantage Are Creating a Generation of Disconnected and Unhappy Kids*. She found that affluent teenagers were the fastest rising population for depression and other mental health problems. At the high school where I counsel teenagers, I meet many who have been pushed too hard and have developed an all-or-nothing approach to school, and life.

Teen years provide a multitude of distractions, and when these erstwhile honor students become unable or unwilling to maintain that level of achievement, they may fall into lethargy, drugs, and depression—they become slackers. They start hanging out with working class kids from other neighborhoods, having nonacademic adventures. One young woman with multiple piercings, silver jewelry, and blue hair said to me, "It's simply a relief to be a failure." Nonetheless, she pontificated on the meanings and symbols in her tattoos and jewelry with elaborate Standard English, complete with citations that would make a graduate student envious: "This one is about—have you read Hegel?—the struggle of opposites leads to a synthesis that surpasses either former position."

When Lareau described to working class parents the busy schedules (including piano lessons) of some of her study's middle class children, they felt sorry for the middle class kids. Some acknowledged that this schedule would pay off later in life, but still said such things as: "I think he is a sad kid"; "He must be dead-dog tired"; "Unless you're planning on him being Liberace as far as piano . . . I think it is a waste of money . . . I think he is cutting himself kind of short. He's not being involved with anything as far as friends" (2003, 251).

The art of concerted cultivation in order to have the best kid has become a national obsession and may be more about parents' self-esteem than their children's welfare. Perhaps the trend of hyperparenting is, at least in part, a result of guilt and internal conflict about ever-rising demands in the work lives of middle class parents. As Arlie Hochschild pointed out over a decade ago in *The Time Bind*, children's time spent in paid child care goes up with the income of parents. Six out of every ten professionals and managers said they regularly averaged over forty hours a week, and one third had kids in child care forty or more hours per week. Eighty-nine percent said they experience a "time famine." They just can't find enough time to do everything in their lives. Only 9 percent (!) felt they balance the demands of work and family "very well." And when asked where they feel more relaxed, at home or work, only 51 percent said "home" (Hochschild 2000).

Rosenfeld and Wise eventually conclude: "Surprisingly, spending unproductive time with our kids turns out to be the best, most constructive thing we can do. We provide evidence of how the whole family benefits when parents take back their lives, and give children a chance to live theirs" (2000, xvii–xix).

Upping the Ante

The cultural focus on individual achievements has ratcheted up intensely over the last thirty-some years. In the 1950s and '60s, when I was growing up in my spontaneous working class world, life for middle class kids was similarly unstructured—though they were coached in expected cultural skills of language, negotiation, and presentation. Likewise, adults in the middle class had more leisure time. Indeed, that was one of the things that distinguished successful people back then, how much leisure time you supposedly had earned. At that time, middle class children, like those working class children who did not have to work, were raised with lots of free time to spend with friends.

At the end of the first decade of the new millennium, middle class people intent on climbing the class ladder, and even their children, rarely have leisure time. The new American Dream, the one that the 1980s and '90s ushered in, appears as pumped up on steroids as the muscle-bound men in American action movies today.

Middle class life has changed since I slipped into it through the backdoor some thirty-five years ago. As individualism in America outstrips community more and more, I think about self-actualization differently than I once did. We have seen that middle class men's developmental models are often not a good fit for women of any class, and they are not necessarily good models for understanding women and men in working class cultures. Increasingly, I think the new hyperindividualism isn't a realistic or desirable goal for *anyone*. For me, coming from a working class world embedded in somewhat overwhelming social connections and expectations, "finding myself"—being allowed to make meaning in life my own way—was new and helpful. As social isolation has reached epidemic proportions in the United States, this goal is not as attractive. Indeed, the last ten years have seen young college students growing more community minded again (Brooks 2001; Putnam and Feldstein 2003; Howe and Strauss 2006 [also 2003, 2000, 1997, 1991]).

In 2000 Robert Putnam's *Bowling Alone* documented with encyclopedic thoroughness a devastating thirty-year decline in community activity in the United States. The trend toward individual striving and competition for social status had only accelerated since Slater wrote his first version of *Pursuit of Loneliness* in 1970. The individualistic America that young people protested in the 1960s and '70s looks like a tribal lovefest compared with what the last forty years have wrought.

On a mass scale, this value of individual becoming has led to a huge loss of community and human connections in the United States as a whole. The loss is great because we have lost the *value* we once placed on community connection as well as, I fear, our sense of common humanity. We have lost a great amount of "social capital," the kind of social connections that facilitate creation of human networks that actually create community, and wealth, through cooperation (Putnam 2000; Putnam and Feldstein 2003).

Social capital accumulates when people interact in communities. Connecting with others, say, in the PTA, leads to other connections, for example, finding work, or an insurance agent, a plumber or auto mechanic, reliable babysitters, also new friends, and bartering services with others. Social connections breed more social connections, creating the self-multiplying personal and economic benefits of community activity. The 1950s, '60s, and '70s were the highest social capital decades of the twentieth century in the United States. According to Putnam's exhaustive research, the last thirty years of the twentieth century found individualism, not community or social capital, reinforcing and reproducing itself. The trend has been accelerating and, if continued, will result in the end of thousands of face-to-face community organizations that have endured for decades, some for centuries, with little to replace them. Among the educated and the middle class, groups that have tended toward structured civic involvement, there has been an especially marked decrease in community activity.

As we saw in chapter 1, the upper middle class sets the standards that the rest of the middle class aspires toward. That means that *normal* is increasingly determined by only 10 to 15 percent of the population, as the rest of the middle class scrambles to keep up with these winners. In her study of a large corporation, economist Juliet Schor found that people frequently came into contact with far-better-paid colleagues, and it was these colleagues' cars, travel plans, and clothes that set the standards that others in the middle class strive (and borrow heavily) to match. She noted in the

1980s that as income inequality has accelerated in recent years, even people with high incomes, relative to the rest of the society, began to feel deprived.

These middle class workers compared themselves with those above them on the class ladder: "They started to feel 'poor on $100,000 a year,' as the well-known phrase puts it, because they were comparing themselves to the Donald Trumps and the other newly wealthy" (Schor, quoted in De Graff et al. 2002, 29). In the new American middle class everyone has their eyes on the rungs above them, spending more and saving less.

Increasingly, the upper middle class is isolated from the rest of the population. In gated communities and private schools, they are so geographically separate from the rest of the country that they have little access to any experiences other than the ones of their class (Lamont 1992, 2000). Thus they compare themselves to one another, or to the upper class, rather than comparing themselves to—or even seeing—the rest of the country, even the rest of the middle class.

When I entered the American middle class in the 1970s, the middle class had leisure time, job certainty, meaningful work, and often more money (than the working class) to hand out to its members. Compared to those few decades in American history, when working class and middle class incomes sometimes overlapped, the new American Dream is a bloated, hypermuscular thing: houses with 7,000 square feet, owning several houses, $20,000 birthday parties, and all the other stuff now expected in upper middle class life. Now even the normal (presteroidal) middle class is threatened with extinction (De Graaf, Wann, Naylor, and Horsey 2002). The mid-twentieth century created very large and overlapping working and middle classes. The 1990s saw an "hourglass" economy, with the middle class shrinking as the number of people at both the top and the bottom of our economy increased. Middle class people were either falling down into the working class or ascending into the ballooning upper middle and upper classes. In 2007, Louise Auerhahn called our economy a "Victorian gown." This means that in the new millennium, following a creeping reduction of middle class jobs since the early 1990s, only the number of people toward the bottom of our economy has grown. While the privileged few—the upper class and the upper middle class—continue to reap outsized rewards, everyone is fall down (from Eitzen and Johnson 2007). That means trouble for both working class and middle class people, as the cascade of mortgage foreclosures and accumulation of overwhelming college debt so clearly demonstrate (Rifkin 1995; Ehrenreich 2006; Zweig 2012).

Middle class and working class incomes may once again overlap, but not like they did in the mid-twentieth century when working class wages and benefits had reached an all-time high relative to other classes. This came after a hundred years of worker strikes and rebellions that started with the demands to limit the workday to ten hours and the right to one day off per week! By the late 1950s working class people had fought long and hard and won a forty-hour week, a weekend, sick leave, medical benefits, pensions, and more (Metzgar 2000; Murolo, Chitty, and Sacco 2001). Today's middle class is increasingly divided into the super highfliers and those who have tumbled down into the already sunken net worth and wages of working class and poverty class folks. Meanwhile, working class folks have lost pensions, medical benefits, predictable pay raises, seniority, and all those other things they fought for and won, once upon a time in America. Doing and becoming are being rapidly replaced with a drive to simply win, at any cost. And failure to achieve, called losing, is more expensive than ever, both in terms of material goods and the psychological toll it takes (Marmot 2004; Levine 2006; Eitzen and Johnston 2007; Zweig 2012).

Crossovers' Crucial Vantage Point

Working class crossovers are likely to experience the psychological problems, and pleasures, that come with their new lifestyle more acutely than their middle class peers because they have something else with which to compare it. The conflicting sets of values they experience mean they are also more likely to be forced to find personal and social solutions that blend aspects of both cultures. Those insights may be instructive to other middle class folks as well. The academic John Koonings articulated the culture clash that some crossovers feel and points to deficits in their middle class lives:

> It seems then . . . that I have alienated myself from my beginnings by moving into a culture that offers me few, if any, binding, sustaining, points of

contact. I do not work as hard as my father did, though I make at least five times as much money as he ever did. But I must admit that there are moments when I believe that those things have cost me the relationships, the cultural ties, the human interactions that define people most humanly. (Ryan and Sackrey 1996, 288–89)

Not to say all is rosy in the working class. If working class life were so great, why would anyone leave it or feel guilty leaving beloved others within it? I return to the notion of survivor guilt, and the class crossovers who mine their conflicted experiences for instruction on how to best live their lives. College teacher Milan Kovacovic vividly underscored the source of his guilt and illustrated that the increasing opulence of upper middle class and upper class people is built on the backs of the working class and lower middle class. For those raised and still living within a middle class bubble, this fact may be invisible. For working class crossovers, it is hard to ignore.

Truly I have no right to complain when I think that so many people earn their living as I once did, from unhealthful if not dangerous occupations, on graveyard, swing, or rotating shifts, in freezing or scorching surroundings, under artificial light and deafening noise, doing repetitive, monotonous tasks, watching the clock tick away the seconds until the first fifteen-minute coffee break, until the thirty minute, unpaid respite of lunch, until the second fifteen-minute break, until quitting time or mandatory overtime, until retirement decades away, and death shortly after. That's for the lucky ones who have full-time jobs with fringe benefits such as health insurance and a two-week paid vacation yearly. . . . [Any problems I have now are not] comparable . . . to the threat of silicosis that I endured for an entire year in my first full-time job immediately after high school at Ace Metal Refinishers in Chicago. . . . This exhausting and filthy work required wading, to the din of compressors, into swirling clouds of pumice powder and lacquer spray in order to clean and refinish the metal surfaces on the facades of various downtown buildings. . . . I can still feel the abrasive dust filtering into my sleeves, down my collar, and through the face mask, irritating my nostrils, and leaving grit between my teeth, my eyelashes itchy from sticky sweat, red hair turned white before mid-shift in the powdery mist. And, supreme humiliation, this was not even a heroic, essential blue-collar undertaking like coal mining or steel-beam riveting but mere cosmetic work to make the metal surfaces shine more brightly, at the expense of my and my co-workers' lungs. (Dews and Law, 236–37)

For working class crossovers who have not swallowed the achievement myth that life in the middle class is wholly earned, rather than awarded, survivor guilt can intensify as successes mount. Robert Lifton suggested survivors need an "animated relationship to guilt" (1983 111–12). When we engage in activities that save others from injustices we have endured, we make new meaning of those obstacles and our lives. When we stop running away from our feelings of guilt, we find the courage to advocate for those whose voices were never meant to be heard. Lifton called this a survivor's mission of illumination (1983).

I'm very grateful that I had the chance to write this book, my own survivor mission. My mother never had that chance, though she dazzled me as a child when she helped with school writing assignments. One of the saddest memories from my sometimes stormy childhood is a very quiet one. I see my mother sitting at the dining room table with a correspondence course writing assignment, the only class I ever knew my antischool mother to take. She just sat there, not writing. Then she quit. That's it. That's the image that still brings tears to my eyes. Not the nights she wept with homesickness for New York, not the ear-splitting battles she and my father sometimes waged, as if raging against it would ease the loneliness. No, it is this image of my mom leaving the table, notebook empty, that brings tears to my eyes. A gifted writer, unable to face the empty page. And no one cared.

It is particularly meaningful for me to make my first book be about class, as I believe class prevented my mom from becoming the writer she could have been.

> Rather than quiet the noise of the working class neighborhood now internalized along with other cultural voices, rather than transmute the distracting din into a convincingly serene Muzak, we might learn to mine such sounds for their worth, their *instructive tension*. . . . I want to suggest that we can't afford to work our psyches into a permanent grimace because of the lack of fit of working-class face to middle-class mask. Instead we need to tell the things we see as what we know: a knowledge that is just as valid as any and possibly more instructive than most. (Mary Cappello, from Dews and Law 1995, 130–31)

When crossovers remember the wisdoms of their working class lives, they can avoid losing these qualities in their new lives—for example, the need for community, talking straight, spontaneity, and heart being at least

as important as mind—as well as inform or remind middle class and upwardly mobile working class folks of these human needs. When I advise
or counsel working class students, I try to help them validate their former
lives and cultures and link this history to new skills and cultural customs
that they are currently learning. I try to help both students and colleagues
to sift through aspects of working class and middle class cultures to pick
and choose the qualities that are right for them.

Crossovers are living testimony to all the incorrect assumptions that
dominate our society's images of and assumptions about working class
people. While we are often used as proof that anyone can do what we
have done, if crossovers can get over ourselves a bit, we can see that luck
and willingness to leave a lot behind played significant roles in our lives.
"Luck" is so frequently mentioned in crossover literature I found it impos-
sible to pick out a single quote. Instead of accepting the tempting label of
exceptional, crossovers can say we really are not so special and we would
appreciate it if people stop referring to people from our homes as idiots,
hillbillies, rednecks, and gangsters. When crossovers occupy positions of
power, we can also make luck happen for those who least expect it.

In Barack Obama's memoir, *Dreams from My Father*, he tells his story of
"race and inheritance," as well as a class-crossover's journey. He describes
going for the first time to the church in Chicago where he would discover
his faith and spiritual community. He flipped through a brochure:

> There was one particular passage in Trinity's brochure that stood out, a
> commandment more self-conscious in tone, requiring greater elaboration.
> "A Disavowal of the Pursuit of Middleclassness," the heading read. "While
> it is permissible to chase 'middleincomeness' with all our might," the text
> stated, "those blessed with the talent or good fortune to achieve success in
> the American mainstream must avoid the 'psychological entrapment of
> black middleclassness' that hypnotizes the successful brother or sister into
> believing they are better than the rest and teaches them to think in terms of
> 'we' and 'they' instead of 'US!'" (2004, 284)

An African American pastor wrote this to his black, urban congregation
about the need for community among black folks of all economic classes.
Much of my working class family of scrappy Scandinavian Americans is as
pale-skinned and blue-eyed as they come, but still I identified deeply with
these sentiments. If I had not gotten over my own middle-classness, that

included the weakening of ties in my extended family, I know I would have missed some of the most meaningful and important moments of my adult life. Top among these moments would be the deaths of my parents.

Were it not for my working class family I would certainly not have had the premature loss of my parents cushioned by their abiding and abundant support. I suspect they don't know it—the many extended family members who reached out to me before, during, and after those deaths—but they carried me back to a world that finally made sense again. Nor could I go now and see my father in their angular faces, their big square hands, or hear him in their voices as they sing. I also would have missed seeing the memory of my spicy, sexy, political mother from Brooklyn in some smiling elderly eyes during the 2008 election season as I argued that there is only one race, the human one.

Because crossovers straddle class borders, we have a crucial vantage point from which to challenge deepening inequality and winners-take-all politics and policies in our nation. We can perceive and explain how class works. We can speak out against the gross inequality the last thirty-five years have wrought rather than falling silent and angling to grab all we can when we have a chance. Most important, we, and our sympathetic friends in the professional middle class, can point America back to "us," to a belief in the common humanity of all Americans and a collective antidote to the runaway individualism that has left most of our collective wealth in the hands of only a very few.

8

GATHERING IN GLENVILLE

The women sit around the old oak table in Auntie Nancy and Uncle Harold's farmhouse. As usual, talking about the things that matter most: people,
relationships, troubles, and anything else that connects us as a family after
months of not seeing one another. Every once in a while, one of the guys
comes in and joins us for a while. Mostly, the men are gathered in the trac-
tor shed, listening and singing to tapes of old country songs by Buck Owens,
Faron Young, Ferlin Husky, Jimmy Brown and the Bells, Patsy Cline, and,
of course, Johnny Cash. They sit with us for a while and listen at the grown-
ups table of my youth. I sit here at the age of fifty-three, still a bit grateful to *not* be seated at a card table in the living room. Thirty years after we
began renting American Legion and VFW halls for our family reunions,
this room, this table, still echoes with the magic and mystery of childhood
and the farm, long after the horses, cows, chickens, and pigs are gone.

"Okay," Nancy finally says, "you're talking about working class." She
raises a painful left hand, gone knobby and arthritic with age, and puts
it on the table. Pauses. "And middle class," she says, and punctuates it by

putting her other crippled hand on the table, too. Those gnarled hands seem to say everything I wish my book could. Hands that show a lifetime of wringing the necks of chickens, shooting rifles, picking up children, and bowling. Hands that made oil paintings, polished rocks, scrubbed floors, and that long ago counted a bank's daily money up the in The Cities. Hands that always were doing some cool thing. Trophies crowd every high-up surface in the old Houg farmhouse, shooting and bowling trophies that she and Uncle Harold have won. A no-nonsense kind of person, Nancy cuts through all the other chatter and says, "What I wanna know is anyone gonna be able to read this thing?"

It was the end of summer, the Labor Day holiday, and time for Auntie Nancy and Uncle Harold's "un-chicken fry." It used to have chickens and it was a chicken fry. But Nancy, who is seventy, stopped raising them a while ago. Everybody, especially Nancy, seemed pleased with the unlikely new name for the not-a-chicken fry. Jensens like to play with words. Around that table, people ask me what I am doing these days. I tell them two things: "I'm writing my book, and my godson moved in with me last June."

"Who is your godson?" The women look around at each other, "Who asked Barbie to be a godmother?" No one here, I suddenly notice. I say, "He's the son of an old friend. He showed up last June with nowhere to live. I'm lookin' for suggestions on raising teenagers." How old is he, they want to know. A young eighteen, I say. Everyone pitches in some comment. We talk about teenagers, raising them right ("get him working, it's the best thing for him"). Then come the life stories I always crave. This time they are about how they have dealt with their kids as teens. My cousin Deb, Auntie Nancy's oldest daughter, who has worked her way into the middle class in sales, had two teen-aged daughters graduate from high school in the past two years, and she has a lot to say.

The book doesn't come up again for a while. But, since reunions last for hours and hours, and this one through breakfast the next morning, someone new always comes into the dining room. "Hey Barbie! What you been up to?"

"Writing a book and caring for my godson."

"Who's your godson?" So I go through the thing again.

Auntie Carol finally says, "Writing a book! To know someone who actually published a book? Well, that's just so . . . so . . . I mean I would feel just so proud just to know you!"

"No," I plead. I feel ill at the thought of her admiring me, knowing she's worked harder than I ever will. I say, "It's not that special. I mean it's just work. You all have worked more than I could ever dream of." Silence. No one disputes this. And, I admit, "It's kind of stupid work because I'm not getting paid for it."

Then the question I always dread, "What's it about?" Two years earlier, around this same table, Lily Jensen, my father's widow and my friend, told them I had written and published a chapter in a book. I told them then I was working on this whole book and that the chapter had come out of that work, and it was partly about us. Auntie Carol asked me then if it was about my family, meaning my immediate family, as the women know my parents had a sometimes troubled marriage and probably also know that I've been in therapy for it, since I became a counselor. "No, not that way," I said. A confused conversation followed, mostly because I felt so uncomfortable being asked to bring my two worlds together. I was also grateful they wanted me to try to do so. But I just faltered and mumbled something on the edge of coherent.

This time, with two more years of writing and a fistful of my dad's siblings' oral work histories under my belt, I take a deep breath and launch confidently into my rap. One thing that buoys me is that during those oral work histories, I found out everyone of their generation identified as working class, not middle class. While my cousins and I grew up thinking we were middle class, the great American myth, our parents knew better.

"So," I say, energetically, "the first chapter is called 'The Invisible Ism.' It's about prejudice against working class people. Just like women can be victims of sexism." And I look around the table at these tough and tender women who have always worked so hard, both in the home and out of it, who have never thought of themselves as victims and realize this is not a great choice of metaphor. "And black people," I say, "are subject to racism" (*really* not a great metaphor, but they nod politely). "People can be punished for being working class. You know, people who don't like to deal with you or even treat you badly just because you're working class." Beneath my words I am saying, "Look, I am writing for you, to defend you." They look puzzled. These women and men told me, in their oral histories, about unions, being working class, about how economics and jobs in this country can't go on like this much longer or our country will collapse. None of them blamed anyone else for anything, and each and every one took full personal responsibility for their lives. I remember, too, how little they cared about class prejudice against them.

Though I tried my hardest to tease it out of them in those taped work histories, they could not come up with examples of how personal classism had hurt them. They knew all about *class* injustice, believed in unions, and, I knew, grasped the plight of working class people better than I ever could. I also remember that not one of them felt bad or ashamed about being working class. They were proud of their hard work lives and knew themselves to be good and valuable people. Who am I to tell them that they are disrespected by those of "higher" classes? It seems almost cruel, but mostly irrelevant. A few had known people who had looked down on them, say at school. But no one cared, then or now. As Auntie Lu had said of "hoity-toity" people "who think they're better than you but they're not. I just like to slide them people by."

Common Ground

I live at the crossroads of two different class avenues in American cultural life. At this intersection, I see two worlds with conflicting worldviews— about manners, values, social attitudes, fashions, and living styles—as to what is considered normal. One is traditional and working class, one is more cosmopolitan and middle class. They point their members in different directions. As an American, my different class worlds are intertwined and complicated with ethnicity and geography, further complicating my class vision. But, inside me, all these qualities blend and come to life. These two selves— Barb and Barbara—dance, tangle, feud, argue, and *conversate* long hours, and some very long nights, year after different year of my life. In moments of clarity and kindness, they find much-needed common ground within me.

I have used stories and studies about class and culture to illustrate a basic point: we are not all one big middle class, but rather, middle class and working class people have different cultural values and customs. I have depicted these cultures in a somewhat artificially stark and oppositional way in order to clarify what I see as foundational differences in approach to identity and life. In real life, people of all classes learn and use different aspects of both working class and middle class cultures. Just as we all pick and switch within a variety of language codes when we speak.

Humans are intensely social creatures. We cooperate in everything from religious worship to building freeways and growing and distributing food and other goods, from playing cards and sharing recipes to canvassing for political candidates and attending funerals. We are a species that depends on collectivity. From tribal groups going out together to kill large animals or dig up potatoes to urban techies and the new millennium's young people surfing cyberspace to find like-minded people all over the globe: human beings look for connections with others. Lack of connection to others creates a necessary distress, an inner warning bell. Therapists' offices are filled with people afflicted with this distress. The remarkable success of community-based nonprofessional 12-step groups in relieving alcoholism and other addictions offers profound testimony to the healing power of people cooperating for mutual aid.

Humans also need a sense of meaning. We have inner lives and conscious selves. We make sense of things. We have interior lives with which we process and evaluate our lives in the outer world. We have talents, passions, interests, and needs. In the modern world, we are called on to make choices about what kind of person we want to become. We also have the remarkable ability to reflect on and direct our own processes (though not as often as we'd like). We make meaning in and of our lives.

Right now in America, social class tends to divide community, with its psychological sense of belonging, from individuality and becoming and assign them to different classes. Both human tendencies—that of belonging and sharing, living, working, and thinking in community and that of individuality and the pursuit of excellence, seeking and making individual meaning of and in one's life—are found across different populations and times in human history. What I am suggesting now is a greater integration of selves, both personally and within our larger society.

The differences I have described in this book are not true for every person or community. In real life these differences are a matter of degree. I have discussed cultural emphasis and focus, not innate ability or needs. People vary in their personal temperament and experiences. Families provide their own unique environments. And each of us has our unique life, experiences, lessons learned, and resiliencies developed. On a societal scale, other broad social factors intrude into the delicate business of personal identity and worldview—gender, race, ethnicity, geography, and much more.

Still, in the lives of most of us, class has exerted its indelible effects. It is unfair to judge either middle class or working class folks by the other culture's mores. But both cultures point to valuable aspects of the human spirit.

In the American middle class, outstanding, publicly recognized individual achievements are the cultural prize, as well as an admission ticket to a life of more control, creativity, and money. Because the upper middle class dominates education, the professions, the world of commerce, and other social locations of power, our larger society's values and customs tend to reflect the middle class and to ignore the insights and values that working class people hold—at least in this historical moment in America.

Individualism is not a life-giving ethic for an entire population. It is a way for winners to win more and for others to try and enter the competition. There is nothing wrong with being an individual, or competing for some things, or taking less-traveled routes. I have enjoyed all this quite a bit. But competition is no way to run an entire society. Competition for basic rights, such as higher education, which is granted as a human right in many other affluent countries across the world, makes the United States poorer, dumber, and less civilized than it could be. Poorer and dumber because, in the long run, it actually costs American society far more both socially and economically to *not* educate its citizens and less civilized, even cruel, because it says people with more money deserve more rights.

Our nation has always rewarded the competitive individual pursuit of success. But over the last thirty-five years, the unfettered pursuit of wealth and power has unraveled the financial safety nets of our larger society. We now face the deepest disparity of wealth since the Great Depression that haunted my parents' childhoods. Without some serious changes, the America I grew up in will continue to erode.

Despite the current trends toward individual competition, mutual aid and cooperation are by far the most common states of human affairs, both historically and even in American life today. Without it we could not survive. The prize for people in working class cultures, and for their agrarian ancestors, has always been the strengths and joys of community life. From building barns and harvesting crops to quilting and cooking meals for community and extended family events, caring for one another's kids, from jobs in machining, automobile assembly, and other trades, on so-called unskilled assembly lines, as hotel clean-up crews or food service, working class people do it together, sharing life's loads and luck within their closely knit communities.

But I can wax enthusiastic for only so long about working class life. I have seen many working class people, including myself, squelch individual talents and abilities in favor of belonging. Also, working class communities are often closed to outsiders. As we have seen, that powerful "us" is particular and personal, not an abstracted "humanity." We can find a wealth of social capital, and everything we need to know about mutual aid, within working class communities. But far too often "eggheads," "sissies," "dykes," and interracial couples need not apply.

Over the last ten years America has seen young people (of all classes) upending the ethic of individuality and the age of avarice by, for example: volunteering, creating organizations, organizing unemployed union workers along with young people and aging hippies into cooperatives in Maine, and winning the right to public health care in Vermont. As activist women (e.g., Women Against Military Madness and Starhawk) in the 1980s did with nuclear power plants, activist young people now lie down in front of bulldozers set to destroy public lands. The new youth movement's massive collective campaigning efforts flooded election primaries and voting stations in 2008, winning Barack Obama the presidency of the United States. Americans came together to elect our first black president because we really needed a change, of heart as well as of policy (Howe and Strauss 2000, 2003, 2006). Now *social capital*, or human cooperation, may be the only thing to help our nation out of the economic hole where decades of unfettered individualism and concentration of wealth in the upper class has left us.

Social Capital: Ways of Belonging

I think the hardest part of crossing classes is that the *kind* of belonging, or sense of place, can be quite different in middle class life than it is in working class community. In *Bowling Alone* (Putnam 2000) and *Better Together* (Putnam and Feldstein 2003), Robert Putnam pointed out two different types of social capital (human connections that are likely to multiply into more connections): bonding and bridging.[1] In terms of class and culture, both working class and middle class people have something to offer to remedy an increasingly divided nation.

Bonders are drawn to informal socializing, from card games to visiting relatives, from going out with friends to bars or restaurants to sending personal greeting cards and remembering birthdays. This is my Jensen family in a nutshell. Putnam used a Yiddish word to describe these folks: *schmoozers*. They have the kind of social capital that is at the heart of working class communities—deep, loyal, we-are-part-of-one-another bonding. For people who leave behind traditional communities, the road "ahead" can be a lonely one. The critique of middle-classness published by Obama's church warned upwardly mobile black folks against losing this informal but life-giving kind of community-mindedness.

Bonding connections are strong ties that connect people in close groups who live interdependent lives. Bonding social capital is having kin, whether literally blood relatives or friends so close they are "part of the family." Bonding social capital is about *us*, personal and particular connections. Bonding connections mean, literally, what's mine is yours. As Auntie Lu admonished me when I asked, "Do you have anything to eat?" after we'd spent hours visiting at the kitchen table. "Well, why didn't you just open up the fridge!?" she exclaimed, as she hustled to it and took out five or six Tupperware containers. "I got all kinds of leftovers!" White, working class, Christian evangelicals were one of the few groups that actually increased social capital in the 1980s and '90s, according to Putnam.

"Bridging" social capital is the kind I found in middle class life. Less personal, it has weaker ties but can unite many people across wide differences: being a psychologist connects me with other psychologists, being Danish American connects me with other Danish Americans, my Jewish mother connects me to other Jews, sending money to the Nature Conservancy connects me with others who also want to preserve our environment—but only superficially. The Yiddish term for those who tend to create organizations is *machers*. Machers start temples and churches, newspapers, magazines and blogs, political action groups, and many other forms of structured human connection. They often organize toward a specific goal, for example, electing someone to public office.

The tendency to be one of Putnam's bridgers increases with higher education, higher income, and higher social status in society, for example, serving on the school board, belonging to the PTA, or attending church meetings. Putnam's bridgers build and attend formal and organizational events and clubs, important in middle class life. They join boards of directors, follow current events, and give to established charities; they participate in many other publicly recognized community-minded activities. After surviving breast cancer, my middle class aunt Flora donated time to helping other victims of breast cancer through the American Cancer Society. After retirement, her husband, Milt, volunteered at the Metropolitan Museum of Art. By contrast, my mother and father rarely, if ever, gave to charities, but they always lent a helping hand if people they knew needed it. Not that Flora and Milt didn't do that, they did, but their culture accentuated certain ways of giving. Putnam's bridging interactions, generally called "networking," invite individuals into new communities and experiences.

"Bonding social capital constitutes a kind of sociological superglue, whereas bridging social capital provides a sociological WD-40," Putnam wrote. Xavier de Souza put it like this, "Bonding social capital is good for 'getting by,' and bridging social capital is good for 'getting ahead'" (Putnam and Feldstein 2003, 2).

We need not choose between Putnam's bonding and bridging, as we all use some of both of these kinds of connections. But conscious awareness of them can help us to increase the tendency to use either or both. Without bridging skills, and access to the mechanics of mainstream America, working class people stay isolated from the mainstream. This was fine, even preferable, at one time, but the last thirty-five years have shown that mainstream values and mechanisms now threaten to destroy working class peoples' way of life (i.e., by lowering working class net worth by some 20 percent and by favoring corporate megafarms over smaller family farms).

Cultural Capital: Ways of Knowing

I want to emphasize the potential for human learning, and integration, of new cultural ways of knowing, learning, and living, for both working class and middle class folks. Another way to describe this is that we could value both *subjective* and *procedural* knowledge, and teachers can use both in our classrooms, neglecting neither way of knowing (Belinky et al. 1986).[2] Subjective knowing is, in part, a result of working class culture's tendency toward bonding connections. By and large, my working class college students demonstrate significant subjective knowledge—they trust their gut—-and like to speak their deeply personal, hard-won truths. Like Shelley, they like to *schmooze* with their classmates and with me.

They have an easy time filling up their weekly journals, where I encourage students to use their usual voices and "just write" about the ideas they are learning, applying them to real-life examples. Their journals sound the way people speak, and, as Bernstein first pointed out, there is a pith and beauty to their metaphoric use of language. In my classrooms, they range from that of Croatian American miners from the Minnesota Iron Range to Southeast Asian Hmong refugees now working in suburban Twin Cities' assembly lines. School did not teach them to trust their own thoughts, experiences, or speech, but it was generally irrelevant enough that it didn't interfere with how they learned to know, through personal experiences and the stories of trusted others in their communities.

My middle class college students, on the other hand, sometimes have difficulty expressing themselves, of finding their own voice in their journal entries. They are not necessarily schmoozers. But they have the *procedural* college knowledge to easily navigate libraries and the Internet, and they write their papers in Standard English. They have the expected analytic skills to compare, contrast, and analyze different ideas. They know how to verify facts, and their papers are filled with references from authoritative sources. But, unless they came from the upper middle class—having attended the schools of Anyon's affluent professionals—and most do not, they may be ill-equipped to assert original ideas, taught to avoid controversial topics, and they may also be at a loss when asked to express their inner life.

Conventional procedural knowledge is what working class children miss out on while being assigned ridiculously simple tasks such as cutting out cowboy pictures and pasting them to a map, or pasting squares of tissue on a cutout of a turkey ("art" in my own elementary school). They do not necessarily learn the specific procedures of abstraction and critical thinking that middle class children routinely acquire and refine both at home and in public education.

Let me be clear—it is not the intelligence or ability to grasp abstractions that working class students lack, but the particular formal language and procedures of the middle class and upper class. Standard English and the many procedures and processes education nurtures in middle class children and young adults are very real access codes to power and mobility in America.

My examination of both cultures leads me to question the whole idea of merit-based competitive education. I want all working class kids to have a real chance to enrich and develop their minds as much as they desire. But what does that mean in a competitive system of education? That they learn not to be concerned about the *effect* of their activity, or wealth, on others? That they reorient their worldview to place themselves at the center of their universe? Must they "outgrow" their deeply held we-are-part-of-one-another ties with other people?

Our education system is class based and class biased, and as such it mostly reproduces inequality. But even a "fair" meritocracy—with equal starting lines for all students, if it were possible—is still not really fair, because it means only the most gifted, talented, and ambitious (or driven?) deserve education, or the "good life" for that matter. Doesn't our very American belief in equality of opportunity for all citizens mean we all deserve the best education we can get? An educated citizenry is a prerequisite for freedom and democracy. Without access to a wealth of information about our complex modern society, we are easily manipulated with TV sound bites.

Capital

In an address to Congress on December 3, 1861, Abraham Lincoln said, "Labor is prior to, and independent of, capital . . . in fact, capital is the fruit of labor, and could never have existed if labor had not first existed. Labor is the superior of capital and deserves much the higher consideration" (quoted in Kelber 2007). While this book has been about cultural divisions, I still want to underline that class is based in real world, material conditions. The dramatic redistribution of wealth since the relatively well-balanced mid-twentieth century is currently giving both working class and middle class people far less than they deserve, less than enough to keep their homes and lives afloat. Economic power is still the spinal column, the nerve center, of class in the America. In 2007, the wealthiest 10 percent of households owned 73.1 percent of all household wealth, up from 68.2 percent in 1983. At the same time the bottom 40 percent of households saw their average net worth drop by 62 percent. From 1983 to 2007, 20 percent of already wealthy Americans gained about 89 percent of the wealth created, and the remaining 80 percent gained just 11 percent of that wealth

(Zweig 2012). Again, from 1970 to 1995, the top 20 percent of the population (by wealth) increased its net worth by some 70 percent, with the most wealth going to the top 1 percent, and the majority of that wealth going to the top half of that 1 percent (Zweig 2000). A radical redistribution of wealth has occurred in the United States; it has only been possible through the loss of working class collective bargaining rights, corporations sending jobs overseas to further undermine labor laws in the United States, and the concentration of extreme wealth on the top half of 1 percent of the population. The stable working class life my parents were able to provide and enjoy is gone.

We can only imagine what that money might have done for working class folks over the last forty years, for those who have lost homes, jobs, and the ability to (ever) have both parents home with their children at the same time (Rubin 1994). Or how some of that wealth might have helped middle class folks over the last decade or two, to say nothing of America's crumbling infrastructure. Instead, as a nation, between 1995 and 2003 we more than doubled the number of millionaires to eight million (Frank 2007, 1), and the number of billionaires went from thirteen in 1985 to more than a thousand by 2006 (11), and created a whole new section in the upper class, what Robert Frank called "Richistan."

Memory

While the 2008 elections put class back on the national agenda, it also uncovered a confusion of class terms, what they mean, and why we use them. Michelle Obama opened the Democratic National Convention with a speech in which she said she was from a working class family in Chicago, that her father worked in a city water plant. Joe Biden said, of friends in his working class hometown, Scranton, Pennsylvania, that "they call themselves 'middle class.'" My working class cousins also mostly call themselves middle class, as I did while growing up. Now everyone, even those in the left wing of American politics, where "working class" is not always a dirty word, is talking about the middle class this and middle class that. As if there were never was, and is not now, a working class at all, as if we are all in the same big culture and it's just that some of us are not as good or outstanding as the others.

Nevertheless, every one of my father's brothers and sisters identified as working class in their oral work histories, when given a choice between middle class and working class to describe themselves: Why the difference? Why do they call themselves working class? Why do I now advocate reclaiming the term "working class"?

Three reasons. Visibility. Pride. Memory.

I have argued that working class cultures have their own cultural logic. Generally invisible to the middle class, working class culture encourages a psychology of sharing and cooperation that becomes integrated into basic psychological processes: "us-ness," use of analogy and metaphor, belonging and connection with others, spontaneity, and a focus on equal or peer relationships, as opposed to power-negotiated hierarchical ones. We have seen that children may be taught to "tune in" to others, to develop cognitive and emotional skills of empathy along with basic language and motor skills. We have also seen that these cultural skills are often valued in working class communities over the learning of school-type ways of knowing. A lack of economic resources in working class and poverty class families also contributes to parents' child-rearing strategies. But studies still find that these kids had more fun and were much less whiney and dissatisfied than middle class children (Lareau 2003; Levine 2006).

In my view, it is not the case that working class children, as many middle class observers have concluded, do not develop much of a self—but that *sense of self is perceived and constructed differently.* I believe that people within working class communities develop an internal sense of self, a sense of identity, that is not defined by how one stands out against others. It does not exist in opposition to others at all, but actually includes—particular, but not all—others.

Generally, working class people are born into cultures that do not encourage them to *outgrow* mutuality, to develop and defend a powerful individual identity. Certainly not to the extent that middle class people are expected, and some would say forced, to do. I have also come to the conclusion that the communal qualities of working class communities guide their members into certain kinds of personal and emotional life experiences that are valuable, but not always available, to all people.

Counseling psychologists often advise folks with workaholism, an addiction to overachieving, to journey deeper into their own inner life. But I think that building nurturing, noncompetitive connections with other people is *at least* as important as searching within oneself. I want the capacity for emotional empathy, to feel deeply connected—*part of* others—encouraged in everyone, regardless of class, talents, or achievements.

Part of the comfort of working class communities comes from their value of peerness, or equal power with others, as my aunt Luella Sharpe explained in chapter 3. There is a relative freedom from having power and role negotiation interwoven with most of one's communication with others. Hierarchies exist in working class cultures, for example, between parents and children, bosses and workers, but most of one's interactions and leisure time is not spent within them. Kids play with kids; and workers talk freely, often quite intimately in my experience, when supervisors and bosses are not around. All this contributes greatly to a comfortable, relaxed atmosphere. Unambitious and unambiguous, with "nothing to prove," people feel freer to just be themselves. It is not difficult to imagine that some psychological freedom from the stress of performance within hierarchical systems would be good for all of us.

Finally, for better and sometimes worse, working class life encourages directness of experience—a powerful present. Middle class people search for this here-and-now experience in psychotherapies, in Eastern and earth-based religions, and in nature. Relatively free of pressures to prove one's originality or superiority—or to identify everything within and around them through proper (but contested) labels—working class people get to enjoy just being there. Children, we have seen, develop considerable resilience and initiative while they invent their own kinds of play with one another, though deprived of the vast array of structured opportunities their middle class counterparts receive. This spontaneity is reflected in working class speech that, though not structured toward universal explication, has much less trouble "telling it like it is" in personal situations than middle class people with far more verbal training.

Working class communities preserve something crucial of human experience: an unearned sense of one's being part of other people, part of the world we live in, part of life—a foundational sense of belonging. While this is in no way absolutely true of all working class cultures, or all people within them, these things seem to occur more freely within working class communities.

Which brings me to pride. My aunts and uncles call themselves working class because they are proud of being workers! They are old enough to remember the savage inequality before workers came together—as workers—to change their lives for the better. They formed workers' unions that changed the desperate plight of manual laborers in the nineteenth- and early twentieth-century's America. They understand the power and pride of what we can only accomplish together, as a working class. In their oral work histories, they associated collective action, in the form of workers' unions, with positive changes for workers. And all of them had plenty of working class pride.

This is not necessarily the case for the generations that came after my now seventy- and eighty-something uncles and aunts. Working class men and women still live within communities and behave pretty much the same as they and their agrarian ancestors always have—with community-mindedness. But too many Americans have forgotten the most important lesson history taught my elders, that being working class is far from embarrassing or shameful. Working class people make our society run. Workers built this country, and to this day everything around you is made by working class people: this book in your hands, the keyboard under mine, the lamps we read by, the food we eat, the houses we live in, our plumbing, cars, every single thing was made by working class people.

As I was growing up, I had the idea that working class men were powerful, even mighty. They did "real work." My father, John "Fred" Jensen, was the embodiment of these powerful "greatest generation" men who went to fight in World War II; built their own roomy additions to tiny tract houses; took apart their cars to learn how to fix them; hunted deer, moose, pheasant, grouse, ducks, and more, then dressed, cooked, and ate them. How and when did society begin to call these mighty men losers? The power of solidarity has almost slipped from view in America.

Both of my grandfathers, one a Dane and the other a Ukrainian Jew, were working class men who came to America for a better life. Both of these men had excellent minds, were avid readers and educated themselves as much as they could without much schooling. On almost opposite sides of the political spectrum, neither held the anti-intellectual attitudes of many working class people today. But then times were different. Grandpa Jensen, a farmer and member of the conservative American Legion, rarely had to deal directly with the snobbishness of a class of people just above him. Grandpa Milstein, a New Yorker who installed and sanded parquet floors for wealthy people, identified as a working class intellectual: he believed workers should rise up and take credit for all the goods and wealth they created. His socialist philosophy made him proud of being working class. Both of them believed, as did their very different communities, that working class people are the backbone of America.

Working class people are ironweeds that sprout out of cracks in the cement of inequality, contorting but continuing to survive. In this historic moment, working class values, psychology, and injuries have no real voice; they have no justification, and they find little justice. They find little context outside their own communities with which to understand or describe themselves and their people, at least few that have their best interests at heart. Class and classism make invisible both the inner and outer lives of more than 60 percent of our population, but they have not always done so.

Let's Go Bowling

Cultural differences, combined with invisible institutional biases, and the American *achievement ideology* that says anyone who works hard enough can achieve anything they wish, conspire to divide working class and middle class people into opposing cultural camps. But together, working class and middle class people make up the *vast* majority of people in this country. Though the upper upper class (about 1% of the population) currently lay claim to over 50 percent of the nation's wealth (Collins and Yeskel 2005), the working class and middle class still are the engine and steering wheel that deliver that wealth and power to the few by doing most of the actual mental and physical *work*. Without all of us cooperating day to day our society would come to a halt.

On personal, cultural, and structural (societywide) levels, both the middle class and the working class are in trouble.

As we have seen, membership in the middle class has been ratcheting up its requirements in terms of individual achievements and destinations of success, so much that only a few can hope to achieve life in the new upper middle class (about 10% of the population), while prospects keep falling for the rest of the middle class (about 26% of population). What was once a concerted effort to teach children to publicly present themselves and master certain middle class skills, leaving them lots of mid-twentieth-century leisure time for unsupervised play, has become an obsession to train them to win and "win big." What was once an unearned advantage has become a burdensome requirement to be almost perfect. The individual achievement imperative, as we have seen, has hobbled many people into believing that, without their meaningful work, they are nothing. We now see a job market where even the middle class can't find jobs (Ehrenreich 2006; Eitzen and Johnston 2007). Where does that leave people whose culture told them they had to prove themselves as people through their work? These days, I find myself reminding middle class people to look for their own families' historical working class roots and connections.

Again, the fortunes of the working class have been falling more than any other group in the United States over the last thirty-five years: at least a 20 percent drop in net worth (Zweig 2000.) Though working class communities have some insulation from society's cultural pressures, indeed often rebel against them, the ethic of individualism has slowly worked its way into the working class as well. While our nation's priorities and policies clearly create the concrete facts of our economy that largely determine what individuals can achieve, individualism insists on personal responsibility above all. White working class men, in particular, have begun to adopt the language of individualism as politicians have infused it with the ethic of personal responsibility (Lamont 2000; Kusserow 2005).

Unfortunately for these men, their individualism is accompanied with none of the tools that middle class individuals receive, nor does it suit their economic interests as a group. As Lamont explained, the language has changed for these men, but the community-based lives they live, for the most part, have not. A focus on individuality has not made many working class folks richer, but it has made very many poorer, due to a corresponding decrease in the idea of direct community and workplace activism.

For the 63 percent of our population in the working class (Zweig 2000, 2012), solidarity and strength is in numbers—belonging is central. Individualism keeps working class people from even seeing that they are still the majority in the United States and that without us nothing runs. Working class cultures preserve mutual aid, but they do little to bring that message to others outside their communities. Alienated from condescending and classist Democrats and used and robbed by manipulative Republicans, working class folks hold fast to the little they have left: their personal families and communities. But the longer they isolate themselves from the rest of the country, the more they will lose.

In February of 2011, in Madison, the Teaching Assistants Association from the University of Wisconsin, with help from the Multicultural Student Coalition and the Student Labor Action Coalition, organized thousands of speakers to protest and stall state Republicans from passing Governor Scott Walker's bill to do away with collective bargaining for government employees, specifically targeting teachers. When the bill's public hearing speakers were dismissed at midnight, a spontaneous decision emerged to occupy the state capitol building. Cell phones and texting technologies allowed them to contact scores of others who brought pillows and blankets and more protesters. An impressive coalition developed between the American Federation of State, County, and Municipal Employees, college students and other young people, farmers' unions, parent's rights groups, building trade union members, Service Employees International Union, the Wisconsin Teaching Assistants Association, college teachers, and many more. After a couple of weeks, they eventually left they building but the spirit of resistance has remained outside it and spread across the nation.

Then came the Arab Spring, during which the Middle East and northern Africa exploded as Arab peoples fought against and wrested control of their countries from wealthy dictators.

By fall of 2011, back in the United States, young people "occupied" a park on Wall Street and have symbolically "occupied" cities and states all across America by demonstrating and even taking up residence at state capitols. Both alike and different from the baby boom generation's coming of age rebellion—against racism, the Vietnam war, individualistic values, the oppression of women, and monopoly capitalism in general—frustrated young people are bent on challenging savage inequality once again.

In the United Kingdom, angry young people have protested and rioted in London, Birmingham, Liverpool, and Manchester. They protested and rioted in Rome and Madrid. They have peacefully demonstrated across the world: from Santiago (Chile) to Zurich and Johannesburg, Frankfurt to Hong Kong, Toronto to Los Angeles, Tokyo to Chicago, young people have spear-headed the protests that claim the name associated with the "occupied" cities and states: 99 percent, a reference to Nobel prize winner Joseph Stiglitz's study that demonstrated that the upper 1 percent of Americans now take in nearly 25 percent of America's income every year.

My generation, that is, the counterculture of the 1960s and '70s, made the mistake of ignoring, or even blaming, regular working class folks.

Since class and the redistribution of wealth are the very subject of the rebellion this time, I can only hope that we do not make the same class(ist) mistakes.

Maybe we can all take a cue from Minnesota's next-door neighbor Wisconsin. Back in February 2011, when the police, who were exempt from the union-busting measure, were ordered to clear the capitol building of protesters, they came in with bullhorns and announced, "We have been ordered by the legislature to kick you all out at four today. But we know what's right from wrong. We will not be kicking anyone out, in fact, we will be sleeping here with you!" There is no way to know how these massive protests will end, but it is just this kind of alliance, between idealistic middle and working class young people, out-of-work or threatened workers, and other Americans who care about the devastating effects of our increasing inequality, that could provide some much-needed common ground in America.

The View from Glenville

I look around again; it's not just my family here, but Glenville friends of the family, too. I realize everyone they know is working class, everyone they have ever really known was working class. The transcripts of my oral work histories reveal that no matter how I approached the subject, none of those I interviewed expressed anything more than a shrug about people with money who may have looked down on them. Some of these women even cleaned houses for rich people when they were young adults, gone to the city to find work. Auntie Lu did, and she says, "They were very nice to me."

I realize and say, "Well, I suppose you see more of the prejudice against people like us when you go into the middle class."

"Yeah, I suppose so," they agree, trying to help me.

"Yeah," I say, "there is a lot of it." I flounder, and that's when Auntie Carol tells me how proud she is to know me. Auntie Nancy, with her clipped bowl-cut hairdo, no makeup, blue jeans and nice sweatshirt, looks and acts like my father, her big brother, gone from all of us forever. I am sitting next to her, eager to hear her quiet opinion while the others talk. I did this as a child, too, waited through my mother's verbal charm, witticisms, and general talkativeness, to hear my dad say some small simple but profound truth. Around this table, we are all reaching across my father's death to keep the circle from being broken. That part is easy, the reaching with love; I love them more than I can say. I feel lost, though, reaching across this class divide.

When Nancy finally says the obvious, "Is anybody gonna be able to read this thing?" I start to hedge. Anybody, of course, is people like us (or like them anyway, I think from my sudden wobbly perch between my working class and middle class lives). I say, "Some of it you'll understand better than anyone. Like roller skating."

And then I tell them that I have responsibilities to my editor and publisher, that it's a university press, and so I need to talk to academic people, too. Everyone nods, everyone knows what it is like to have bosses that one must take into account.

I say, "I want to tell those people what this life is about." People nod to encourage me, but they also look at one another like "Why bother, who cares about them if they're that way?" I say a few more sentences, and Nancy takes me off the hook, pointing out that "Louis L'Amour writes novels but he has a lot of history in them, too, and he writes real good." She continues, "We got some down at Seniors, but they go fast."

My father Fred, then Auntie Nancy, was president of the Glenville Senior Center. My family here, including Lily, Lu, Nancy, Cheryl, and Shirley and uncles Harold, Mike, and Rick, keep that center going. My seventy-something family takes care of Glenville's eighty- and ninety-something seniors. Glenville, like my family's rural farm, is old and forgotten by modern times. Seniors gather there each morning for coffee and rolls and games of whist. We still fill the Glenville Community Center with our family for Christmas each year. All of us come back to Main Street once a year, the place where I wandered alone as a small child, going in and out of businesses, meeting the proprietors, finding conversations and penny candy. I want the vitality back in this town. I don't want it to die, this place where everyone knows everyone, where all I have to do is say I'm a Jensen and everyone knows me, too. I want to tell them we need to protect this, that the life they had will no longer be possible for working class people, but I tumble into the chasm between my two lives and fall silent. While they still talk and talk and talk.

Notes

3. Belonging versus Becoming

1. They were G.K. Piorkowski's "Survivor Guilt in the University Setting," R. Gould's "Dr. Strangeclass: How I Stopped Worrying about the Theory and Began Treating the Blue Collar Worker," and J.D. Meltzer's "A Semiotic Approach to Suitability for Psychotherapy."

2. These codes are artificially stark and, as Bernstein (1971) said, a "crude index" due to class mobility in our society and frequent hybrids of the language codes in real life. I return to the notion of cultural, now linguistic, clouds or fields that overlap. Indeed, these areas of overlap are crucial to understanding the codes because the edges are dynamic locations of conflict, oppression, and change. Nonetheless, in the extremes of the codes we find the roots of the different cultural underpinnings. As such, the cultures stand in sharp contrast to each other. Whatever variation may be woven into the basic patterns, they point their members in different, and even opposing, directions.

3. The term "restricted" also carried an implicit negative meaning in the United States, as it was used, prior to the 1960s, to indicate that Jews were not welcome at an establishment. This implication was clearly not Bernstein's intention, himself a Jew.

4. He referred to Emile Durkheim's notion of organic and mechanical solidarities, pointing out these were the initial basis for his codes.

5. It is very tempting to try to illuminate the proper meaning of his entire body of his work and to write about the debate that arose around his early work and the supposedly contrasting theory advanced by William Labov (1970). I have read both Bernstein and Labov extensively, and clearly Labov's criticisms were both wrongly conceived and constructed. Indeed, he had to

write an apology in *Atlantic Monthly* for misrepresenting Bernstein. The competitive nature of academic discourse, however, has molded their images. I believe both of these men deeply shared the same concern I bring to this book: the illumination of working class cultures and the rescue of them from the solipsism of the dominant middle and upper classes, as well as the material conditions of their lives.

I would also like to note that the "deficit versus difference" debate that arose around them has used Bernstein to personify a particularly American confusion between class and race, and that it has labored under an ignorance of Bernstein's work. He has stated, over and over, that when he initially said working class children were at a disadvantage he was only referring to education systems, not the inherent worth (or complexity) of working class language or culture. In spite of his many attempts to clarify this, American theorists continue to go back to his early work to challenge him, ignoring thirty years of subsequent theory he developed. His most recent books, still refining his theory of class, education, social control, and inequality, were published in 1990 and 1996. Though it is beyond the scope of this chapter, a properly detailed look at this debate is at least as relevant now, as the age of multiculturalism reaches its zenith, as it was forty years ago when it began.

6. I am *not* saying that in American history working class people have never learned and loved formal or classical music or played instruments by reading musical notation. My godmother, Aunt Mary, loved to read music and play the piano, and she taught me to do the same, at least until she had five children to look after. Rather, in my own Midwestern rural family and working class suburban experience, this has not *generally* been the case.

4. Behaving versus Blooming

1. The science of sociology and community psychology is about finding, or disproving, general trends in populations. I point to cultural tendencies that are *more likely than not*, not to how each and every person (or subgroup) deals with them. These categories are not (and should not be) proposed to pigeonhole or define people but, rather, to provide patterns of human behavior and questions to explore. Theory is merely a simple line drawing to be held up against the rich color and texture of real life. Only then do we see what holds true and what does not. Particular individuals, families, whole neighborhoods, or intentional communities and ethnic groups can vary wildly in how they adopt or reject cultural norms.

2. I chose this highly respected work because of the great care Heath took in recording speech and tracking community customs through it, as well as her outstanding ability to analyze and theorize from her material. Her work also encompasses the three levels of influence I have mentioned earlier: that of particular people and families (personal), community or cultural, and societywide institutional or structural influences. Finally, she demonstrates successful cross-cultural practices derived from her work that has helped teachers, administrators, and students.

3. With these very different religious foundations, it's easy to see how working class white and black folks might see the other group as having bad manners. But the similarities between them still outweighed the differences when compared to the middle class children of Laurenceville.

4. Virtually *all* of the other wealthy democratic nations, as well as many poorer ones, expect their society to offer excellent educational opportunity to all children, not just those from the middle and upper classes. They believe an educated citizenry benefits their whole society, and there are many indicators that this is true. We, too, could offer better education to all our children, regardless of their social class.

5. Identity and Resistance

1. I am *not* saying that attention deficit disorder is a clinical fiction. I am saying that, in my clinical experience, it is overdiagnosed by professionals who do not do adequate neurological

screening, relying solely on reports of behavior and teachers' and counselors' subjective judgments about that behavior. We have seen that a student's behavior can be easily misunderstood.

Chapter 6. Across the Great Divide

1. I use the name *crossover* to describe the experience of those who are crossing classes. Al Lubrano (2004) uses the term *straddler*. Neither term is particularly precise, and I suspect at some point we will find a better one. But both describe the experience of being in two different class-related worlds.

2. I write "so-called" here because I am challenging the notion of a ladder of achievement that includes the myth that we all start in a similar place. I object to the term lower class, preferring the term working class because it is the name workers gave themselves, not how sociologists label them, and it is more accurate.

Chapter 7. Pain in the Promised Land

1. Carl Rogers wrote in 1967 of the Wisconsin project: "In those cases where the patient enters therapy with a fair degree of expressive capacity and/or motivation for self-exploration, the therapist's corresponding involvement may be enhanced. . . . on the other hand, patients lacking these capacities will generally fail to evoke similar therapist involvement. That is, the unmotivated, defensive and reluctant patient from a different (lower) socioeconomic background may not provide the therapist sufficient opportunity to deepen the relationship, and thus may severely limit the therapist's ability to communicate and function effectively" (1967, quoted in Jones 1974, 308–9). Talk about blaming the victim!

2. Another problem with this group (I am in it, so I am admitting this tendency myself) is that our desire to be on an intellectual cutting edge can hinder our students. I call this the *amnesia of cultural capital*. In this postmodern age, many intellectuals long to see beyond systems, beyond social structures or institutions (which they see as too static) and to focus scholarly inquiry into processes. We like to think and teach beyond "the canon" (the accumulated and recorded knowledge of human scholarship). I have prided myself on teaching outside the box, beyond the limits of a falsely named objective truth that is, in historical fact, filtered through the lens of monied white men. Postmodern, noncanonical teaching has validated the experiences and different *ways of knowing* of women and minority students. But here's the rub: many working class (and some middle class) students, including women and people of color, also have a need to *understand formal systems* before moving beyond them. Their entry point may differ from that of traditional students, and they are rightly changing the biases of higher education. But still, many miss out (as I once did) on formal training in seeing and thinking about systems in general, not just the ones that touch your personal life, as well as other crucial pieces of traditional education that can get overlooked.

3. I have purposely blurred the lines between poverty class and working class folks in this book, as I believe they generally have more in common than not. With the exception of some generational poverty, the difference between poverty class and working class people is far less than either of them as compared with the middle class (Heath 1996; Lareau 2003; Lareau and Conley 2008). Culturally—language styles, recreational activities, manners, fashion, kinds of work, and family values—they have many similarities. Also, most poverty class people work much of their adult lives, but they have seasonal or other short-term jobs, which are more likely to dry up for long periods of time. Especially in the new millenium's economy, with so many so-called skilled-labor (all jobs require skills) and pink-collar working class jobs sent overseas by "our" upper class, the difference between poverty and working classes have become increasingly indistinct. Home-ownership was a mid-twentieth century distinction that our upper class has removed from the "skilled" working class almost entirely, and so with all the material extras—to say nothing of the

right to sick pay, vacation pay, and pensions—that came with higher wages and other aspects of the American Dream that were hard-won by organized workers by the 1960s.

That said, there can still be significant differences between those raised poverty class and working class that may be invisible to those not raised poverty class. Although beyond the scope of this book, these differences are important and instructive (Lavell 2011).

Chapter 8. Gathering in Glenville

1. This is a different use of the term "bridging" from the way I used it in chapter 6.

2. In *Women's Ways of Knowing* (1986), Belinky et al. described five different *ways of knowing* that they found in their study of differences between men and women. They are hardly universal, as they are based on mostly middle class American college students, but they still provide a framework for understanding differences in ways of learning and thinking. They called them "phases," like stages but more fluid, of cognitive (mental) development. The five ways of knowing are: (1) silence, that is, unthinking acceptance of roles prescribed by powerful others; (2) received knowledge, that is, finding the one right answer; (3) subjective knowing, that is, gut or inner knowledge; (4) procedural knowledge, that is, processes that take people beyond the subjective, such as original and library research, critical thinking, debate; and (5) constructed knowledge, that is, an individualized choosing and blending from the other four. I mention this model to help explain and express the validity of and potential for blending both subjective and procedural ways of knowing. This work also helps me to explain the mixture of subjective, procedural, and constructed (intentional mixing of all of the above) "ways of knowing" from which I have gathered my ideas about working class life.

References

Adlam, D.S., G.J. Turner, L. Lineker. 1977. *Code in Context.* London: Routledge.

American Psychiatric Association. 1994. *Diagnostic and Statistical Manual of Mental Disorders: DSM-IV.* Washington, DC: American Psychiatric Association.

Anyon, J. 1980. "Social Class and the Hidden Curriculum of Work." *Journal of Education* 162 (2): 67–92.

———. 1981. "Social Class and School Knowledge." *Curriculum Inquiry* 11 (1): 1–42.

———. 1997. *Ghetto Schooling: A Political Economy of Urban Educational Reform.* New York: Teachers College Press.

Auerhahn, L. 2007. "Our Society's Middle Is Shrinking from View." In *Inequality: Social Class and Its Consequences*, edited by D.S. Eitzen and J.E. Johnston, 69–70. Boulder, CO: Paradigm.

Belenky, M.F., B.M. Clinchy, N.R. Goldberger, and J.M. Tarule. 1986. *Women's Ways of Knowing: The Development of Self, Voice, and Mind.* New York: Basic Books.

Bernstein, B.1958. "Some Sociological Determinants of Perception: An Enquiry into Sub-Cultural Differences." *British Journal of Sociology* 9 (2): 159–74.

———. 1962. "Linguistic Codes, Hesitation Phenomena and Intelligence." *Language and Speech* 5:31–46.

———. 1971. *Class, Codes and Control.* Vol. 1. *Theoretical Studies towards a Sociology of Language.* London: Routledge.

———. 1973. *Class, Codes and Control.* Vol. 2. *Applied Studies Towards a Sociology of Language.* London: Routledge.

———. 1977. *Class, Codes and Control.* Vol. 3. *Towards a Theory of Educational Transmissions.* London: Routledge.

———. 1990. *Class, Codes and Control.* Vol. 4. *The Structuring of Pedagogic Discourse.* London: Routledge.

———. 1996. *Class, Codes and Control.* Vol. 5. *Pedagogy, Symbolic Control and Identity.* London: Routledge.

Black, L. J. 1995. "Stupid Rich Bastards." In Dews and Law 1995, 13–25.

Bourdieu, P. [1979] 1984. *Distinction: A Social Critique of the Judgment of Taste.* Translated by Richard Nice. Cambridge: Harvard University Press.

Bowles, S., and H. Gintis. 1976. *Schooling in Capitalist America: Educational Reform and Contradictions of Economic Life.* New York: Basic Books.

Brantlinger, E. A. 2003. *Dividing Classes: How the Middle Class Negotiates and Rationalizes School Advantage.* New York: Routledge Falmer.

Brooks, D. 2000. *Bobos in Paradise: The New Upper Class and How They Got There.* New York: Simon and Schuster.

———. 2001. "The Organization Kid." *Atlantic Monthly*, April.

Bruni, F. 2006. "A Buzz Saw of Buzzwords." *New York Times*, December 24.

Cappello, M. 1995. "Useful Knowledge." In Dews and Law 1995, 127–36.

Chodorow, N. J. 1989. *Feminism and Psychoanalytic Theory.* Cambridge: Polity.

Christopher, R. 1995. "A Carpenter's Daughter." In Dews and Law 1995, 137–50.

———. 2009. *A Carpenter's Daughter.* Boston: Sense Publishers.

Collins, C., and F. Yeskel. 2005. *Economic Apartheid in America: A Primer on Economic Inequality and Insecurity.* New York: New Press.

Conarton, S., and L. K. Silverman. 1989. "Feminine Development through the Life Cycle." In *Feminist Psychotherapies: Integration of Therapeutic and Feminist Systems,* edited by M. A. Dutton-Douglas and L. Walker, 37–67. Norwood, NJ: Ablex.

Dahrendorf, R. 1979. *Life Chances.* Chicago: University of Chicago.

De Graaf, J., D. Wann, T. H. Naylor, and D. Horsey. 2002. *Affluenza the All-Consuming Epidemic.* San Francisco: Berrett-Koehler.

Dews, C. L. B., and C. L. Law, eds. 1995. *This Fine Place So Far from Home.* Philadelphia: Temple University Press.

DiMaggio, P. 1982. "Cultural Capital and School Success." *American Sociological Review* 47 (April 1982): 189–201.

Easterbrook, G. 2007. "Cheapskate Billionaires: The Super-Rich Have More Than They Can Ever Possibly Spend, So Why Do They Give So Little?" *Los Angeles Times*, March 18.

Ehrenreich, B. 1989. *Fear of Falling: The Inner Life of the Middle Class.* New York: Pantheon.

———. 2006. *Bait and Switch: The Futile Pursuit of the American Dream.* New York: Henry Holt.

Eitzen, D. S., and J. E. Johnston. 2007. *Inequality: Social Class and Its Consequences.* Boulder, CO: Paradigm.

Finn, P. 1999. *Literacy with an Attitude: Educating Working-Class Children in Their Own Self-Interest.* Albany: State University of New York Press.

Frank, R. 2007. *Richistan: A Journey through the American Wealth Boom and the Lives of the New Rich*. New York: Crown.

Freire, P. 1970. *Pedagogy of the Oppressed*. New York: Herder and Herder.

Fussell, P. 1992. *Class: A Guide through the American Status System*. New York: Touchstone, Simon and Schuster.

Gans, H. J. 1962. *The Urban Villagers: Group and Class in the Life of Italian-Americans*. New York: Free Press of Glencoe.

Garger, S. 1995. "Bronx Syndrome." In Dews and Law 1995, 41–53.

Gilligan, C. 1982. *In a Different Voice*. Cambridge: Harvard University Press.

Gini, A. 2001. *My Job, My Self: Work and the Creation of the Modern Individual*. New York: Routledge.

Giroux, H. A. 1983. *Theory and Resistance in Education*. London: Heinemann Educational Books.

Golden, D. 2006. *The Price of Admission: How America's Ruling Class Buys Its Way into Elite Colleges—And Who Gets Left Outside the Gates*. New York: Crown.

Gould, R. 1967. "Dr. Strangeclass: Or How I Stopped Worrying about the Theory and Began Treating the Blue-Collar Worker." *American Journal of Orthopsychiatry* 37:78–86.

Greene, D. 2003. "The Matrix of Identity Revisited." Paper presented at the Sixth Biennial Conference of the Center for Working-Class Studies, May 15, Youngstown State University, Youngstown, Ohio.

Heath, S. B. [1983] 1996. *Ways with Words: Language, Life, and Work in Communities and Classrooms*. New York: Cambridge University Press

Heath, S. B., L. Mangiola, S. R. Schecter, and G. A. Hull. 1991. *Children of Promise: Literate Activity in Linguistically and Culturally Diverse Classrooms*. Washington, DC: NEA Professional Library, National Education Association.

Heath, S. B., and M. W. McLaughlin. 1993. *Identity and Inner City Youth: Beyond Ethnicity and Gender*. New York: Teacher's College Press.

Hochschild, A. R. [1997] 2000. *The Time Bind: When Work Becomes Home and Home Becomes Work*. New York: Metropolitan Books.

Hollingshead, A. B., and F. C. Redlich. 1958. *Social Class and Mental Illness: A Community Study*. New York: John Wiley and Sons.

hooks, bell. 2000. *Where We Stand: Class Matters*. London: Routledge.

Howe, N., and W. Strauss. 2000. *Millennials Rising: The Next Great Generation*. New York: Vintage.

———. 2003. *Millennials Go to College: Strategies for a New Generation on Campus: Recruiting and Admissions, Campus Life, and the Classroom*. American Association of Collegiate Registrars and Admissions Officers and LifeCourse Associates, Great Falls, VA.

———. 2006. *Millennials and Pop Culture*. Great Falls, VA: LifeCourse Associates.

Howell, J. T. 1973. *Hard Living on Clay Street*. Garden City, NY: Anchor.

Jensen, B. 1998. "The Silent Psychology." *Women's Studies Quarterly* 261 and 262: 202–15.

———. 2004. "Across the Great Divide." *What's Class Got to Do with It? American Society in the Twenty-first Century,* edited by M. Zweig, 168–83. Ithaca: Cornell University Press.

Jones, E. 1974. "Social Class and Psychotherapy: A Critical Review of Research." *Psychiatry* 37:307–19.

Joos, M. 1961. *The Five Clocks*. New York: Harcourt, Brace and World.

Kegan, R. 1982. *The Evolving Self*. Cambridge: Harvard University Press.

———. 1995. *In over Our Heads: The Mental Demands of Modern Life*. Cambridge: Harvard University Press.

Kelber, H. 2007. "Lincoln Had It Right: Labor Is Prior to Capital; But Where Is Labor NOW?" *Labor Talk* (October 24). http://www.laboreducator.org

Kozol, J. 1995. *Amazing Grace: The Lives of Children and the Conscience of a Nation*. New York: Crown.

Kusserow, A. 2005. "The Workings of Class: How Understanding a Subtle Difference Between Social Classes Can Promote Equality in the Classroom—and Beyond." *Stanford Social Innovation Review* 3 (3): 38–47.

Labov, W. 1969 and 1970. *The Study of Nonstandard English*. Champaign, IL: National Council of Teachers of English.

———. 1972. "The Logic of Nonstandard English." In *Language and Cultural Diversity in American Education*, edited by R. D. Abrahams and R. C. Troike, 225–61. Upper Saddle River, NJ: Prentice Hall.

———. 1972. *Sociolinguistic Patterns*. Philadelphia: University of Pennsylvania Press.

Lamont, M. 1992. *Money, Morals, and Manners*. Chicago: University of Chicago Press.

———. 2000. *The Dignity of Working Men*. New York: Russell Sage Foundation; Cambridge, MA: Harvard University Press.

Lareau, A. 2003. *Unequal Childhoods: Class, Race, and Family Life*. Berkeley: University of California Press.

Lareau, A., and D. Conley, eds. 2008. *Social Class: How Does It Work*. New York: Russell Sage Foundation.

Lavell, F. 2011. *Counseling for the Working Class: Weaving Authentic Practice*. Presentation at the Working Class Studies Association conference in Chicago, June 24, 2011.

L'Engle, M. 1962. *A Wrinkle in Time*. New York: Ariel Books.

Leondar-Wright, B. 2005. *Class Matters: Cross-Class Alliance Building for Middle-Class Activists*. Gabriola, BC: New Society.

———. 2011. "(More) Classist Comments: New Responses to the Survey on Classism." *Class Matters*. Critical Literacy. http://www.classmatters.org/2005_07/more_classist_comments.php (accessed May 5, 2011).

Lerner, M. 1991. *Surplus Powerlessness: The Psychodynamics of Everyday Life—and the Psychology of Individual and Social Transformation*. Atlantic Highlands, NJ: Humanities Press International.

Levine, M. 2006. *The Price of Privilege: How Parental Pressure and Material Advantage Are Creating a Generation of Disconnected and Unhappy Kids*. New York: HarperCollins.

Levison, J. 2007. "(More) Classist Comments: New Responses to the Survey on Classism." *Class Matters*. Critical Literacy. http://www.classmatters.org/2005_07/more_classist_comments.php (accessed October 30, 2008).

Lifton, R. J. 1967. *Death in Life*. New York: Random House.

———. [1976] 1983. *The Life of the Self*. New York: Basic Books.

Lubrano, A. 2004. *Limbo: Blue-Collar Roots, White-Collar Dreams.* Hoboken, NJ: John Wiley and Sons.

MacLeod, J. 1995. *Ain't No Makin' It.* Boulder, CO: Westview Press.

Marmot, M.G. 2004. *The Status Syndrome: How Social Standing Affects Our Health and Longevity.* New York: Times Books.

Marmot, M.G., C.D. Ryff, L.L. Bumpass, M. Shipley, N.F. Marks. 1997. "Social Inequalities in Health: Next Questions and Converging Evidence." *Journal of Social Science and Medicine* 44 (6): 901–10.

Meltzer, J.D. 1978. "A Semiotic Approach to Suitability for Psychotherapy." *Psychiatry* 41:360–75.

Metzgar, J. 2000. *Striking Steel.* Philadelphia: Temple University Press.

———. 2005. "Politics and the American Class Vernacular." In *New Working-Class Studies*, edited by J. Russo and S.L. Linkon, 189–208. Ithaca: Cornell University Press.

Miller, J.B. 1977. *Toward a New Psychology of Women.* Boston: Beacon.

Modigliani, K. 2008. "(More) Classist Comments: New Responses to the Survey on Classism." *Class Matters.* Critical Literacy. http://www.classmatters.org/2005_07/more_classist_comments.php (accessed October 30, 2008).

Motley, W. [1947] 1989. *Knock on Any Door.* DeKalb: Northern Illinois Press.

Murolo, P., A.B. Chitty, and J. Sacco. 2001. *From the Folks Who Brought You the Weekend: A Short, Illustrated History of Labor in the United States.* New York: New Press.

Obama, B. 1996. *Dreams from My Father: A Story of Race and Inheritance.* New York: Three Rivers Press.

Payne, R.K. 1998. *A Framework for Understanding Poverty.* Baytown, TX: R.F.T.

Peckham, I. 1995. "Complicity in Class Codes: The Exclusionary Function of Education." In Dews and Law 1995, 263–76.

———. 2010. *Going North, Thinking West: The Intersections of Social Class, Critical Thinking, and Politicized Writing Instruction.* Logan: Utah State University Press.

Pegueros, R.M. 1995. "Todos Vuelven: From Potrero Hill to UCLA." In Dews and Law 1995, 87–105.

Peltz, W. 1995. "Is There a Working-Class History?" In Dews and Law 1995, 277–85.

Phillips, D.B. 1995. "Past Voices, Present Speakers." In Dews and Law 1995, 221–30.

Piorkowski, G.K. 1983. "Survivor Guilt in the University Setting." *Personnel and Guidance Journal* 61:620–22.

Putnam, R.D. 2000. *Bowling Alone: The Collapse and Revival of American Community.* New York: Simon and Schuster.

Putnam, R.D., and L.M. Feldstein. 2003. *Better Together: Restoring the American Community.* New York: Simon and Schuster.

Register, S. 2000. *Packinghouse Daughter, a Memoir.* St. Paul: Minnesota Historical Society Press.

Rifkin, J. 1995. *The End of Work.* New York: Tarcher/Putman.

Robbins, H. 1966. *The Carpetbaggers.* Montreal: Pocket Books

Rodriquez, R. 1982. *Hunger of Memory: The Education of Richard Rodriquez.* New York: Bantam.

Rose, F. 2000. *Coalitions across the Class Divide: Lessons from the Labor, Peace, and Environmental Movements.* Ithaca: Cornell University Press.

Rose, M. 2004. *The Mind at Work: Valuing the Intelligence of the American Worker.* New York: Viking.

Rosenfeld, A. A., and N. Wise. 2000. *The Over-Scheduled Child: Avoiding the Hyper-Parenting Trap.* New York: St. Martin's Griffin.

Rubin, L. B. 1976. *Worlds of Pain: Life in the Working-Class Family.* New York: Basic Books.

———. 1994. *Families on the Fault Line.* New York: Harper Perennial.

Ruddick, S. 1989. *Maternal Thinking: Toward a Politics of Peace.* New York: Ballentine.

Russo, J., and S. L. Linkon. 2005. *New Working-Class Studies.* Ithaca: Cornell University Press.

Ryan, J., and C. Sackrey. [1984] 1996. *Strangers in Paradise: Academic from the Working Class.* Lanham, MD: University Press of America.

Sadovnik, A. R., ed. 1995. *Knowledge and Pedagogy: The Sociology of Basil Bernstein.* Norwood, NJ: Ablex.

Sarason, S. B. 1988. *The Psychological Sense of Community: Prospects for a Community Psychology.* Cambridge, MA: Brookline Books.

Schatzman, L., and A. Strauss. 1955. "Social Class and Modes of Communication." *American Journal of Sociology* 60 (4): 329–38.

Schwalbe, M. 1995. "The Work of Professing: A Letter to Home." In Dews and Law 1995, 309–31.

Seligman, M. 1992. *Helplessness: On Depression, Development, and Death.* New York: W. H. Freeman.

Sennett, R., and J. Cobb. 1972. *The Hidden Injuries of Class.* New York: Vintage.

Slater, P. E. [1970] 1990. *The Pursuit of Loneliness: American Culture at the Breaking Point.* Boston: Beacon.

Strauss, W., and N. Howe. 1991. *Generations: The History of America's Future, 1584–2069.* New York: Quill William Morrow

———. 1997. *The Fourth Turning: What the Cycles of History Tell Us About America's Next Rendezvous with Destiny.* New York: Broadway Books.

Torlina, J. 2011. *Working Class: Challenging Myths About Blue-Collar Labor.* Boulder, CO: Lynne Rienner Publishers.

Vanneman, R., and L. W. Cannon. 1987. *The American Perception of Class.* Philadelphia: Temple University Press.

Willis, P. 1977. *Learning to Labor: How Working Class Kids Get Working Class Jobs.* Westmead, UK: Saxon House.

Wilson, J. E. 1996. "Balancing Class Locations." In *Strangers in Paradise: Academics from the Working Class*, edited by J. Ryan and C. Sackrey, 199–209. New York: University of America Press.

Withers. J. 2010. "Hey Teacher Leave Them Kids Alone." *Touchy Subjects in Education.* http://touchysubjectsineducation.blogspot.com/2010/06/hey-teacher-leave-them-kids-alone.html (accessed October 30, 2010).

Yates, M. D., ed. 2007. *More Unequal: Aspects of Class in the United States.* New York: Monthly Review Press.

Zweig, M. 2000. *The Working Class Majority: America's Best Kept Secret.* Ithaca: Cornell University Press.

———, ed. 2004. *What's Class Got to Do with It? American Society in the Twenty-First Century*. Ithaca: Cornell University Press.

———. 2005. "Class as a Question in Economics." In *New Working-Class Studies*, edited by J. Russo and S. L. Linkon, 98–112. Ithaca: Cornell University Press.

———. 2007. "Six Points on Class." In *More Unequal: Aspects of Class in the United States*, edited by M. D. Yates, 173–82. New York: Monthly Review Press.

———. 2012. *The Working Class Majority: America's Best Kept Secret*. 2nd edition. Ithaca: Cornell University Press.

Index